The Morning
Of The White Stone

Revelation 2:17

And to him who overcomes

I will give him a white stone.

Patsy J. Lewis

Page left Intentionally Blank

Copyright © 2025

Patsy J. Lewis

Dedication

DEDICATED TO JESUS,

FOR WITHOUT HIM,

I CAN DO NOTHING

Acknowledgments

First and foremost, I want to thank the Lord for giving me His Holy Spirit to dwell within this body and making it His temple. Writing about my life experiences has been a spiritual journey of healing for me.

The struggle between light and darkness is a reality. This book is fact and fiction, interwoven, so that all those who read it may experience the emotion that prompted the writing of it.

Regardless of how many midnights one encounters in a lifetime, there is always that moment when, looking through the window of the soul, we perceive a glimmer of difference in the intensity of the darkness. Jesus said, "I am the light of the world." In Him there is no darkness. When we walk in the light of his Spirit, there will be no darkness in our soul.

Thank you to my lifelong church family, the wonderful Pentecostals of Alexandria, Louisiana. All my love goes to my five children, ten grandchildren, and ten great-grandchildren. You are the treasures I hold dear.

I am so grateful for my dear friends: Wanda, Diane, Vivian, and Patricia, who read my first drafts and encouraged me to press on to the end.

PROLOGUE

She knows she is dying. There's something very important she must do. If only she could hold on long enough. Opening her eyes with great effort, she looks into the eyes of her husband, who is leaning over her, his eyes anxious and afraid. He sees her lips moving and he puts his ear close to her mouth. He listens closely, and then nods in agreement. Her hand grows limp in his warm grasp. He can hear her breath rattle and he knows she's leaving him. Bowing his head over their clasped hands, he began to weep. When he raised his head, she was smiling her beautiful smile and her eyes were wide open and filled with wonder and excitement. Her face was radiant with joy. Her spirit rose up to meet her Lord. Her body remained, to be buried by those who loved her. Later, after the funeral, he found the small metal box where she had said it would be. Inside he saw a feather, a coin, and a smooth white stone with some strange sign etched into it. He put it with the baby's things. His baby son lay on the bed where his mother had died, kicking his little feet, gurgling and chuckling. Coal back hair framed his head and his dark eyes were alight with laughter. The man looked at him with sorrow. Then, he picked him up and went out to the waiting buggy.

Table of Contents

Introduction

Matthew

At first glance, you could not see the boy. His sun browned skin blended with the color of the fresh-turned-earth. Skinny, with no shirt, his slick, black hair hugged his small head, curling around his ears. His bare feet sank into the moist earth at each step, as he plodded slowly behind the big mule. His sturdy little arms are strained to their limit. His small hands grip the plow handles determinedly. The loamy soil folds itself to each side of the furrow as the plow cuts its way up and down, traversing the length and breadth of the field. He does not know his destiny, but circumstances have already set him on a course. Each event, each interaction with the other molding characters in his life, and each choice made are moving him along towards disastrous consequences. Fate has him in her grasp but, if at this point in his life, he could know and understand this fact, perhaps he could extricate himself. For now, at eight years of age, his heart is still tender enough to be touched, his mind still pliable enough to be redirected, and his life new enough to be set on a different course. Who is wise enough to discern how easily a life can be set in a pattern, either for good or for evil, and put forth the effort required to "train up a child in the way he should go." Who in his life has the insight to see that with the training there must be tenderness, affection, acceptance, and much love? There is no such person in Matthew Carlisle's life, as, on this beautiful spring morning he resolutely plows his uncle's field.

Chapter 1

Early County, Georgia

Matthew, Five years later

Matthew! Matt! Where are you, boy? Come here, now! Where in tarnation is that boy? Never around when you need him. Off somewhere gitten' into trouble, sure as my name is James Carlisle." Cursing in impatience, James stomped across the yard and into the kitchen, his anger growing. "Martha, where's Matt? He knows it's milking time and May needs milk for her kids. It'll be dark soon. That boy will feel my stick on his backside when I get hold of him."

Martha eyed her irate husband. "James, don't get yourself all worked up. You know your heart is weak. Matt's probably fishing. If he doesn't get back, make him milk in the dark. Then, he'll learn to come home on time."

"You're right, Martha. Where's the girls?" he's still irritated at Matthew's absence.

"Kate and Annie are weeding the vegetable patch. I sent Millie to gather the eggs." Martha's agile hands kneaded the dough skillfully, forming it into loaves, and then greasing the waiting pans.

The door opened quietly and Matthew padded in on bare, dirty feet. Grasped in one filthy hand is a string of three catfish.

He grinned proudly, as he held them up to Martha. "Look, Mama, I caught these for you. This one must weigh at least three pounds!" He exclaimed excitedly, his eyes shining with pride at his accomplishment.

"Take them outside, Matthew. She turned away, ignoring the expectant look she saw in his dark eyes for her approval.

"Well, boy, I'll tend to you later. Get to the milking. May needs milk tonight." James ordered brusquely. Matt's shoulders drooped and the sparkle died from his eyes. Turning, he went toward the door. Leaving the fish on the porch, he returned for the milk buckets, and then continued toward the barn, bare feet dragging in the dusty yard. Martha stood for a moment, watching his forlorn figure, then shrugged her shoulders and turned back to her chores. "Why does Matthew seem to purposely bring punishment on himself?" she wondered, "It seems as though either James or I have to punish him continually."

She remembered the day her sister-in-law passed away, finally, after much suffering. The helpless baby boy was doted on by all the girls, even Millie, who was only two years old. With his Indian mother's black hair and expressive eyes, he was a beautiful baby, continually laughing. Now that Matt is an awkward boy, always seeming to be involved in some mischief, he is constantly irritating her. As she covered her fresh bread with clean napkins and set it aside to rise overnight, Martha remembered the catfish Matthew had so proudly shown her.

"I'll fry them up with some potatoes for supper," she decided. Just then, the door opened to admit Kate and Annie.

"Girls, start peeling potatoes and I'll have Matt clean those catfish as soon as he finishes the milking. I'll get the skillet hot and we'll have supper so he can run over to May's with the milk." Her tone brooked no argument.

In the barn, Matthew gave vent to his frustration by milking furiously, dreading the whipping he felt sure Uncle James meant to give him. A dark resentment fills his heart every time he thinks about the circumstances that have made him an orphan in this house comprised of women.

"If only my Mama hadn't left me. If only my Papa had not given me away! I hate all of them, especially Millie, always tattling on me. Someday, I'll leave this place. I'll show them, all of them! Someday Uncle James won't be able to whip me, ever again. He'll be sorry when I'm gone." At this thought, Matthew finished up in the barn and hurried to the house, knowing he still had to ride to May's before dark. Entering the kitchen with the foaming buckets of warm milk, he remembered the catfish he still must clean and went out again.

"As soon as you finish with those fish, Matt, get the mare and go on to May's. You can eat when you get back. Otherwise, you'll be going in the dark." Matt looked up from his chore as Martha spoke to him from the doorway."

"Okay, I'm almost finished. You can take those two. I'll bring this one in just a minute" he replied.

A few minutes later, swinging one wiry leg over the back of his mare, Firefly, Matt held out his hands. James placed a jug of fresh milk in his arms, cautioning him, "You be careful, Matthew, crossing the creek. Don't be losing this milk, now. May needs it for that bunch of kids."

Nodding in agreement, Matt turned the mare. Holding tightly to the milk, he headed for the stretch of woods bordering James's land. A trail leads through the trees, crosses a creek, and goes on to the homestead of May, the oldest of James and Margaret's daughters. Living in the drafty old house with three small children, May is constantly in need. Her husband, a happy-go-lucky type of young man, works away from home. Matthew cuts wood for the fire and makes frequent trips to deliver milk, eggs, and other items sent from Aunt Martha to May. Shadows are lengthening this evening as Matt nears the thick woods. Here and there through the trees, the crickets begin their evening song. Soon, the bass section, comprised of big old bullfrogs will join in the chorus. Having made this trip countless times, Matt nevertheless does not relish being caught by nightfall in the woods. Stepping daintily along the trail, the little mare knows the way. Just before reaching the bank of the creek, she suddenly stops dead still. Caught off guard, Matt almost lost his seat on her bare back. Gripping the milk close to him, pressing his knees into her sides, and clucking encouragingly to her, he urged her forward. Instead of going on, though, the mare squealed shrilly, whirled around, and dashed back down the trail toward home. Clinging on with all his strength, Matthew laid down on her neck as she galloped headlong through the trees. He feels low branches scrape across his back and hopes he can stay on until they are out of the woods.

Reaching the open trail, the mare raced towards the barn, not pausing until she was brought to a stop by Matt at the big barn door. Sliding off, his heart racing, he looked anxiously at his mare. Her sides are heaving and her eyes are wildly dilated. What in the world could be wrong with her? She has never acted like this. He knows her well, having raised her from a colt. Must be a wildcat in those woods, or maybe even a bear! Yeah, she probably smelled a big old grizzly, just waiting to jump out and chew me up! Patting the mare's slender nose, he dashed for the house to tell Uncle James about the bear down by the creek.

"Uncle James! Uncle James" Matt jumped onto the porch, still holding the jug of milk. Thank goodness, he didn't drop it when the mare bolted!

"What in tarnation is wrong with you, boy, yelling like that? Seeing Matt's eyes, huge and dark in his white face, James rises from his chair in alarm.

"What's happened? Why didn't you take the milk to May?" he questioned immediately.

"There's a bear down by the creek! The mare wouldn't go through. She ran away with me. Ran all the way home. I didn't drop the milk, though!" Matt's words tumbled over each other in his excitement.

"Go hitch up the wagon. We'll go take the milk to May. Come morning, we'll check out this story of yours." Matthew raced back to the barn at James's words.

Within a few minutes, Matt climbed into the wagon beside Uncle James, still holding the jug of milk. His heart seemed to be beating up in his throat and his hands were wet with nervousness. Uncle James slapped the reins against the old horse's back, forcing him to pick up a little speed as they started for the dirt road leading to May's house.

The road is narrow and bordered by thick stands of trees and underbrush. Matthew strained his eyes, trying to see into the darkening thicket, sure there were yellow eyes, staring back at him. Thankful that his uncle is with him, he cannot relax until they reach the clearing surrounding the house where May lives, along with her husband, Duncan Hanks, and their three small boys, Jeremy, Johnny, and Sam. Guiding the horse up to the porch, James speaks at last.

"Take that milk in there, Matt, so we can get on back. It's getting late."

Matthew could hear the sounds of the boys playing as he knocked on the door. May stood in the doorway, a baby slung on her hip.

"Hello Matt, come on in."

Leaving the door ajar, she put the baby down onto the floor.

"I'm sure glad you made it with the milk. The boys can have some with their supper."

"Well, I would've been here before now, but something scared my mare when I was going through the trail down by the creek. I couldn't get her to cross the creek. She ran away with me, ran all the way back to the barn before she would stop." Matt's voice rises in excitement as he relates the events of the past hour.

The little boys listened in admiration, eyes growing bigger at each word. Matthew is their hero. He has taken care of them many times when they visited their Grandma. He even let them sit up on Firefly, his mare, leading her around the barnyard, patiently teaching the older ones how to ride. Jeremy, the oldest of the trio, now grabbed Matthew around his legs.

"I'm scared, Matt," his voice quivered. "Will the big bear come and eat us up?"

"Heck, no, Jeremy. Why, that old bear knows better than to mess with you. Your Mama will shoot him with your Daddy's gun if he even comes near the place."

Matthew winked at May as he reassured the small boy. Then, tickling him in his ribs, causing him to dissolve in helpless giggles, Matt turned to go, for he knew Uncle James was growing impatient.

"I'll come over before long and take you riding on Firefly," he promised. "See you, May," he called from the door, as he went out.

"Thanks for bringing the milk. Duncan's coming home tomorrow. He can take care of the wood cutting. No need for you to worry about it." May followed him to the doorway. "How you doing, Daddy?" she called to James.

"Fair to middling. When's that husband of yours goanna be home?" James asked brusquely.

"Tomorrow, Daddy, he'll be home tomorrow. Tell Mama we'll be up there to see her as soon as Duncan gets back. Good night and watch out for the bears." May laughed good-naturedly as she closed the door.

As the wagon rolled towards home, Matt was silent, fearful of the promised whipping, hopeful that in all the excitement, Uncle James would forget. The stars have appeared, sparkling pinpoints of silver light. A huge golden moon peeps over the treetops, lighting their way. Gathering his courage, Matt breaks the silence.

"What do you think it was, Uncle James that spooked the mare? Could it be an old grizzly, right close to the house, you think?"

"Now, boy, don't be scaring Martha and the girls with that bear talk. Come daylight, we'll check for tracks. It's probably nothing but your imagination. You're something of a scaredy cat, anyway. Put up the horse and wagon."

James climbed stiffly down off the wagon and left Matthew alone. Quickly unhitching the old horse, and throwing the harness over the fence post, he measured out a little feed into the trough. Firefly, cropping grass in the moonlight, nickered and trotted over to Matt. Laying his face against her velvety nose, he wrapped his arms around her neck. Her warm breath blew on his face as she nuzzled in his shirt, looking for a treat.

"What did you see, girl, down by the creek? Did you smell an old' wildcat, or was it just a coon in the bushes?" He whispered.

He Scratched between her pricked ears, feeling his chest tighten and his eyes burn with emotion. He loves this horse. She returns his love. Not like people! It seems like animals are better friends than humans. Even his own Pa had given him away when he was a baby. Matt's thoughts went back to the day a couple of years ago when his Pa had come for him. He had just rode up to the porch on his big roan gelding and called Matthew from the house.

"Get your clothes, son. You're coming home with me." he had told the astonished boy.

Hearing his voice, Martha and the girls had all come running out to greet him. When Matthew obeyed his Daddy, going to his room, and gathering up his clothes, they all began to cry and beg him to stay. Matt wanted to go with his Pa. His heart beating fast, he hurriedly tried to pack his belongings in the old valise before his Aunt Martha talked his Pa into leaving him there.

"My daddy does love me. He wants me to live with him. "Oh boy!" Matt's heart sang excitedly as he ran out onto the porch."I'm ready, Pa," he cried happily.

Aunt Martha stood quietly, hands in her big apron, a strange look on her face. Looking from one to another, Matt was shocked to see tears in Millie's eyes.

"What's going on here?" He thought, "What's Millie crying about?" He hadn't seen her cry since he pushed her face into the cow pile after she tattled on him to Uncle James, causing him to get a whipping.

"Uncle Wiley, please let Matt stay," Katherine had begged.

Matt's heart had almost stopped as he saw his daddy hesitantly look his way. "Well, my goodness, Matthew. I didn't know you were so important to everybody. I might have to reconsider taking you away. It seems like your Aunt Martha and the girls will be heartbroken at your leaving them."

Wiley Carlisle did not notice that Annie remained silent. If he had been a perceptive man, he would have seen the message she tried so hard to send to him, the same message so plain in the dark eyes of his small son. The message was lost on Wiley, for, looking at Matthew once more, he made his decision.

"You stay here for the time being. Looks like you're well tended, well fed, and with all these womenfolk to look after you. You come down and play with Robert any time, you hear?"

Then, reining the horse around, he was gone, without giving Matthew a chance to speak his feelings, if he had even had the courage to speak out in front of Aunt Martha. In spite of the whippings, the lack of outward affection, and the reserve exhibited by Aunt Martha, she is yet the only Mother he has ever known. He remembers how different she was when he was small. Now, it seems she does not love him. He remembers loving her then, but now he only feels unwanted.

Matthew remembered standing on the porch, his clothes in his hand, a terrible feeling of betrayal silencing his cry as a great anger engulfed him. Two years have gone by, but he has relived that moment over and over. He wishes now he had spoken up for himself, run after his Pa, ignoring Aunt Martha and the girls. They didn't want him to leave. Not from any love for him, though. He wasn't fooled by Millie's tears. And that Katherine! She had a certain way of making him feel like an outsider, barely tolerating him, it seems, talking down to him, as though he had no feelings. They wanted him to stay, alright. They needed him to cut wood for the three fireplaces, milk cows, plow, and do all the other chores allotted to him since he was a small boy. Kicking the churned-up dirt with his bare foot, he blinked back hot tears of frustration and pain. Someday, he will control his own life. Someday, he will be big enough to stand up for himself, he vowed.

Turning toward the house, now, Matt latched the gate carefully behind him. Firefly followed him, hanging her head over the fence. Once more, Matt presses his face against her soft neck. Walking across the yard, he heard her soft nicker behind him. "I love you, girl." The words are only a whisper from his hurting heart.

Sleep will not come to James Carlisle, lying on his bed in the room he shares with Martha. His leg throbs. The pain, always with him, since his accident, many years before, is relentless. It is for this reason that he and his wife no longer share a bed. Many nights, he lies awake, staring into the darkness, suffering in silence, lest he disturb Martha. Tonight, hearing the soft closing of the back door, he remembers the events of the day. His thoughts are on Matthew. "I should have taken my cane to him right off when he came in late for the milking. I can't let him think I'm weak. This infernal leg of mine! Can't let on to him how much it pains me. He's getting bigger and stronger all the time. Figure I won't be able to bluff him into obeying me much longer."

Realizing a confrontation is inevitable; James nevertheless determines to administer his usual punishment for Matthew's disobedience. Attempting to get up, he moved his good leg to the edge of the bed. Sitting up with great effort, grasping his other leg with both hands, he tried to maneuver himself onto the edge of the bed. Suddenly, excruciating pain assaulted his body. With a gasp of agony, he fell backward, as waves of nausea washed over him. Beads of perspiration formed on his face and he cannot move or call out to Martha.

But, she has heard his barely audible gasp and is beside him, her face full of concern. "James, James, what is it? Oh, Dear Lord, don't let him die!

God have mercy on my husband." She prays as she wipes the perspiration from his face with a cool cloth. "Where is the pain, James? Is it your leg?"

Hoping it is his leg and not his chest causing such agony, Martha can only wait, for James seems unable to respond to her question. He seems to have passed out, for he is very still, his hand clutching the bedcovers in a death grip. Fearing the worst, she began to call out for help, hoping Matthew or the girls will hear and come quickly.

Coming in a few minutes earlier, Matthew had eaten the beef stew and cornbread left for him, washing it down with milk he had retrieved from the spring house. Putting away his dishes, he is startled by a desperate cry coming from his aunt and uncle's bedroom. Hearing his name called in Aunt Martha's voice, he quickly crossed the short distance and entered the room without knocking, for her voice was frightening. A terrible scene met his eyes and sent fear through him. Uncle James lay dead on the bed and Aunt Martha is kneeling beside him, weeping. Hearing him enter, she raised her head and he saw the desperation on her face. "Matt! Oh, Matt! What can we do?"

Seeing him rooted to the spot in the doorway, paralyzed by fear, she jumped up and rushed to him. Grabbing his arm, and shaking him hard, she pulled him over to the bed.

"Help me get him straight in the bed. Let's see if his heart is still beating." Martha forces herself to speak calmly, for she sees that Matthew believes James is dead.

Attempting to move his uncle, Matt realizes what a big man he has become. Due to a forced inactivity in the last few years, James has put on quite a bit of excess weight. Now, he and his aunt can barely budge his inert body, as they try to lift him higher onto the pillows.

Grunting with the exertion, they manage, finally to get James straight in the bed. Applying cool cloths to his clammy face, Martha feels a feeble pulse beating in his temple. Weak with sudden relief, she sank to the floor beside the bed.

"Thank God, thank God, he's still alive." she cried to Matt.

Standing awkwardly, his eyes glued to his uncle's prostrate body, Matthew feels moisture fill his eyes at her words. Blinking back the tears, lest Martha notice them, he can only shake his head in answer. Just at that moment, James moans weakly, though his eyes are still closed. Springing up from the floor, Martha leans over her husband.

"James, James, can you hear me? Are you still in pain? Tell me what to do for you." she pleads anxiously.

"Be still, Maggie, just be still a minute. Let me rest a minute. Thought I was gone, there for a while. I must've passed out. Terrible pain. Worst I ever had. I could use a sip of water. Tongue's kind of thick." James struggled weakly to raise his head. Martha held a glass of water to his lips. He took a swallow, then closing his eyes, James murmured, "Tired, so tired. Need sleep."

Looking up at Matthew, Martha motioned him towards the door. Relieved at being dismissed, he went out without saying a word. As he turned towards his own room, the door opened quietly behind him.

"Matthew, James is not as strong as he makes himself out to be, you know. Please try not to rile him. His heart is mighty weak. I thought sure he was gone tonight. If anything happens to him, I sure would be glad for you to stay here with me and the girls, at least until you marry."

Hearing his "Mama" express her feelings to him creates a conflict in Matthew's mind. He really wants to believe she wants him because she cares for him. Then, he is reminded of all the work that is expected of him, the harsh words spoken, the feeling of only being tolerated, and not loved by all this family. The softness that had touched his heart evaporated in an instant and his response was abrupt.

"I'll decide on that when the time comes." Turning away, he went on to his room. Martha is touched by a pang of regret as she goes back to see about James. Matthew has done practically everything that needed to be done around the place since James' health had declined. Now, facing the prospect of a future without either him or her husband, she knows a moment of fear. She must begin to think about how she will manage, should the unthinkable become reality.

James is sleeping, it seems. Still nervous about him, Martha lays down on her bed, positioning herself so she has a clear view of her husband. Seeing the rise and fall of his chest as he breathes, she finally drops off into an uneasy sleep, awakening off and on throughout the night.

After he left Aunt Martha in the hallway, Matthew had gone thankfully to bed. 'What else could happen,' he thought. 'What if Uncle James had really been dead? How would I feel about it? Would I be sorry?' the question hung in the air, demanding an answer. Matthew dared not answer himself, for he remembered his uncle's white, still face when he thought he was dead. At the moment, he had been numb, scared, not really thinking of how James's death would affect him. Now, searching his heart, he realized his true feelings. He could never wish his uncle dead. He could only wish that he could have loved him. Almost asleep, Matt is startled by a faint sound, seemingly coming from underneath the bed. He rose up on an elbow to hear better. There IS something under the bed! Lying flat, hanging his upper body over the edge of the bed, he peers into the darkness beneath. He can barely make out two white spots.

"Tippy!" he whispers in astonishment. "What are you doing under there? Aunt Martha will skin you alive, you silly dog. You know you're not allowed in the house."

Hearing his voice, a small black dog, sliding on his stomach, tail thumping on the wood floor, appeared at the edge of the bed.

"Come here, Tippy, boy," Matt whispered, scooping the little dog up into the bed. "Settle down, now, go to sleep," he cautioned the excited dog, who now eagerly licks his face. Then, scooting under the covers, snuggling against Matt's knees, he is still. Smiling, Matthew is finally able to sleep.

It is still dark the next morning when Matt hears Aunt Martha calling his name. Struggling up through a fog of sleep, he realizes someone is knocking on his door. "Come in," he calls and is amazed when his aunt sails into the room, a steaming cup of coffee in her hand.

"Matthew, I know we're all tired this morning, but I brought you coffee because I need to talk to you privately before the girls get up."

Martha's hair is freshly combed, and her dress neat as always. Only the dark circles under her eyes and the determined set of her lips belie her calm exterior.

"I want to caution you not to say anything about James's attack to Katherine, Annie, or Millie. I intend to speak with May, myself as soon as I see her. I don't want them having an attack of nerves, making matters worse for everybody." Martha paused, swallowed hard, as though dreading what she must say next, and then plunged right in, as is her customary manner. "I'm asking you to help James as much as you possibly can. I realize you already do more than most boys your age, but Wiley has never offered to give us any help in your raising. Having no sons, we've come to depend on you more than I guess we should, seeing as how we're not your true parents. We've always looked at you as the son we never had. What I'm trying to say, and having a hard time saying it right out, is, hold your tongue around James and don't provoke him into losing his temper. He may not live through another attack such as the one he had last night. God spared his life, that's all I can say. Perhaps, to give him time to get right with his maker before he does go. Hopefully, he will make good use of the time he's been given. If you appreciate anything that we've done for you, since you were an infant, I'm asking you to go along with me on this."

Matthew is silent for so long, that Martha grows impatient, waiting for a response from him. This is possibly the longest conversation she has ever had with him in all the years he has lived in her home. Most of the communication between them has been superficial, to say the least. She has given him orders and instructions and berated him for his acts of disobedience. Many times, she has provoked James into whipping him with her complaints about some small indiscretion not worthy of such severe punishment.

"Do I have a choice?" he finally asks.

Somewhat taken aback by his response, Martha is for once at a loss for words. Seeing her confusion, Matthew relents.

"Don't worry, Mama. I'll help you." At his words, Martha felt a lifting of the burden that had been on her all night. She quickly rises and leaves the room, lest Matthew see her emotion.

Calling over her shoulder to him, "Breakfast is ready," she returned to the kitchen.

Matthew finished his coffee, and then quickly dressed. About to leave the room, he remembers Tippy hiding under the covers from Aunt Martha. Grinning, he drags the culprit out of the bed, whispering conspiratorially into his ear.

"Tippy, you stay under the bed and be very quiet. I'll come back and get you as soon as everyone is out of the way."

Licking Matt's face in reply, Tippy squirms excitedly. Sticking him up under the bed, Matt goes out, closing the door tightly. The smell of frying ham fills the room, along with the aroma of baking biscuits. With his stomach growling in response, Matt headed for the back porch to wash up. Returning, he stops in surprise, for there is Uncle James in his usual place at the table. Very white and drawn, seeming to have shrunk overnight, he nevertheless has managed to make it to the kitchen. Seeing Matthew, he spoke quickly.

"Well, boy, I never could stand to eat in the bed. I've always said that's for women and weaklings, not for real men."

In spite of his brave words, Matthew notices how weak James's voice sounds. Remembering his promise to Aunt Martha, he only nods his head in agreement. "You feel better?" Matthew asks, almost as an afterthought.

"Feel like death warmed over. That's how I feel. Thought I would feel better if I got out of bed, but I'm not so sure. You know what to do today. Just remember, I'll be checking up on you. As soon as you finish breakfast, the cows are waiting to be milked. Then, get to your other chores."

James applied a generous amount of homemade butter to a hot biscuit and began to eat.

Matthew feels the anger tie his stomach in knots as his uncle talks. Same old mean way of talking to him. Nothing changed. Not even almost dying last night could soften him. Well, promise or no promise, he wouldn't be here much longer. "I've paid for my keep in hard work," he says to himself. "I don't owe them a thing. Let Katherine and the other girls do the work if he can't do it. Then they'll get a taste of what I've been doing all my life." Keeping his eyes on his plate, Matthew cannot enjoy the delicious breakfast for the rebellious thoughts filling his mind. Anxious to escape from the house, he finishes quickly, gathers up the milking pails, and goes to the barn.

Watching the warm milk foam into the pail, Matt leaned his head against old Sadie's lean flank. There's something comforting that makes him feel happy when milking, early in the morning with the sun coming up all slow. The cow smell of the barn, the foamy milk rising as his strong brown fingers expertly draws down on the long teats of the familiar old cow calms his mind. This morning, though, his thoughts are too black to be affected by the familiar ritual of the milking. Turning Sadie out so her calf can finish off the milk, he repeats the procedure with Daisy, being careful to watch her hind leg. She loves to kick the bucket over when it's about half full, so there's no restful leaning against her side while milking. She only tolerates the milking as long as her feed lasts. Matthew has learned to time himself so they both finish at the same time, thereby avoiding a fight with her. Opening the lot gate, he watches the calf rush to its mother and greedily begin to nurse. Then, a brimming bucket in each hand, he heads for the house, walking slowly, so as not to spill the milk.

Entering the kitchen, finding it empty, he grabbed a biscuit from the plate and quickly went out again. Making a wide circle, so as to avoid being seen from any of the windows of the house, Matt crossed the field behind the barn and entered the woods. Nearing the creek, he walked very slowly and quietly, for this is where Firefly bolted and ran home last night. He would have felt better about returning here with Uncle James but since the events of the night, he figures it will be quite some time before his uncle will be able to walk this far.

Listening for any unusual sound, he begins to examine the soft earth around the creek. Yes, here are Firefly's hoof prints. Here's where she whirled around, almost causing him to fall off, and then, these deep prints are where she galloped back up the trail, at full speed. His heart beating in excitement, Matthew goes further into the undergrowth, looking for any sign that a large animal had been there recently. Going down on his knees, moving the pine straw aside, he examined the ground, and then crossed the creek, careful to watch where he steps.

"Oh, my gosh!" Matthew dropped down on one knee, hardly believing his eyes. There it is. The biggest cat print he has ever seen. Not that he has seen very many, but this one is really big. Gripped by a fearful fascination at being so close to something totally wild, he followed the prints along the creek, then up into the woods leading away from the trail. The track is plainly visible as long as the cat had remained in the open, but soon, he loses it totally, as it takes to the denser growth of bushes, briars, and honeysuckle vines. Standing, finally, Matthew looks all around, as far as he can see. Evidently, the big cat had come down to the creek to drink. It may have already been gone when he got there last night. He knew just the scent of the big animal would have been enough to send Firefly into terror.

Promising himself to look for the big cat another day, Matt loped down the trail towards home and his chores.

In spite of his brash talk, James has been forced to return to his bed after eating only a few bites of breakfast. Even with the persistent pain in his leg, he dropped off to sleep.

Annie was making her bed and straightening up her room in preparation for the day. Noticing movement through the window, she saw Matthew sneaking towards the house from the woods leading to the creek.

"What's he up to now?" she wondered. "Probably doing something he's not supposed to be doing, as usual."

Annie, out of all the girls of Martha and James has the most sympathy for Matthew. Being a straightforward person, she readily admits to herself the partiality of her parents' treatment towards them, especially Millie. Lacking the courage to ever speak out in his defense, she does, however, treat him as a real brother. Annie is always kind to him, for she senses the hurt inflicted on him as a young boy from the circumstances that brought him to live with them. Now, hoping he's not getting himself into another punishable situation with her Daddy, she says a quick prayer before leaving the room.

Martha looked up as Annie came into the kitchen. "Good morning, Mama. How are you this morning?" Annie greeted her mother, and then poured herself a cup of coffee before sitting down across from her at the big oak table.

"I'm well, Annie. A little tired. I didn't sleep well last night." Looking at her Mother, Annie notices how drawn and weary she looks.

"Mama! What's wrong?" she exclaimed, immediately concerned. Then, "Where's Daddy? Has something happened? Don't try to spare me. I'm not a child."

Reaching across the table, Annie grasped her Mama's arm. She is astonished to see tears shining in Martha's eyes. Very seldom has Annie ever seen her Mother cry. Sometimes, when they had attended revival meetings, or at a funeral, but never like now, for some unknown reason. She feels a touch of real fear, now, sure that something bad has happened and her Mother is trying to keep it from her.

"Annie, Annie, calm down. I wasn't going to tell you girls, because I didn't want you to worry unnecessarily. Seeing as how I've given myself away with these foolish tears, I'll have to tell you straight out. Your daddy had a bad spell with his heart last night. I thought we had lost him. I called for help and Matthew heard me and came. There wasn't much we could do, except pray. He's resting this morning. Looks rather the worse for wear and lack of sleep, as I know I do, too, but at least he's alive. Now, don't go fussing over him. You know he won't like that. Try to keep Millie from knowing how bad he really is. I don't want him to get upset about anything. He may not come through another such spell."

Martha got up from the table and began to bustle about the kitchen.

"Katherine and Millie will be in for breakfast soon. I had planned a trip into town this morning, but I'm nervous about leaving James.

School will be starting and Millie needs shoes and material for a couple of new dresses. I don't know what to do."

Annie thought for a moment. "I could take Millie and Katherine could go along with us. I can handle the wagon, I think. Would you trust me with the buggy?"

Annie knows how particular her parents are about the buggy. Not especially fancy, but the nicest means of transportation they had ever had, it had been purchased at great sacrifice for her Mother as a gift from her Daddy on their thirtieth wedding anniversary. No one other than Mama ever drove the buggy. Now, Annie waited for a response to her question.

"Let me give it some thought," Martha finally answers. "We'll see what Millie wants to do. I'm going to look in on your daddy. Breakfast is in the warming oven."

Left alone, Annie poured herself another cup of coffee and wandered into the front room of the sprawling old house. Through the years, rooms had been added as needed. Now, though finished roughly, the house is spacious and sturdy. Small luxuries have been added to make it more comfortable. Annie's favorite room, the parlor is also the nicest room in the house. Overstuffed chairs and a comfortable sofa are arranged around a low mahogany table. Crocheted doilies abound, along with small figurines and keepsakes. Lace curtains cover the windows and a large flower-patterned rug softens the bare boards of the pine floor. An old rocking chair, with well-worn cushions, sits beside the empty fireplace. It is here Annie seats herself. Taking the family Bible onto her lap, she turned to the record of marriages, births, and deaths. Some of the entries are barely legible, faded from time and much handling. As she runs her fingers down the pages, touching each name as though touching the person represented there, the past comes alive in her mind. Some are well known to her, some strangers.

Her expression becomes dreamy as she looks into the past. There's her grandmother, Louisa Eliza, in her crisp, white apron, neat black hair coiled atop her head in a crown of shiny braids, bustling about the kitchen, rolling out pie crust. Grandmother Louisa, with her strong faith in God and her own stout body, was always humming under her breath as she worked or rocked a fretful baby in this old rocking chair.

As her finger moves along the page, Annie hears the voice of Grandy, her big, boisterous grandfather, who filled the house with his robust presence. She felt his big hairy arms against her face as she sat on his lap in this chair, the creaking of the runners lulling her to sleep as a little girl. A feeling of loss steals over her and tears puddle in her eyes as she recalls the love of these two special people, now gone forever from her life. Will she ever see them again, hear their voices speaking loving words, and feel the touch of gentle hands upon her face? "Oh, Jesus, will I once again be caught in a strong bear hug by Grandy?"She whispered.

If this Bible is true and the faith of her grandmother and mother real, her grandparents are not lost to her forever, only until she passes from this life and into the heavenly city described in God's word. Smiling through her tears, Annie hugged the big Bible close to her chest as she rocked back and forth in her grandmother's old rocking chair. "I wonder if Mama will let me have it when I marry," she muses to herself.

Hearing her sisters talking in the kitchen, Annie laid the Bible aside. With a resigned sigh, she returned to the kitchen.

"Good morning, Katherine, Millie. Looks as though your plans for the day will be changed," she informed them immediately. "What do you mean?" Katherine snapped. "Mama is taking us into town today"

"She sure is" Millie adds. "In fact, where is Mama, anyway? I'm hungry."

Annie laughed out loud at her sisters. "I wish you two could hear yourselves. You sound like spoiled brats instead of grown women. Do you ever think of anything other than satisfying yourselves? Do you even care to know why a change of plan is necessary? Suppose someone died or became sick suddenly. Would you two still insist on carrying out your plans?"

Annie looked from one to the other of her sisters, her face stern.

"Oh, Annie, you make me tired with your preaching. You're not our Mother." Katherine replies quickly. Then, as a thought seems to occur to her, she asks, "Is Mama sick?"

"Why didn't you say so right off, Annie, instead of beating around the bush? If Mama's sick, maybe she'll let us go by ourselves." Katherine interjected.

Millie's brown eyes lit up excitedly at the prospect of going off on her own. About to enter her last year of school, she is anxious to assert her independence. A really pretty sixteen-year-old, she has an eye for the young men and the feeling is mutual on their part.

"You never did say, Annie, whether Mama's sick, or what's going on that she has changed her mind about going to town, Katherine said.

Katherine has filled her plate and now sits down to eat. She looked inquiringly at Annie, waiting for her answer. Just then, the door opened with a bang and Matthew came into the kitchen. Three pairs of eyes turn his way, momentarily distracted by the interruption.

"What are ya'll staring at me for?" he asked with a frown. He stared back at each of the girls in turn. "What will they accuse me of doing now?" He wondered. Uncomfortable at their silence, he ignored them, picked up a biscuit and began to butter it.

"What are you doing in here, Matthew? Don't you have work to do?" Millie sounded just like her mother, Matthew realized.

"I've been working. I was working when you were still in the bed. I don't answer to you, anyway." Matthew replied quickly, giving Millie a black look.

"You need to go do your chores. You don't need to be sitting around listening to our talk. We have things to discuss that are none of your business."Katherine gave Matthew a stern look, hoping to intimidate him into leaving them alone.

"Matt, you don't have to listen to Millie and Katherine. We were only talking about the trip into town. Nothing secret about that, for sure." Annie saw the rejection on his face.

Entering the kitchen just at that moment, Martha heard the last words. "What secret are you talking about?" she asked.

"There is no secret, Mama." Annie replied. "What have you decided to do about the shopping trip?"

"You girls may go in the buggy. I've discussed it with James. We feel all of you are responsible adults. You do need to get going as soon as possible so that you will be able to get back before dark. We certainly don't want any more excitement any time soon." she paused, suddenly aware she has said too much, as Millie and Katherine look inquiringly at her. "Your Daddy has had a spell with his heart. He's resting up, but I need to be here in case he needs me today. He's rather weak, still, but I believe he'll recover his strength in a few days. He just needs to take it easy for a while. Now, you girls quit dallying around here, wasting time, and get yourselves ready to go. Matthew, I plan to make some soup for James. Run out to the garden. Gather me up some onions. There should be enough green beans and okra ready to pick. Just get the small pods of okra, now. See if there are a few tomatoes left on the vines, too."

Martha issued orders right and left, as she began clearing the breakfast table remains away, hoping to bring normality back to the day.

Knowing better than to argue, her daughters left the kitchen quickly. Matthew took his biscuit and went out the door towards the garden. Crossing the yard, he looked towards the pasture. Firefly raised her head and nickered, then started toward him. The sun turned her dark bay coat to red. He hurried on to the garden, for a daring plan has suddenly occurred to him. Picking beans with nimble fingers, his mind raced as fast as his hands. Snatching the okra, he goes on to the tomato vines, gathering what remains of the season's fruit. His heart beats faster as he quickly finishes and forces himself to walk back to give the vegetables to Aunt Martha. He can't let her suspect anything. If she thinks he has nothing to do, she'll come up with something to keep him busy the rest of the day. Then, he won't be able to carry out his plans, which don't include any more work.

"Here are the vegetables, Mama. I'm going down to check the fence in the back of the pasture. Uncle James told me to do it. I've cleaned the barn, like he said."

Matthew hopes she doesn't remember all the chores Uncle James has assigned to him.

"That's fine, Matthew. You go on. Take one of those fried pies in case you get hungry before you get back." Preoccupied with her own thoughts, Martha offers no objections.

Delighted to be free, Matthew is quick to exit the house and hurries out to the pasture. With a sharp whistle, he summons Firefly. Suddenly, he dashes into the smokehouse, where he cuts himself a generous piece of smoked beef. This, along with the fruit tart, a piece of bread, and a ripe tomato, would have to do him a long time. He has decided on a daring escapade, one that could very well be his undoing, even end his life. Knowing his uncle is sick and Aunt Martha is occupied with concern for him, Matt realizes this is the perfect time to take advantage of the situation to pursue adventure on his own. Astride his mare, his small store of food slung around his neck, he trots Firefly out of view of the house, and then gallops headlong across the pasture. At that moment, a big, ugly black dog, lying under the house in a hole he has dug for himself to escape the heat, raises his head. As though considering his options, he slowly crawls out from his cool retreat. He stands for several minutes, watching the horse gallop away. The boy had not called him. An instinct tugged at him. With a low, imperceptible sound deep in his chest, the black dog streaked out of the yard and across the pasture, following the horse, now out of sight.

After seeing Katherine, Annie, and Millie off, Martha busied herself preparing the soup she hoped would be appealing to James. She could not help but worry about him, in spite of her brave talk to the girls. When the soup was bubbling fragrantly on the stove, she peeped in on her husband. Seeing his eyes closed and his even breathing, she quietly withdrew. Going into Annie's room, she lay across the bed, feeling suddenly very tired.

The sun made its way across the sky and then began its westward descent. Annie, Katherine, and Millie, their buggy loaded with purchases, talked companionably as they neared home in the early afternoon. Their day had been pleasant, in spite of getting off to a bad start. Millie, excited over her new shoes and the prospect of new dresses, was in a very good mood. As they rolled up to the front porch, she jumped down and rushed into the house, eager to show her Mother what she had bought. Not finding Martha in the kitchen, wondering, she looked out the back door into the yard. Then, not wanting to disturb her daddy, she didn't call out but went from room to room. Finally, opening Annie's door, she is surprised to see Martha sound asleep, lying across the bed.

"Mama? Are you all right Mama?" Millie called softly. Coming slowly awake, Martha looks surprised to see Millie. "I thought you were gone into town, Millie," she said.

"Mama! Wake up! We've already been to town and we're back. It's four in the afternoon." Millie replies impatiently. "I want to show you what I bought to make my dresses."

"My goodness! I must have slept a long time. Let me go check on the soup. I need a cup of coffee. Come into the kitchen with me and I'll see what you bought."

Martha slid off the bed and led the way into the kitchen. Annie and Katherine are already there. Annie has put the coffee on and set the soup aside. She now ladled some into a bowl and sliced thick slices of homemade bread. Seating herself, she bowed her head briefly, and then began to eat.

"I'm sorry, girls, Mama, but I'm absolutely starving." she apologized, as she took the first bite.

"I'll have some of that, too." Katherine also helped herself and sat down at the table. "This is delicious, Mama," she smiled at Martha, savoring the first bite of the soup.

As Millie spreads out her material and tries on her new shoes, Martha sipped her coffee gratefully, feeling much refreshed after her long nap.

"Well, girls, you did very well without me. I'm so glad you made it home before dark. By the way, have you seen Matthew? He went back in the pasture to do some work on the fence and I don't know if he's gotten back yet."

Going to the window, she looked across the yard and into the pasture, half expecting to see Matt riding up. It'll soon be dark and the cows will need to be milked. Why does he pull these stunts, over and over, when he knows his duty, she cannot understand. Sighing, Martha finished her coffee. She then prepared a tray for her husband, wondering if he might feel like coming to the table. She turned to Annie.

"Annie, go ask your daddy if he wants me to bring his tray to the bedroom, or if he is able to come sit at the table."

When Annie tapped on the door of her parents' room, she heard her daddy's low response.

"Daddy, are you feeling well enough to come to the table?" she asked.

"Well, girl, I sure will try. This room is looking mighty close, after being in here all day." James's voice sounds much stronger and he begins to prepare to rise from the bed. This is a procedure, due to his bad leg.

"Can I help you, Daddy?" Annie feels helpless as she watches her daddy struggle.

"If you'll take hold of this infernal leg and swing it around, I can make it. Guess I'll have to start sleeping sitting up. Seems like I get stiffer by the day." James replies, irritably. Finally, with Annie's assistance, James makes it to the kitchen, where he drops heavily into the chair held for him by Martha. Setting the soup and bread before him, Martha bowed her head, asking for a blessing on the food. Then, seating herself, she, too begins to eat. "Daddy, are you feeling better today?" Millie's tone is concerned.

"I'll make it, I guess. Wasn't so sure last night, though. Don't know what brought on such a spell. I never have felt quite that bad before." James spoke slowly.

"It's probably that Matthew, aggravating you all the time. Not doing what he's supposed to do." Millie suggests, ignoring Annie's kick under the table.

"By the way, where is Matthew? It's about milking time, isn't it?" James glanced out the window as he spoke.

Everyone is silent, afraid to answer him, knowing what his response will be. Looking around the table, James' eyes rest on his wife. "Well? Martha, what are you keeping from me? What's the boy done now?"

"James, I don't know that he's done anything, yet. He just hasn't returned from checking the fence in the back pasture. He left on Firefly before dinner today." Martha's reply is an attempt to mollify her husband and delay a reaction that would be harmful to him.

"Well, you and the girls will have to see to the milking. If you have plenty of milk, just let the calves have it tonight. I don't feel up to it myself.

He'll come dragging in with some wild story, I'm sure."

James' attitude is surprising, to say the least. The girls are not pleased that they will have to do Matthew's job, especially Millie.

"Daddy, I don't want to fool with the cows. Let Annie and Katherine do it. They don't need me, anyway." Millie said You're right, Millie," Annie replied, rather sarcastically, for her. "Katherine and I can manage perfectly well without you. You would just get in the way. Come on, Katherine. Let's get it done before it gets too dark to see in the barn."

Giving Millie a scathing look, Katherine followed Annie out the door.

"That Millie! She's so afraid she'll have to do a little work. She's a spoiled brat!" Katherine angrily expressed her feelings once outside the house.

"I agree wholeheartedly, but right now, we need to try and keep Daddy calm. What he doesn't know won't hurt him. All we have to do is let the calves in with the cows. We won't feed them tonight, just let them graze. I'm sure Matt will be home to do the milking tomorrow."

Annie's voice is conciliatory; for she knows her sister has a bad temper and is not afraid to say what she thinks, regardless of the consequences.

Left alone with her parents, Millie is a little ashamed of her outburst, especially after her Mother had asked them to do nothing to upset her daddy. Her jealousy of Matthew overcame her desire to obey her mother. She enjoys getting him in hot water with her daddy and seeing him punished. Through the years, when they were both younger, they had a brother/sister relationship. However, as Millie grew up, being two years older than Matthew, he became a source of constant irritation to her. She did not care to share her parents with him and consistently tattled every small act of a mischievous boy to them. Needless to say, over the years, he has developed a deep animosity towards her. He never misses an opportunity to play a prank on her, thereby bringing more punishment down on himself. Now, rising from the supper table, Millie gathered up her purchases and retired to the room she shares with Katherine, leaving her parents alone.

"James, do you think something could have happened to Matt?" Martha nervously questions her husband.

"Probably not, he's pretty tough, you know," James replied.

Getting up with difficulty, he went to the back door and out onto the porch, gazing out into the distance.

A thought has been nagging at him ever since he discovered Matthew had not returned. Remembering the boy's excitement over the prospect of checking out the possibility of tracks by the creek, he is faced with the fear that Matt has gone off on his own, trailing some animal. Giving a low whistle, he summons the big black dog they have raised from a puppy. With the unlikely name of Black Beauty, given him by Millie, the dog is an excellent tracker. Making up his mind, James whistles again, wondering why the dog doesn't come crawling out from under the house. He looked around the area surrounding the house and outbuildings, and then whistled again. No big black dog appeared in response to his whistles.

"Well, I guess the dog has either followed him or is off hunting on his own." James said to Martha when he returned to the kitchen. Feeling helpless, he sat down at the table. Martha has cleared away the supper dishes and now sits at the table, the big family Bible open before her. Glancing up at James, she notices the distracted look. Immediately, she realizes he is beginning to worry about Matthew's continued absence. Meeting her eyes, he said, "Do you think we might have a sip of coffee? We may be facing a long night." Needing something to occupy her hands and mind, Martha quickly goes to prepare coffee, adding a few sticks of fresh wood to the stove.

At the very moment his family was having supper, Matthew was miles away, getting hungrier by the minute. After leaving the house, he had taken a little used trail that led away from the settled areas and into the denser wooded hills. He had never been this far alone before. Excited at being off on his own, he urged Firefly into a fast trot, until the terrain became too rough for speed. Then, sure he was on the trail of the big cat, he finally dismounted and led the mare through the thickets of briars and vines, until finally coming out into the open, where the land began to rise and fewer trees grew. Astride Firefly again, he carefully made his way farther and farther into unfamiliar territory.

After several hours of going up and down hills, he noticed the sun was starting to move towards the horizon. Realizing how hungry he was, he dismounted and led the mare under a big outcropping of rock, which afforded some shade.

Taking out his sack of food, he quickly made short work of finishing it off. Firefly found a few sprigs of grass growing among the rocks. Matthew felt a little breeze move across his face. Laying back, his head pillowed on his arms, he closed his eyes. Without meaning to, he fell asleep. Firefly continued to crop the sparse grass, moving farther and farther away from Matthew.

A short distance from where he slept and Firefly grazed, a natural formation of rock had created a shallow cave. Over the years, underground water, continuously flowing, had gradually worn away the solid rock. At different times, the cave had harbored many occupants. Indians had camped overnight here, sheltered from the elements, on their way to somewhere else. A lone man, running from his past, had roasted a rabbit over the coals of his fire, and then moved on. More recently, a large cat had sought refuge here in its cool depths, moving about the territory of its hunting ground late in the evening. Standing at the mouth of the cave, her yellow eyes narrow slits in her black face, she surveys her kingdom. The same breeze blowing across Matthew's face brings his scent to the keen nostrils of the panther, as she sniffs the air. Not accustomed to the smell of humans, curiosity more than anything else causes her to cautiously make her way toward this different smell. Sleek and black, she is awesomely beautiful. Powerful muscles ripple beneath the skin with each step of the padded feet. The sinking sun cast shadows over the ground as she moves in and out of the shade, moving down the hill, towards the unusual smell. The scent becomes overpowering, then mixes with another smell, that she recognizes instantly. Coming out upon a slight ridge, there below her she sees the source of the smell that has drawn her. A motionless figure lies on the ground. A short distance away, a slender mare crops grass. Sinking to her belly, tail switching slowly, the big cat watches the scene below with narrowed eyes.

The wind has been blowing away from Matthew and Firefly. Suddenly, with a swirl of dust, the breeze changes direction. With a startled cry, the mare's head came up, her ears pricked, and her eyes began to roll in fear. She called shrilly to the sleeping boy. Instantly awake, Matthew jumped to his feet, looking wildly around for whatever has spooked the mare. Calling to her in as calm a voice as he can manage, he walked slowly towards her. Now prancing around nervously, Firefly pawed the ground. Then, she raised her head, looked straight up the ridge, and screamed a warning. Afraid that at any moment, she may bolt and leave him afoot, Matthew grabbed the hanging reins and threw himself on her back. He is almost unseated when she whirls, then does a repeat of the action by the creek. In an instant, she is off, hooves striking against the rocky soil, as she flees for her life. As before, Matthew can only cling to the mare, praying she won't stumble and pitch them both headlong down the hill.

Finally, losing the scent of the big cat, the mare allows him to bring her to a trot, then a walk. Sweat covers her sleek body and her sides are heaving. She begins to calm down. Matthew is shaking like a leaf in a strong wind. Sliding off the mare, holding tightly to the reins, he finds his legs won't hold him up, they're trembling so much. Sinking to the ground, he just sits there, trying to recover from his frightening experience. His terror, he feels, is justified, for just before Firefly took off in her wild gallop, he, too had looked up at the ridge. His eyes had met the narrowed yellow eyes of the biggest, blackest wild cat he ever hoped to see. Suddenly struck by the thought that it could be on his trail right now, he forced his legs into a standing position. Leaning against Firefly's wet side, he looked back in the direction of their mad flight. Reassured by the emptiness of the land, he remounted his horse. Noticing the sun barely above the horizon, he felt a touch of nervousness at being caught out here with darkness approaching. Realizing he had somehow lost his bearings, he could not tell which direction he should go. He could not retrace his path through the hills, for that would bring him back into the big cat's territory. He would have to make a wide circle, hoping to find something familiar eventually, to point him in the right direction.

"Firefly, do you know how to get home?" At the sound of his voice, the mare pricked her ears, swinging her head around in his direction. Then, dipping her head up and down, as though to say "yes," she whinnied, looking towards the East. Matthew, too, looked in that direction. Surprised, he looked again, thinking he must be mistaken. Something black is coming towards them. For a moment, fear gripped him again, then since Firefly didn't show any fear, he knew it couldn't be the cat. The speck got larger. Suddenly, letting out a loud whoop, Matthew kicked the mare, urging her forward to meet the black animal, moving towards them, now running, too. Throwing himself to the ground, he is knocked flat by Black Beauty. As he grabbed the neck of the dog, Matthew felt a rough tongue licking his face. Feeling weak with relief, he laid his face against the big dog and almost cried. Then, astride his horse once more, following the big dog, they struck out for home.

When darkness fell and still there was no arrival of Matthew, James, and Martha had decided to wait until morning and if Matthew had not returned, they would seek Duncan's help the next morning. Wondering why May and her husband had not come to visit as they usually did, the moment he returned home, they determined to ride over there as soon as daylight showed in the sky. Meanwhile, they both lay down, thinking to get a little sleep before facing whatever lay ahead.

"Martha, Black Beauty is gone, too. I have a feeling he followed Matthew."

James knows Martha is severely agitated over the boy's absence and tries to make her feel better.

"But James, where could he be that he couldn't get back? You know he's afraid of the dark. What could cause him to stay away like this? You know he wouldn't go to Wiley's and stay without our knowing. We'll have to go down there and get him and the boys to help us look, if Matt doesn't show up by morning." Martha is searching for a reason for Matt's prolonged absence, but finding no easy answer.

James keeps silent about the incident at the creek, for were he to relate this to his wife, she would become hysterical, for sure, knowing

Matthew was trailing some kind of wild animal, with no weapon of any kind.

Finally, with a prayer for Matthew's safe return, Martha dropped off into an uneasy sleep.

James, having slept quite a bit during the day, lies awake as the minutes tick away.

"What if something has happened to the boy?" he questions himself. "Have I been too hard on him? No, No, he needs a strong hand. I can't afford to be soft. If he were truly my own son, would I treat him the same way?"

James will not answer this question, even to himself. Even in the midnight hours, even though Matthew may be hurt, or even dead. He still cannot let such an answer plague his conscience. Better to leave it unanswered. Dozing off and on throughout the night, James drops into a deep sleep towards dawn, just about the time Martha is waking up.

Slipping quietly from the room, she built a fire in the stove and put the coffee on to boil. Standing at the window, she searched the horizon with anxious eyes. Fear grips her for there is still no sign of a small boy on a bay mare. With a sigh, she poured a cup of the freshly brewed coffee. Walking out onto the porch, Martha feels a lightening of the worry that has plagued her since last night. The sun is coming up, the night is over. The sky is streaked with color. A fresh, cool breeze speaks of fall days ahead. Closing her eyes for a moment, Martha sends a petition to God.

"Please, God, bring him back safe." Seating herself in an old rocking chair, she sipped her coffee, enjoying the peace of the morning.

A few miles away, his head resting on the big black dog, Matthew sleeps the sleep of the young and tired. Nearby, Firefly lies dozing, her head bobbing. Darkness had overtaken the trio last night. Not knowing how far he still had to go, Matthew had sought shelter underneath the low-hanging branches of a small live oak tree. Gathering up pine straw and fallen leaves, making a bed for himself and Black Beauty, he fell asleep, feeling safe with the dog and his horse nearby.

A rustling in the leaves awakened Matthew a little after daylight. Raising his head, realizing where he is, he looked in the direction of the sound. Grinning sleepily, he sees a possum, rummaging around the base of a tree. At the sound, Black Beauty raised his head, giving a sharp bark. Jumping up, he dashes at the possum, who takes off at a fast waddle. All this commotion causes Firefly to spring to her feet. Fully awake, Matthew is anxious to get home, for his stomach is in knots, partly from hunger and partly from fear of the welcome awaiting him. Calling the dog, and then jumping astride the mare, he moved out of the trees, still trusting the dog to lead him home. Black Beauty returns, having treed the possum.

"Let's go home, boy, come on, now." Matthew's tone is commanding and the dog obeys. With his nose to the ground, he follows his own trail through the woods and soon, the cornfield of their nearest neighbor is visible. Realizing he is still a long way from home, Matthew urges Firefly into a fast trot, covering the distance between the homesteads in a short while.

Racing ahead, the black dog arrived first, barking furiously at the back door. Rushing out onto the porch, the whole family is standing there, when Matthew rides up. He seems a bit startled to see them all. His eyes are anxious, knowing he's in trouble again. Steeling himself for the whipping he knows will follow his escapade, he nevertheless is not sorry he went. He will tell this story of his adventure to his brothers, he decides, anticipating their astonishment. Facing Martha and James, he slid off the mare, too proud to ask for understanding.

"Matthew! Where have you been? We've been so worried. You've put us through some kind of night. What do you mean, going off like that without a word?"

Martha's questions are fast and furious. Her anger hides her relief and thankfulness that he has returned unharmed. She thinks of putting her arms around him, but refrains herself, feeling he would not like it. Seeing his streaked face and dirty clothes, she ordered him to clean up before coming into the house.

"Breakfast is ready, Matthew. Wash up, then you can tell us all about where you've been." Turning, she went inside.

The girls, seeming to have nothing to say either go back inside also. Only Annie, catching Matt's eye, gives him a smile and a quick wink.

Encouraged by James's silence, Matthew takes the bar of lye soap and the bucket of water to the wooden trough behind the partition on the back porch. Stripping off his clothes, he lathered himself from head to toe with the strong-smelling soap, and then doused himself with the cold water. Aunt Martha has thrown fresh clothes over the top of the partition and a rough cotton towel, which he uses to rub himself dry. Clean and anxious to get to breakfast, he comes out from his bath only to find Uncle James waiting for him, seated in the rocking chair by the door.

"Did you find the cat, boy?" James' voice is low and confidential. Putting a finger to his lips, he nods towards the kitchen.

"You should have seen it, Uncle James.! It was big and black, with yellow eyes. It was lying up there, just watching me and Firefly. If she hadn't warned me, I might have been eaten up by now."

So relieved that his uncle is not angry, Matthew's words tumble over each other as he shares his news with him.

"You know you have just about worried Meg to death, don't you? I ought to give you the whipping of your life, just for that. The only reason I'm letting you by is that I can't afford to get my dander up about things right now. I would have done the same thing when I was a boy. You wouldn't be worth much if you didn't have a little daredevil in you. Now, let's figure out what we can tell Meg and the girls. We sure can't tell them the truth. They'll be afraid to go outside the house."

As Matthew listened closely to his uncle, he could hardly believe his ears. Maybe it was a good thing that Uncle James almost died. Maybe when people almost die, they try to do better. "I sure do hope so." he thought. "I sure hope Uncle James is different."

Later, having eaten a huge breakfast, Matthew resumed his chores, the first being to milk the cows. Coming from the barn with the fresh milk, he saw Duncan's wagon sitting at the gate. Delighted at the prospect of relating his adventure to the receptive ears of the three boys, he hurried into the house.

The kitchen is noisy and full of people, all trying to talk at once.

As soon as Matthew enters the door, he is smothered by all three of the little boys, who have been anxiously waiting for him.

"We want to ride Firefly, Matt. Can we ride now, please?" Jeremy has him around the legs so tight; he can't even take a step.

Laughing, Matthew scoops him up, first handing the milk to Aunt Martha, who rescued it just in time. With the baby in his arms, the other two trailing behind, he goes back outside, taking them to ride the mare.

*****

After an hour of circling the yard and corral, slowly, so as not to unseat the excited trio of small boys, Matthew tried to coax them off the mare's back. Sammy, the youngest, barely two, kicked and began to scream, chubby legs trying to cling to Firefly's back.

"One more time, Matt, just take us around one more time," Johnny pleads.

"Yeah, Matt, just one more time," Jeremy adds his plea to his brother's. His big brown eyes begged Matthew.

"Okay, Okay, everybody simmer down, now. Once more, then let Matt have a rest. You boys could ride all day." Duncan walked out to the fence rail. Matthew turned with a grin. Then, he led Firefly around once more, with three happy little boys laughing with glee. Finally, with promises of sugar cookies and milk, Duncan and Matthew persuade the boys to relinquish their seats on the mare's back. As they walk across the backyard toward the porch, Duncan's voice is low and confidential. "What's this James is telling me about a big cat hanging around?" he questions. "Man, if May knows about that, she won't let the boys out of the house, for sure."

"Well, Uncle James wanted to keep it between us, you know. He figured Aunt Martha and the girls would be awfully nervous, too, if they knew. The only thing, though, if they don't know and he does happen to come back down to the creek, one of them could run into him unprepared.

Course, I kind of doubt that happening, seeing as how none of them venture out late in the evening. I think it had already moved out when I was taking May's milk. Firefly smelled it because it had been down to the creek. I'm telling you, Duncan, it's some kind of a big thing. Coal black, yellow eyes just glowing. There I was, just sleeping. The next thing I knew, there it was, looking right at me. Thanks to Firefly, I got out of there in a hurry."

Engrossed in relating his adventure to Duncan, Matthew failed to realize the two oldest boys are listening, wide-eyed, their mouths hanging open in fearful excitement. Reaching the back porch, Duncan sat down in the rocking chair, Sammy on his knees. Dropping down onto the step, Matthew continued his tale of adventure with the panther.

"You see, I followed its tracks away from the creek as far as I could. Then, I lost them in the thicket. I figured he had taken to the higher ground, so the first chance I got, I struck out on Firefly to try to get a glimpse of him. I went farther than I realized and couldn't make it back before dark. Would you believe that Black Beauty trailed me and Firefly and caught up with us just when I decided I was lost? I spent the night in the woods, bedded down on the ground with him and Firefly. It wasn't too bad, either. If I had just had more food, I could have stayed out there a lot longer." Matthew paused for breath.

Duncan looked at him a little strangely at hearing his last words. "Why would you want to stay out there by yourself, Matt? Is there anything you want to talk about, just man to man, you know, between you and me?" his voice is kind, inviting confidence.

Just about to share his feelings with Duncan, the door opened and May stepped out onto the porch. With a smile, she joined her husband and Matthew. Feeling the tension, she raised an eye brow questioningly. "How about some coffee, honey? She asked Duncan, laying her arm affectionately on his shoulder. "And how about some cookies and milk for you cowboys?" she adds to the three little boys.

Scrambling quickly to the door, the trio ran into the kitchen, not needing a second invitation for a treat. Laughing, May turned to Matthew.

"Well Matt, how are things going for you, lately?" she asked "If you run out of something to do, you can always come and keep those boys occupied." she teased, good-naturedly.

Annie joined them on the porch, a tray in her hand holding cups of coffee, which she offers to

Duncan and May. Setting the tray down, and taking a cup for herself, she dropped down on the edge of the porch, leaning her back against a post. "I can feel a touch of fall in the air today," she remarks, as they all sip their coffee contentedly.

"Yes, it won't be long we'll need a fire in the mornings." May agreed. "We intend to have plenty of firewood laid aside this year. We almost froze last winter. With the snow so unexpected, we used up all we had early in the winter. If it hadn't been for you, Matthew, I couldn't have made it." she smiled at him, but he only nodded his head.

"I plan to get quite a lot of wood cut next week," Duncan looked at Matthew. "Think you might give me a little help, Matt?"

"You'll have to talk to Uncle James, Duncan. He keeps me busy with all the chores around here. I imagine I'll be cutting wood for these fireplaces from now all through the winter. You know he doesn't do much anymore." Matthew's tone is resentful.

"Matthew, you know Daddy has that bad leg, and now Mama told me about him almost dying. It's no more than right for you to take over the work, seeing as how he's given you a home." May said sternly in defense of James.

At her words, Matthew jumped up from the porch abruptly. As they stared after him in surprise, he went all the way across the yard, into the pasture and jumped astride his horse. Without a backward glance, he galloped off towards the woods.

May looked at Annie and Duncan in confusion, speechless for a moment.

"What in the world has come over him?" she asked no one in particular. Duncan only shrugged his shoulders and said nothing. Annie kept her thoughts to herself, wondering if May saw what she glimpsed in the dark depths of Matthew's eyes before he left.

The door burst open and Jeremy and Johnny ran out onto the porch. Stopping in surprise, they looked across the yard, expecting to see Matthew and Firefly. Disappointed, turning to May, they began to tug on her hands, urging her out into the yard.

"We want Matthew to ride us some more, Mama." Jeremy pleads.

"Yeah, Mama," Johnny repeats his brother's words. "We want Matthew and Firefly."

"Boys, I'm sorry, but you'll have to find something else to do. Matt is gone."

"Where did he go, Daddy?" Jeremy asked Duncan, putting his arm around his neck.

"I don't know, son. He'll be back later, I'm sure. Then, he'll ride you boys some more." Duncan reassured the small boys. "Why don't we go down to the creek and all of you can splash around in the water awhile? What do you think of that idea? Summer's about gone and this will probably be the last time you can play in the water. Mama and Annie may want to go with us." he looked questioningly at his wife and sister-in-law.

"Oh, no," May quickly responds. "I have them all the time. It's your turn. Take Sammy, too. He's big enough to go with you. I'm going to enjoy this."

"Well, boys, you heard your Mama. It looks like it's just us men. Where's Sammy?" He asked.

"I'll get him." Jeremy quickly answers and goes inside the house to find his baby brother. He returned in a few minutes, with Sammy in tow, a cookie in each hand.

"My goodness, Sam. Are you still eating cookies? You're liable to pop wide open, you know, eating so many." May exclaimed.

At his Mama's words, Sammy looked a little concerned. Pulling up his shirt, he examined his fat little stomach. "No pop," he said in relief.

When the adults burst into laughter, he grinned happily, pulling up his shirt again, he repeated "No pop." Then, delighted at the response his antics have caused, he does a little dance, whirling around, repeating, "No pop, no pop."

Duncan swung his baby up astride his shoulders, gave May and Annie a wink, and walked off toward the creek. Jeremy and Johnny followed on his heels, along with Black Beauty, awakened by all the noise.

Watching her family from the porch, May heaved a sigh of relief. "Oh, how wonderful to have a little while away from them all." She said, as she turned to Annie. "Okay, what's going on with Matthew?" She demanded.

When Annie doesn't answer immediately, May frowned impatiently. "Well? Are you going to answer me, or do I need to ask Mama?"

Quickly, then, Annie replied, "For heaven's sake, May, don't go asking Mama anything. She has enough to worry about. There's nothing wrong with Matthew that hasn't always been wrong. He's a motherless boy who feels like a motherless boy in spite of the presence of all the women in this house. You can take up for Daddy, that's your privilege, but he's always been too hard on Matt. Oh, you can shake your head all you want, May, but you know what I'm saying is true. I really dread to see what lies ahead when he gets big enough to stand up to Daddy." Annie's eyes are full of concern as she continues. "He has such a little bit of childhood left to him. I wonder if he will hate us all or forgive us for not sending him to live with his Daddy when he got old enough. That has always bothered me. I can still see the look on his face the day Uncle Wiley came for him. Why Millie cried, I'll never know. She makes his life miserable. I think, and this is just my thinking, not anything that I'm positive about. But, there's darkness, emptiness in Matthew. He may not be aware of it himself. What he will do to try and dispel that darkness and fill that emptiness when he is able to name it will likely bring him more pain than he's already suffered."

May stared at Annie, shocked by what she has heard from her sister. Resisting the truth of Annie's words, she never the less, knows, deep inside her soul, that all she has said is true. Now she understands the look Matthew gave her before he so suddenly left earlier. A prick of real fear had touched her when she looked into his dark eyes.

What she saw there did not belong to the sweet baby boy who had been raised in this house, loved by them all. An involuntary shudder passed over her body as she tried to put a name to her feelings. Looking at her sister in dismay, she saw the same response in Annie's eyes, as she slowly shook her head.

Chapter 2

Matthew galloped full speed across the pasture, leaving Duncan, Annie, and May staring after him. Reaching the back of the pasture, wild in his rage, he pushes the little mare straight at the fence. She has never been ridden like he is riding her now. Always, he has treated her with love and she has given him all she possessed of loyalty and love in return. Now, he is seemingly expecting more than she can possibly give.

The fence loomed closer and closer. There is no turning back, now. Matthew's heart feels a stab of regret. What is he doing to his mare? Too late to change course, he feels her muscles knotting beneath him. Making himself as light as he possibly can, he lifts up, up, and up, willing her to rise above the top rail. Valiantly, she responds to the urgency in his legs and voice. Leaving the ground in a heroic effort, the little mare rises, higher and higher, and then, they're airborne for a few glorious seconds. Wonder of wonders, her forelegs hit the ground on the other side of the fence. "She did it! We made the jump!" He cried

"Yahoo! Good girl!" Matthew's yell of triumph echoed across the fields. But, he is trembling from head to toe, as he pulls Firefly down to a walk. Sick with relief, he can hardly keep himself from falling off her back as he guides her to his destination.

Deep in the woods, Matthew slid off the mare and stood for a moment. This is his secret place. The chirping of the birds and the sound of the creek flowing over the rocks and tree branches never fails to soothe his troubled mind.

"You're a beauty, Firefly. You flew, didn't you girl? I was sure scared there, for a little while, but you pulled it off."

Talking low, he stroked her neck and sleek little head, between her eyes, down to her velvety lips. Seeming to understand his emotion, she nibbles at his face carefully; blowing her warm breath, she butts him playfully with her head. Giving her one last rub down the deep crease of her rump, he looped the reins around a low bush and left her to eat the lush grass growing near the creek.

Carefully making his way down the steep bank, he walked across the fallen tree to the other side, where he suddenly disappeared, seemingly into the bank of the creek. Under the huge roots of the tree is a small cave that Matthew has enlarged by digging it out a little at a time.

He quickly recovered the oilskin pouch holding his fire-making implements. Gathering up dry leaves and pine straw, forming a little hollow, he prepared to build a fire, using the same method his Indian ancestors used for generations. Patiently, he worked, until he is rewarded by a puff of smoke, then a tiny flicker of flame. Feeding the feeble glow with the dried leaves until it begins to burn brightly, he gradually adds twigs, then small sticks, and finally some larger branches he has stored in the back recesses of the cave.

Leaving the fire, he went to the very back of the small space. Underneath a pile of twigs and leaves, moss and pine boughs, he dug carefully in the soft dirt. He lifted out a small metal box. Listening intently for a moment, he hears nothing but the murmuring of the creek outside the cave entrance. Sitting cross-legged beside the fire, he opened the box, peering at the contents. A single coin, a feather, and wrapped in cloth, an object, which he removes carefully, almost reverently.

Holding the small oval stone in the palm of his hand, he gazed intently at it for several seconds. Then, closing his hand tightly for a moment, he feels the coolness against his hot skin. Upon the wall of the cave, the flickering light creates shapes and images. He sees a raven-haired, slender Indian princess with tender, smiling lips. Beside her is a proud, hawk-nosed chieftain, stern and solemn. Closing his eyes, Matt hears the beat of many feet as the flames seem to leap higher against the cave walls. There are the warriors, in war paint and feathers, dancing as they surround the fire. The longing to know his people overwhelms him as his heart beats in time with the drums. His body swayed from side to side. He stared fixedly beyond the walls of the cave imagining the past from which he came.

Suddenly, a face appeared at the entrance of the cave. "Matt! Matt! What are you doing in there?" An astonished voice exclaimed.

Startled out of his trance, Matt turned to see his brother's scared eyes staring at him. "I'm remembering, Rob, just remembering, that's all. It's nothing to be afraid about. I like to come here, think about our Mother. Makes me feel less like an orphan, I guess, to think about her people, wherever they might be, as my people, too. Do you ever think like that, Robbie?" He looked earnestly at Rob, his words, soft, hopeful, begging for understanding.

"Aw, Matt, what good can it do? She's gone. Gone forever." Seeing the disappointment on Matt's face, he adds quickly, "I used to think about her a lot, too, you know. When she first went, I cried so much, I got sick. Then, one day, Aunt Martha told me to stop crying and start living like she would want me to live. Told me she was in Heaven and I could be with her again someday if I lived by the same Book she lived by. I'm trying to do that, but sometimes I wonder if anybody can be as good as that Book says we should be. I really want to see our Mother again, though, so I have to keep trying. I think about Rance, too, you know, whether he's with her. I hope so. I sure do want to see him again. I wish he never would a' took that dare. Old' dumb Rance, always taking dares, trying to be better at everything than everybody else. Who would expect anyone to swim that lake anyway? I would a' never thought he was a coward if he couldn't have done it. Would you have thought bad of him, Matt, if he had not taken the dare?"

Looking at Robert, Matt sees his eyes redden. Not wanting to embarrass his brother by noticing his tears, he looked away, slowly shaking his head.

"Heck, Rob, I would a' never thought nothing bad about Rance. He had to prove nothing to me. I know he was the bravest brother any boy could have. If he was here, I bet you I could live with him. Uncle James wouldn't be using his old walking cane on me. Yeah, I know Rance would take care of that walking cane, real fast. He could fight, run, swim, shoot, and track anything better than anyone. I wish he had listened to Paw and not gone swimming that day."

Matthew stared into the fire, saying nothing, and then looked at Robbie.

"Robbie, what are you doing here, anyway? How did you know I was here?" He asked.

"Paw and Becky and I rode over to visit ya'll. Robbie replied. "You had lit out like a wild bronco. I figured something must have riled you up, for you to take off like that. I just naturally knew this is where you would end up."

Robert's eyes filled with affection, waiting, but not requiring an explanation of his sudden departure from the house. He knows about the whippings Uncle James administers and has great sympathy for Matt's plight. Now that he is practically a grown man, he has questioned his Pa's reasons for leaving Matt with Uncle James. He could understand his Pa giving an infant into the care of a woman when their mother died, but now that Matthew is big enough to care for himself, he can see no reason for the continued separation from his real family. He and Matthew, he remembers, when both were very young, spent a lot of time together. Matthew had slipped off many times from Aunt Martha and run through the field to his Daddy's house. He had gotten many whippings for these excursions, but the times the brothers had spent together seemed worth the consequences he had suffered. Not willing to leave his brother alone, he got to his feet.

"Matt, whatcha say we go back to the house. Aunt Martha was cooking some mighty good-smelling food. I hate to miss out on that. I ain't complaining 'bout Becky's cooking, 'cause she does pretty good, but boy, can Aunt Martha turn out some delicious goods." He suggested, with a grin. "My stomach is already growling, just thinking about it."

He watched as Matthew replaced the contents of the metal box without a word. He then went to the back of the cave, carefully hiding his treasure under the pile of leaves and moss. *What does he have in that box that is such a secret?* Robbie wondered. *Well, if Matt wanted him to know, he would tell him, sooner or later. Must be something really important, though, for him to hide it so carefully.*

Matthew returned to the fire and put dirt on the flames, quenching them quickly. Looking around once more, he nodded to his brother.

"I guess I'm bout ready for some food, too. Let's go," he said, leading the way out of the cave, across the tree trunk, back to the waiting horses.

As they mounted up, Matt began to fill Rob in on all that has happened since they were last together. As they rode slowly back, Rob listened in amazement to the tale of the panther, from the bolting of Firefly by the creek to the escapade up into the hills.

"I wish you had come and got me, Matt. I would a loved to go with you, hunting' that cat. Man that was something! You saw him looking at you?" Rob asked again.

"Sure did, just before I galloped off. I looked straight at him. Biggest, blackest, scariest cat I ever saw."

Matthew's dark eyes sparkled with satisfaction at the respect he hears in Robbie's voice. Now, he wishes he had thought to ask his brother to go with him. It would have been good to have had company.

"Next time I go off, I'll come by and get you, Robbie," he promised, as they neared the house.

Taking the bridle off Firefly, Matthew rubbed her down, gave her fresh water and then he and Rob quickly headed for the dinner table, hoping there's plenty of food left.

The big table in the kitchen is full of people, eating and talking. Some have moved out onto the front porch, taking their plates, sitting in the porch swing, in the rockers, on the steps, wherever they can find a place. Matthew and Robbie quickly filled their plates and after waving a hello to his Pa and Becky, Matt joined his brother on the porch.

After eating in silence for several minutes, Robbie paused long enough to ask Matthew a question. "You planning on going back to school this year, Matt?"

"I might not. I sure get tired of hearing all that stuff that doesn't seem to be much use to me. You know, like history and all the people, dead so long. What's the use in knowing about a lot of dead people, I want to know." Matt replied.

"Well, Matt, you ought to try to learn how to figure and write well. You never know what you might be able to do when you become a man. Why, you might want to go to another territory. What if you have kids of your own and need to teach them yourself? Yeah, it's good for a man to know how to figure and write." Robbie concluded.

"I can figure and write already, Robbie. I want to be on my own, someday." Matthew leaned close and lowered his voice in confidence.

"Why don't you come on down and live with us? What's stopping you, anyway?" Rob asked.

Surprised by the question, Matthew thinks for a moment. What IS stopping him from leaving Uncle James and Aunt Martha? Would they try to make him come back if he did just go? Would his Pa even allow him to move in with him? Seeing his thoughtful expression, Rob waited patiently for an answer.

"Why don't you talk to Pa, Matt? If he were to tell Uncle James he wants you to come home, there wouldn't be anything he could say, would there?"

Rob pressed Matt for an answer. Watching his brother closely, Rob saw excitement light up his eyes when he finally answers him.

"You're right, Robbie. What could Uncle James say if Pa told me to come live with him? He's my real Daddy. He could take me away from here if he just says the word. Yeah, who could stop him?" Matthew's voice is intense in his longing for such a thing to happen. "Would you talk to Pa for me?"

"Sure, Matt, I'll talk to him as soon as we get back home today. Don't worry little brother. I know he'd be glad to have you. He probably just feels he owes Uncle James and Aunt Martha, seeing as how they've provided for you all these years. Course, as I see it, you've paid for your keep with all the work you do around here." Robbie added.

Elated at the prospect of going to live with his brothers, Matt grinned in genuine happiness. For the first time in a long time, he sees a way out for himself.

"I sure have, Robbie. I don't owe them anything." he quickly agrees. "How about a piece of hickory nut cake?" Matt asked, getting up from the steps.

"Sounds mighty good to me. Haven't had any since the last time we ate here. Wish Becky would get Aunt Martha's recipe." Robbie followed Matt into the house.

Later that evening, having milked the cows so Duncan and May could take some of the still-warm milk home with them, Matthew waved goodbye to the three boys and their parents with something akin to relief. Aunt Martha and Uncle James, along with Annie, Katherine, and Millie lined the porch as the wagon rolled down the road, all waving and calling goodbyes. The last sight they saw was little Sammy, blowing kisses until the wagon turned the corner at the end of the road. Heaving a sigh of relief, Martha sank into the porch swing, wiping her face with her apron.

"I enjoy company, but this has been a long day," she said. "I think everyone enjoyed the dinner. I know there's very little left. Maybe enough for a light supper," she added, looking at the girls. "You girls can fix your daddy a plate if he wants anything. I'm going to rest. I think my feet are swollen from standing all day in the kitchen."

"Mama, we have eaten all day. I don't need anything more." Annie answered. "Daddy, do you want me to fix you something now?" she asked, turning to James.

"No, if I get hungry before bedtime I'll eat some bread and milk," he replied. "I'm going to lie down myself, get off this leg. It's paining me something fierce." James limped across the porch and into the house.

Seeing Matthew sitting on the steps, Martha asked, "Have you gotten me some firewood for the cook stove, Matthew? What about the chickens? Are they shut up in the chicken house? You need to get your work done before you sit around."

At the scolding tone in her voice, Matthew got up abruptly, without replying. His expression, though, spoke volumes, as he walked quickly away around the corner of the house. *"Can't stand for me to sit down for a minute, always fussing at me. Well, just a little longer and I won't be around for her to order to work. Let Miss Prissy Millie bring in the firewood."* He told himself.

Matthew felt the same old blackness fill his mind as he closed the latch across the door of the henhouse. Does Mama hate him? Is that why she is seemingly angry or irritated with him so much? He knows that much of his problem with Aunt Martha is just downright contrariness on his part. But, as far back as he can remember, hard words have been his lot. In turn, he has purposely, for some reason he doesn't understand, done things that brought her anger down on him. Her constant complaining to Uncle James has provoked action from him, which without her prodding would never have taken place. As he thinks of the severe beatings administrated to him, even as a small boy, his fist clench and he feels such anger, he just wants to hit something. *Do all children get whipped so hard? He wonders. I'll soon be big enough to leave Uncle James. Is there really a Heavenly Father somewhere that cares about me?* "If you care about me, God why did you let my mother leave me alone?" He looked up into the sky of endless space, waiting, but no voice answered his questions.

Gathering an armload of small sticks and short stove wood, he stacked it neatly next to the wood stove in the kitchen, ready for Martha's use the next morning. Going back outside, he drew a bucket of water from the well and carried it, too into the house, setting it on the table. Standing for a moment, in the kitchen, Matthew felt undecided as to what he should do next. Slightly hungry, he crumpled a left-over piece of cornbread into a bowl, and then poured milk on top of it. Going onto the back porch, finding it empty, he sat down in the old rocker and began to eat the bread and milk. Black Beauty, sprawled in the dirt beside the steps raised his head expectantly. Having received a pile of scraps from the big dinner earlier in the day, he really doesn't care whether Matt throws him a crumb or not. Seeing nothing is coming his way, he laid his head on his paws again and dozed contentedly.

"I wonder if Robbie has talked to Pa yet about me going to live with them?" he wonders out loud. At the thought, excitement fills him again. Hopefully, Robbie will come tomorrow, giving him the good news. Oh, it's got to happen; it's just got to happen!" Anticipating the moment of his departure and the surprised reaction of everyone in this house, Matthew rocks gently back and forth, a little smile of satisfaction tugging at the corners of his mouth.

Sometime during the night, the weather changed. A cool front moved in, bringing first a lightning storm, then a drop in the temperature. The whole countryside received a drenching rain, which was welcomed as a blessing after the hot summer. Everyone awoke to the sound of rain dripping off the eaves of the house and much cooler temperatures.

Snuggled under the covers, with Tippy beside him, Matthew awoke with a feeling of expectancy. Hugging the little dog in glee, an unusual happiness rose up in his heart and he found himself grinning uncontrollably. This could be the day! His last day in this room, in this house! So caught up is he in the thought of leaving, Matthew has not even considered that there is anything he would miss when he walks away from uncle James's house. Suddenly, hugging the squirming little body of his dog, an unpleasant thought hit him. He just took it for granted that Tippy would go with him. Tippy had been given to him, a little runt from a large litter, by his Aunt Wilhelmina and Uncle Buck, who lived a day and a half ride away across the river. He would certainly be taking his dog and horse with him, Matthew vowed, as he got out of bed, shivering a little in the unusually cool room.

School would be starting soon and so far, he had no shoes. Aunt Martha had made him two shirts, but his pants from last year were above his ankles. He would just as soon go barefoot all year round, but sometimes the weather got mighty cold and wet. If he went to his Pa's before school began, he might not have to go at all. With this thought in mind, he finished dressing, then, barefoot, as usual, went into the kitchen. The kitchen is warm and inviting on this cool morning, the heat from the wood stove taking the chill from the air. Martha bustled about, from stove to table, preparing breakfast for the family, as usual.

"Well, Matthew, looks like fall has come in sudden like after all the hot days we've had lately." She placed a plate of flapjacks, eggs, and fried potatoes before him, as he sat down at the table.

"Feels good in here. Wonder if this cool snap will last till school starts." He replied, taking a bite of his food.

"Matt, you know better than to eat without giving thanks. You could show a little appreciation for the food being provided." Aunt Martha scolded.

At her words, he paused, his fork halfway to his mouth, as she asks the Lord to bless the food. With her eyes closed, she failed to see that he neither closed his eyes nor bowed his head as she prayed. Unaware of this, with a hearty "Amen", Martha sat down across from him and began to eat her own breakfast.

"You'll have to get started mighty soon on the wood cutting, Matthew. If this cool weather holds, we could have some really cold weather early this year. School's about to start and you won't have as much spare time as you've gotten used to this summer. You need to get the ax sharpened as soon as this rain quits, take the wagon and old Bill to the woods." Martha gave him his orders, as he finished his breakfast in silence.

They looked up as Uncle James came into the kitchen. "How about some coffee, Meg? It will be mighty welcome this morning. There's a little chill in the air. I guess winter is right around the corner." He said, rubbing his hands together. He went to stand before the stove, warming himself.

As Martha started to rise, he motioned her back into her chair and poured himself a cup from the pot on the stove, then dropped heavily into a chair, grimacing in pain.

"I might need another quilt on my bed tonight if this cool spell holds. This leg seems to be worse in the cold."

Regarding him anxiously, Martha went to the stove, dished up a plate for him, placed it on the table, and then reseated herself to finish her own breakfast.

"Well, Matthew, school is about to start again. I hope you intend to do better this term than you did last year. You know what to expect if I get a bad report on you. I hear a woman teacher will be boarding with the Walkers and riding to school with their children. We don't want you mean boys scaring her off before the term is out." James's voice is stern, demanding Matthew's attention.

"I've been thinking that I don't need no more schooling," his voice low, Matthew doesn't look at James, waiting for the reaction to his words.

"Your thinking doesn't matter, boy. Are you hearing me?" James face flushed with anger. Looking at the half-grown boy he has lived with since he was brought into his home as a baby, he raised his voice in rage at his rebellion against his authority. "You'll do as I say. You're eating' my food, living on my charity. Your thinking don't amount to a hill of beans in this house. Do I make myself clear?" Matthew's silence seemed to infuriate James even further and his voice has grown louder with each word.

Suddenly, unexpectedly, Matthew jumped to his feet, overturning his chair, which crashed to the floor behind him. With clenched fists, he faced his uncle, daring him to raise his hand against him. Knowing himself close to losing control, he only wants to escape from James, before he commits an irrevocable act against him.

"You make yourself clear." the words are forced past his lips, and his eyes are smoldering pools of blackness in his flushed face.

"You ungrateful whelp! You don't appreciate anything that's been done for you all these years. Shame on you for talking like that to your uncle." Martha's voice rose shrilly, adding to the tension mounting in the room.

"Martha, fetch my strap. Seems to me I need to make myself real clear to Matthew just who is in charge here." James told her. He looked straight into Matt's angry eyes. "Down on your knees, boy. Let's see how tough you really are." he commands.

Instead of obeying James, Matthew ran to the door, jerked it open and left the room. He jumped off the porch and into the yard. As Martha and James watched in helpless anger, they saw him disappear into the darkness of the barn. Looking at each other, they see their own thoughts mirrored in the eyes of the other. What should be done about this boy, so close to becoming a man? James feels his control over him slipping away with each confrontation. Martha knows sudden fear, realizing that up to now Matthew has allowed her to whip him, that at any time, he could easily overpower her and possibly do her injury.

All of this, James sees in her face, but will not allow her to know his own similar feelings. The door, standing open, gives them a clear view of the barn and the yard. The scene appears as a painting in a frame, except the figure of the boy mounted on the bay mare is not a figure painted on a canvas. With legs gripping the sleek body, his head lying close to her mane, he is one with her, as they move quickly out of the frame and out of view of those watching.

The figures in the kitchen are still, frozen in time and the tension of the moment. The warm, comfortable room has the feeling of unresolved anger, violence barely avoided, and human emotions allowed to get out of control. James and Martha, each feeling justified in their treatment of the boy they have raised, are unaware that the angry young man that faced them down this morning is their own creation. Even now, perhaps, the course of events could be altered. With the right words, wrongs may be set right, offenses forgiven, and relationships set on a different plane. The two people who could make a difference in the future of all involved, have no such thoughts, as they finally turn from the open door.

Unaware that anyone else had witnessed the violent scene in the kitchen, James and Martha are startled to see their youngest daughter standing transfixed in the doorway to the kitchen. For once, Millie is speechless. Confusion, disbelief, and anger all vie for dominance in her expression, as she faces her parents.

"Are you going to let him get away with that?" she finally gets out the words, demanding an explanation from them.

"Now, Millie, this is none of your concern. Leave Matthew to me. I can handle him." James's tone is reassuring, more confident than he feels at the moment. "He'll have to come back, sooner or later. I'll be waiting for him, you can be sure of that."

"Well, I sure hope so. He needs a good whipping. Talking like that to you and Mama. He's gotten too big for his britches, lately. He's mean too. No telling what all he has done that we don't even know about," She finished ominously; delighted to see Matthew in trouble with her parents again.

Going to the stove to get a cup of coffee, she smiled to herself in satisfaction, her back turned away from the two at the table. "Where do you think he ran off to?" she asks, seating herself across from her mother, sipping the strong coffee.

"Probably off to his hideout in the woods. I know he has a place somewhere out there. Just where it is, I don't know. Since I can't ride anymore, it's hard for me to go past the yard." James replied to Millie's question.

"I can find out, Daddy, if you want me to. I'll find him and make him come back and take the whipping he deserves." Millie eagerly offers her help in bringing Matthew to face up to her daddy and the strap.

"Millie, do you really think you can make Matthew do anything he doesn't want to do?" Martha laughed nervously, still upset by all that has taken place.

"No, Millie, you leave Matthew alone. You'll only make matters worse." the words came from Annie, who has heard the last of the conversation, as she walked down the hall from her room. Everyone turned at her words, her father a little irritated at her show of authority.

"I'm not listening to you, Annie," Millie is quick to put her in her place. "I only listen to Mama and Daddy."

"Oh my, aren't we the good little girl? What's this all about?" Katherine's voice interrupted the conversation as she went to the stove for her morning coffee. "Are we having a family gathering this morning? Why didn't someone let me know sooner? What have I missed?" her tone is slightly mocking, as she faced her family, her eyebrows raised questioningly.

Martha and James look from one to the other, wondering just how much of the morning's events they need to reveal. Deciding to keep most of the situation to themselves, James puts an end to the bickering. "Matthew and I have had a little difference of opinion. It's none of your concern, any of you. Now, let's have our breakfast and get busy on the chores."

At his words, Martha began to dish up the food, as Annie stood and silently gathered up eating utensils, placing them on the table. Glancing at Millie, as she set the table, Annie received a glare in return. Unperturbed by her sister's bad temper, Annie smiled serenely back at her, only making Millie angrier. Unconcerned, Annie finished her task, and then seated herself, as Martha asked the blessing over the food.

About a mile away, Matthew sat beside the creek, Firefly nearby. Helpless fury, robbed of an object upon which it can be vented, boils like bile in his throat. Physical nausea overpowers him and he heaved convulsively, throwing up his breakfast. Then, disgusted at himself, he stumbled down to the creek, bathing his burning face in the cool, running stream. Kneeling in the damp sand, oblivious of everything except the pain in his heart, his mind is void of clear thought or purpose. Quenching his aching thirst in the crystal waters, he finds a shady spot on the grassy bank and throws himself down, face up, his upraised arm shielding his eyes.

Suddenly, he feels velvety lips move across his arm and a soft breath blows across his face. Removing his arm,

Matthew looked into the gentle, concerned eyes of his mare. Big and luminous, he sees himself reflected in their depths. Reaching up with both arms, he grasps her mane. The desolation that is threatening to choke him finally overpowers his restraint. He feels the dam break within his soul and for the first time since he was a small boy, racking sobs break forth from his clenched lips. Laying there, his hands entangled in the mane of his patient friend, he is overcome by the emotions so long held at bay by his determination to let no one see his feelings.

The violence of his weeping frightens the birds to halt their twittering and singing. There is no human for miles around. There is no sympathetic ear to hear his weeping. Finally, his eyes swollen and burning, his chest hurting from the effort, he lies spent, drained of strength. Closing his eyes against the light, relaxing his hold on the mare, he dropped off into a weary sleep, blessed oblivion from unanswered questions.

Firefly, standing beside the sleeping figure, dropped to her knees, then stretched out, with all four legs thrown out beside her, head lying on the ground. The breeze stirred the tree tops, and then moved gently across the still figures. The birds, inquisitively, move closer. A few feet away, the creek flows silently through the open places, then splashes and talks to itself as it moves over the rocks and pieces of half-rotten logs lying in its path.

The breeze takes on substance and form, becoming visible to the human eye. A tall, handsome man stands near Matthew, looking down on him. Firefly senses his presence, for she raises her head, and then sits up, gazing at the stranger. She makes no sound, for something prevents her alarm. She only watches in silence. Then, the air is filled with motion and suddenly, there are many others, similar to the first man. They form a circle around the boy and the mare and the beauty of their faces shines as the first light after a dark night. A rush of power emanates from their bodies as the first man stands silently beside the sleeping boy. The beauty of his face is unearthly, as he gazes on Matthew. Compassion and love flow from him upon the prostrate form.

Reaching out with a tenderness surpassing that of a mother, he touched his head. Opening his eyes sleepily, Matthew sees a shadowy form kneeling over him. He feels no fear, as he gazes into the most loving eyes he has ever seen. The face above him is perfect, unbelievably beautiful. The lips curve in a reassuring smile, and then the figure rises and joins the others. Turning his head slightly, Matthew's eyes blinked in astonishment. All around the grassy bank, he sees beautiful beings, their faces shining. Unable to believe his eyes, he rubbed his face vigorously, and then looked again. He can no longer see the men. He must have been dreaming.

The creek flows serenely between its banks, and the birds are singing again. A wonderful feeling of peace has filled Matthew's heart. Suddenly, he knows what he must do. He must go back and face Uncle James. He doesn't want to, but for some reason, he knows that this is the best thing for him to do. He will probably get a terrible beating, but, that's the chance he'll have to take. Leading Firefly down to the water, the two of them drank thirstily. He sprang onto Firefly's back and , rode up the slope away from the creek. Just as he reached the stand of trees where the woods began, he turned suddenly and looked back at the spot where he and Firefly had lain only a few minutes ago.

Something had brought him up short, causing him to pull her to a sudden halt. A whisper. What did it mean? Who said it? Just a phrase, floating through his mind. Something about angels. His mind was filled with the scene he had just witnessed. He urged Firefly forward, as the cool fall breeze moved through the tops of the trees, setting them in motion again.

The little mare trotted briskly towards home, knowing the way, even without the guidance of the reins. Matthew paid little attention to his surroundings, beginning to question his decision to face Uncle James.

"I could go to Pa's, just for a while, until things simmer down," he reasons to himself, as each moment takes him closer to a confrontation with James's anger. "I don't even know why I'm going back. I hadn't planned to go back." he talks out loud, as Firefly's ears prick, thinking he's talking to her.

Making a decision, he jerked on the reins, turning the mare off the trail they are following and guiding her into the woods. After a short walk through the undergrowth, they emerged at the edge of a field, across which he sees a chimney. Maybe he wouldn't have to face Uncle James, after all.

"I'll stop by and see Robbie. Maybe he's already talked to Pa. Maybe I can just stay with them and I won't ever have to go back." He decided.

Resolutely, Matthew guided the mare across the field, now stripped of the corn, which has been picked by his daddy and brothers. The mare's dainty hooves sink into the wet earth, made muddy by the recent rain. Finally, they reached the yard of the house. Reining up at the gate, Matthew is greeted by a mongrel of a dog, who rushed out from under the steps, barking and then wagging his tail as he recognized the visitor. Dismounting, he quickly looped the reins over the fence and closed the gate behind him, as the front door opened. "Hello, Pa" Matthew greeted Wiley as he mounted the steps.

"Well, Hello Matthew. What brings you over here in the middle of the day like this? Nothing wrong, I hope." Wiley waited anxiously for Matthew's reply.

Unsure just how to approach his Pa with all that has happened, Matthew dropped silently into one of the old chairs on the porch. Concerned at his silence, Wiley seated himself, figuring Matthew will talk when he gets his thoughts together.

"Pa, do you believe in angels?" The question popped out of Matthew's mouth, surprising him, for that is certainly not what he had planned to say.

Wiley said nothing for a minute, looking at his boy. It's been a while since he really looked at his youngest son. He sees a boy on the brink of manhood, with the potential of being a big man, once he fills out. He sees the dark eyes of his wife looking out from the face of his son. His eyes filled with tears, remembering the beautiful Indian woman who had made him the happiest man on earth. In a gesture as unfamiliar to him as to his son, he stood, and wrapped his arms around Matthew's shoulders. So unexpected is his Pa's embrace, Matthew sat immobile, unable to respond. Wiping his eyes, Wiley returned to his chair.

"Son, you don't remember your mother at all, do you? She had beautiful black hair, just like yours. You have her eyes, too," Wiley concluded.

Shaking his head, he seems to have forgotten Matthew's question, lost in his memories. Unsure how to respond to this mood of his Pa's, Matthew waits for him to recover his composure. His Pa is so different from Uncle James. Slow to anger, more gentle, his Pa is easier to talk with. Once more, Matthew posed his question.

"Pa, I asked you if you believe in angels." he reminded Wiley.

"Matthew, I sure do believe in angels. The Good Book tells all about them, you know. They even have names, some of them. There's Gabriel, he's the one who will blow the trumpet on judgment day. Then, there's Michael, he's the one that fights. Yes, sir, I sure do believe in the Good Book." Wiley assured him.

"Have you ever seen one? What do they look like?" Matthew pursues the subject relentlessly, wanting an answer.

"I can't say as I've ever seen one, myself. I've heard other people tell of seeing them, though. From what I've heard, they have big wings and look like men." Wiley replied, his face showing his curiosity at Matthew's questions.

"Are you sure they look like men, just ordinary men, like you and Uncle James?" Matthew seems a little disappointed at this information. "Well, maybe not just like ordinary men, but, you know, bodies like men." Wiley is silent, searching for an answer, wondering what all this is leading to.

"If I was to tell you, if, now, just supposing," Matthew is very earnest, as he moves closer to his daddy's chair, "what if, I told you I had seen, not just one angel, but a whole bunch of angels, all around me, in a big circle. Would you believe me?" Seeing his daddy's eyes fill with tears again, Matthew stopped in confusion. "Pa, what's wrong? Do you believe me?"

"Son, nothing's wrong. I'm just a man who had a wife who meant more to me than anything. She died, but I know she lives forever in heaven. You were just a tiny baby, so you have no memory of her. I see her, now, lying in that bed, wasting away right before my eyes. I prayed and prayed and trusted God to save her, to let me keep her with me. She held you in the bed with her, right up to the last. Her tears fell on your face, for she was concerned about you being left without her. Martha was good to her, nursing her, and helping.

At this point in his narrative, Wiley stopped, put his head in his hands, slowly shaking it from side to side.

"I didn't know what to do. I couldn't care for a tiny little baby. For days, I couldn't eat or sleep. I walked these woods and fields, searching for answers as to why my wife had to die, leaving my children motherless and me, alone in the prime of my life. Finally, exhausted with grief, one night, I dreamed about her. We stood beside a river. I picked her up in my arms, carried her across the river, set her down on the other side, and then left her there. After that dream, I had peace in my heart. I know that someday, I will see her again and she will be just as beautiful as she was when she left me."

Looking directly into his son's eyes, Wiley continued, "You asked me if I would believe that you saw a whole bunch of angels, all around you, in a circle. Yes, son, I believe you. Your mother used to read her Bible a lot. She knew a lot of the verses by heart, and could just say them, any time, for any occasion. One of the verses she used to pray over you was, *'And He shall give His angels charge over thee.'* Then, she would pray, *"God, send your angels to guard my baby. I won't be there, to watch over him, so you just let your angels be all around him, protect him and help him, as he grows up without me."* Tears streamed down Wiley's face, unchecked, as he is reminded of all he has lost.

Matthew is overwhelmed with conflicting emotions. Never has he seen a man weep like his daddy is weeping now. He has grown up believing it unmanly to cry. Men who cry must surely be weaklings, soft. Now, seeing his daddy weep, knowing what a strong, vigorous man he is, seems to put the lie to this belief. Venturing to reach a hand towards him, he awkwardly patted Wiley on the back, unsure just how to comfort him.

"Pa? Don't cry. I did see them, Pa. Big, tall men. One of them knelt down beside me, right there on the ground. He touched me." Matthew shivered, remembering. "I never saw anybody like that, before. I had a really strange feeling when he touched me. There was something about his eyes I've never seen. They were different." Groping for words, he is at a loss to describe his experience.

At his words, Wiley's tears dried on his cheeks, as he listened attentively. Looking at his boy, something like awe filled his heart. He's heard some tales, through the years. The scriptures are full of humans seeing angels and God sending angels to carry messages. Never has anything like this come so close to him. He does not doubt that Matthew has actually seen what he has related to him. Whether he was dreaming, or awake, Wiley believes the experience to be the direct result of the prayers of his wife over her infant son, knowing she was about to die. Getting up from his chair, he gripped Matthew on his shoulder.

"Son, I believe every word of what you say. It's your mama's prayers. She loved God and was filled with His spirit. Her prayers were for all her children, but especially for you, for she knew she would not be with you as you grew up. Those men you saw were the angels that are always with you, everywhere you go. You can't always see them. Just remember, they are always there. When you get into danger, they will protect you." Wiley released Matthew and returned to his chair, falling silent, deep in thought.

Matthew too is silent, trying to absorb all that has happened to him since he got up this morning. What a strange kind of day it had been, that's for sure. Who would believe him? Well, his Pa does, but his Pa is kind of religious. Everybody would not be so quick to swallow such a tale as he just told. Knowing it to be true, though, Matthew suddenly realizes what an unusual thing has happened to him. Maybe his Pa is right. Awe overcomes him, as he considers the magnitude of the event. Angels, from somewhere way up there. Looking upward, searching the blue, limitless sky, he wonders how far the angels had to travel and how long it had taken them to get to him, there beside the creek. The biggest question, though, that remains unanswered, is why? Why had they chosen today, to come? Why not yesterday, or tomorrow? What is so different about today that a whole bunch of big angels would suddenly show up, all around one boy and a horse? What kind of danger could he have been in that he needed that many angels, all at one time? Unable to answer this, Matthew finally got up from his chair.

"Well, Pa, I guess I'll be seeing you. I just wanted to ask you about them, you know, the angels." Matthew's face is young, and vulnerable, as he starts to leave.

"Wait, son. Are you hungry? It's about dinner time. I've got some mustard greens and Becky has probably got the cornbread made. You need to come in and see her. She'll be hurt if you leave without speaking a word. The boys will be back tomorrow. They've gone off with a load of corn, to get it ground into meal."

Without waiting for an answer, Wiley led the way into the house, expecting Matthew to follow, which he does, gladly. He had been hoping his daddy would offer him something to eat. His stomach had been growling for quite some time. The aroma of freshly baked cornbread filled the house. The moment he crossed the threshold, it brought a response from his empty stomach.

His sister, now twenty-three, bears a striking resemblance to her mother, also. Her black hair is coiled atop her head. Damp from the heat of the stove, her face is very pretty, with high cheekbones and a small, delicate nose. Her eyes are the same color as Matthew's, but smaller, with black brows arching naturally above them.

Turning from the stove, she smiled shyly, her face lighting up at the sight of him. Smiling in return, he pulled up a chair and sat down at the table. Becky is not a very sociable young woman. The death of her mother had left such a huge void in her life that she has never fully recovered from it. A child of eleven at the time, her grief was so deep and the loss of the most important person in her world so horrendous, that her immature mind was unable to cope or deal with it. Her daddy, oblivious to all except his own despair, had failed to give her the explanation and comfort she so desperately needed at the time.

Becky, in her childish mind, knew only that her beautiful, gentle mother was now in a hole in the ground. Nightmares had assaulted her. Horrible scenes played themselves out through night after night of grief, as she wept and moaned in despair. She saw her mother, trying to get out of the wooden box under the ground, clawing and crying, begging her to help her. One night, she had run out of the house in her nightgown, screaming to her mother that she was coming. When Wiley and the boys were awakened by her screams, they had caught up with her, only to find themselves at a loss as to how to deal with her terrible condition. Finally, understanding her incoherent sobs, Wiley had taken his daughter up in his arms and carried her back to the house, his own tears mingling with hers. Sitting in the rocking chair beside the cold hearth, he had held her through the night.

The next morning, white and shaken, he told her that her mother was no longer in the box in which they had laid her when she died. He showed her the Bible; her mother's Bible, the verses about heaven, and read about the streets of gold and the gates of pearl. He told her that now her mother was there, not sick anymore, waiting for all of them to join her someday. Comforted by his words, yet brokenhearted and still motherless, the little girl remained silent and withdrawn much of the time.

She very seldom left the house and had no friends her own age. She did go to school, which she had always loved. Always one of the best students in the school, she excelled in spelling and was the winner in most of the spell-downs. After her mother's death, she continued to excel at school; she just didn't play and have fun like a young child. She began to try to be the mother of the house. Cooking and cleaning and even scolding her brothers and daddy for dirty boots and messy ways, she seemed content with her life. She had wanted to keep Matthew with her, for she loved him to distraction. She had been her mother's right hand when he was born. Then, as her mother grew weaker, she tried to be his mother. Losing her mother, and her baby brother, all in one terrible blow, proved disastrous to the little girl.

Her behavior at times seemed erratic and irrational. Her shyness and way of secluding herself were misconstrued as a mental condition by many of those who did not know the circumstances of her life. Greeting Matthew today, her manner is more open and normal than he has seen her exhibit in a long time. "Matthew, where have you been?" She exclaimed. Before he can reply, she threw her arms around him. Taken by surprise, Matthew is speechless. Becky released him quickly and then turned back to the stove.

"Becky, that smells mighty good to me. I'm hungry as a bear, I know that." Matthew spoke to her back, covering his embarrassment at her show of affection.

Smiling eagerly, his sister set the dishes on the table, then an iron pot containing mustard greens, seasoned with big pieces of cured ham. Then, with a little flourish of pride, she set the cornbread, brown and fragrant, before them. Standing with her hands on her hips, she looked expectantly from one to the other.

Wiley exclaimed, "Girl, you've outdone yourself with this bread. It's just like your mother used to make. Let's pray and get started before it all gets cold." Smiling with satisfaction, Becky bowed her head, along with Matthew, as her daddy prayed a simple prayer of thanks for the food, asking a blessing on her, whose hands have prepared it.

"Matt, I'm mighty glad to see you. I didn't get to talk to you when we visited Uncle James and Aunt Martha." Becky spoke with a soft wistful expression.

Matthew, thoroughly enjoying his food, looked up at her words. Her eyes spoke a longing that he recognized.

"I know, Becky." He replied, sudden compassion for her disturbing his own thoughts. "I'm sorry I haven't been around more."

"Daddy, could I maybe go back with Matthew and visit Annie?" She turned eagerly to Wiley.

"Well, you wouldn't be able to come back by yourself," he reminded her." Supposing you and I both ride back with Matthew and visit awhile this evening. Would that make you happy?" His voice broke with emotion.

Her eyes sparkled with excitement, giving him the answer. Watching her, Matthew felt an emotion he could not name. Regret? Pity? Maybe. Something else.

Something that tugged at his heart, bringing tears to his eyes again.

"My gosh, what a crybaby I've become in one day." he thought. *"What's wrong with me anyway?"*

Not realizing he was staring at his sister, he was unaware of Wiley's eyes resting on him with a strange expression on his face. *"They should be together. They hardly know each other. Brother and sister, growing up in different houses, hardly ever seeing each other. Almost like strangers. Becky might have been better if she had been able to care for Matthew after her mother died. What can be done about it now, he asked himself.*

Becky, anxious to be off to see Annie, seems oblivious to both of them. Suddenly, she turned to Matthew, her eyes shining.

"I love you, Matt."

Enjoying the meal, Matthew's face registered surprise at her unexpected words.

"I love you too, Becky." The sound of his own words sounded foreign to his ears. The realization that he had never thought about his feelings for his sister brought a burning in his chest. Maybe that is the feeling he has for Firefly. Maybe it's the painful longing that grips him some time. Maybe that's how love feels, he remembered with a shock. Maybe it's the way he felt when he looked into the eyes of the man beside the creek. Was it love?

Seeing the happiness on his sister's face, he grinned back at her, and then turned his attention to finishing the good food.

Hearing the dog bark, Martha went to the front door, just as Wiley pulled up in his wagon. Seeing Matthew trailing along behind the wagon, Martha's lips tightened in anger. I guess he thinks Wiley's going to keep him from getting a whipping, she thought. Well, we'll just see what happens.

"Ya'll light down and come on in," she called out to Becky and Wiley. "I'll put the coffee on and let James know you're here."

She totally ignored Matthew, who lagged behind as Becky and his Pa entered the house. Seeing how angry his aunt still appeared, Matthew chose to remain on the front porch, as the door closed on his Pa and Becky. Now what would happen, he wondered. He never had told his Daddy about what had happened this morning. Somehow, he had forgotten about it, while they were eating, then, riding alongside them in the wagon, he really didn't want to bring it up, because of Becky. Now, he had missed his chance to get his daddy on his side before Uncle James and Aunt Martha told their side.

Inside the house, Becky quickly sought out Annie, whom she had always favored over the other girls. In her room, Annie was displaying her quilt top, which she was piecing as part of her hope chest.

James had been lying down but made an appearance when he heard his brother had arrived.

Now, they all sat around the kitchen table, cups of fresh coffee before them. Noticing James's drawn face, Wiley was concerned.

"James, how you doing, you know, since that bad spell you had?" He sure doesn't look too good, Wiley is thinking, waiting for his brother to respond to his question.

"Have to admit, Wiley, haven't been myself for weeks, now. I can't seem to recover. There's still a lot to do around here, too, what with the fall plowing of the pea field, planting the greens for the winter, and all the wood needed to keep the fire going through the cold weather." James looks worried.

"Well, I guess this is not a good time to bring up the subject that's brought me here today, seeing as how your health is bad and all."

Wiley hesitated, undecided whether to go on or wait for a better time.

"What are you trying to say, Wiley? Just spit it out, man, and no use beating around the bush. I'm not dead, not yet, anyway." James' voice is impatient.

"I'm thinking of taking Matthew back home to live. I've come to realize that I should have done it a long time ago. He's grown up with you and his own sister is almost like a stranger to him. Becky might have been a different girl if she had been able to take care of Matthew. You know, when Elizabeth died, she was left alone with just me and her older brothers. It was mighty hard on a little girl." Wiley's voice broke with emotion.

James says nothing for some minutes. He is stunned by Wiley's words. If Matthew is taken away, now, he knows he will be faced with a bad situation. He was planning on Matt to take care of the place, for at least another few years. He figured the girls would be married and he could parcel off some of the land to them, and he and Martha could just raise a small garden, for their vegetables. Not looking at Martha, who is also shaken by Wiley's words, he cleared his throat, knowing he must give his brother an answer.

"You've caught me by surprise, Wiley. I didn't know you had these thoughts. I guess this is about the worst time you could have come to this decision, though. With my leg and now this other problem, I'm just about worthless when it comes to fieldwork, plowing, planting, gathering the hay; you know what I'm talking about. I depend on Matthew heavily, as I thought you knew. We've had our differences, but I've tried to do right by him. If you feel you must take him, I really can't stop you. He's your boy, but you will sure be leaving me without help just when I need it the most."

James knows his brother. He knows Wiley is tender-hearted to a fault. He is not really worried that he will take Matthew, now, for he sees the concern written all over his brother's face. Knowing he has won out, James relaxes inwardly. Outwardly, he displays an anxious expression, watching the struggle Wiley is going through.

"James, I would sure be a sorry brother, if I took the only help you have at a time like this. I guess I wasn't really thinking how much you depend on Matthew. I know I'm disappointed. Of course, I haven't mentioned my thoughts to either him or Becky. It just came to me today, seeing them together, how comforting it would be to have all my children together. It won't be long before they'll all be going off on their own. I felt like this was the last chance to have them all together, for a while, anyway."

Wiley's tone is regretful, as he falls silent.

In spite of herself, Martha feels sorry for Wiley at this moment. He's got plenty of help, though, she thinks. He doesn't need Matthew, too. Let the boy work, and pay us back for his clothes and food. It's no more than right. Thinking it best not to voice her thoughts, she stood up and refilled the coffee cups.

Outside the kitchen window, his bare feet making no sound, Matthew slipped off the porch and quickly moves around the corner of the house. Reaching the mare, patiently standing at the gate, he gathered up the reins, jumped on her bare back, and quietly walked her out of view of the house. His face is the face of one betrayed. Clenching and unclenching his fist, he feels a terrible pressure building up in his mind.

The mare, receiving no guidance, chooses her own way, taking the well-worn path toward the creek. The tension in the boy is felt in the pressure of his legs against her sides and she is unsure of what is expected of her. A terrible wildness invades Matthew's body. Suddenly, without warning, pulling hard on the reins, stopping Firefly in her tracks, he slips from her back. Going only a short distance off the trail, crazy in his pain and rage, he attempts to rid himself of the awful emotion possessing him. He rammed his doubled-up fist against the trunk of a tree, screaming in pain, physical and mental. He finally collapses, pitiful in his helplessness against controlling forces in his life.

****

With a cup of coffee in her hand Martha quietly opened the door to Matthew's bedroom. The occupant of the bed is sound asleep, the homemade quilt pulled up around his head. She stood for a moment, studying the sleeping face on the pillow. Long black lashes, unusual for a boy, lay against skin turned dark from constant exposure to the sun. The thick, dark hair lay over his forehead. "What will become of him, Lord?" She asked. "Have James and I been too hard on him? Should we let him go to Wiley? How can we manage without his help with James unable to do the work? Martha hears no answers to her questions.

Watching him sleep, she can't help but remember the terrible scenes of the last few weeks. That day, he had come in on Firefly, slumped over, his hand bleeding, busted, his eyes glazed and unseeing. The mare had walked into the lot just before sundown. Slowly and carefully, she had come to a standstill, seeming aware of the condition of her rider. Hearing Black Beauty bark and then begin to whine strangely, Annie glanced out the window. Then, running out the door, leaving it standing open, she had rushed into the yard, catching him in her arms as he rolled of Firefly's back. Unable to support his body, she had sunk to the ground, tears streaming down her face. Seeing her rush out of the house, Martha fearfully followed her. Not knowing what to expect, she sank to the ground, seeing Matthew lying across Annie's knees. Trying to discover exactly what had happened to him, they could see no injury other than his hand, the knuckles split and bleeding profusely. Running to the well, Martha quickly drew the bucket up. With water sloshing over the sides, she hurried back and began to bathe Matthew's battered hand in the cold water; then, grabbing the first thing she saw, the coarse towel off the porch, she wrapped it around his hand to soak up the blood. Annie had looked at Martha, then quickly away, but Martha had seen the anger in her daughter's eyes. Seeing the battered and bleeding hand and the lost look on Matthew's face, feelings of guilt pierced her as she stared at him. Getting the blood stopped they had looked for other injuries. He seemed almost unconscious as they knelt beside him as he lay on the porch. Gently bathing his face, Annie began to call his name softly, urgently.

After some time, the glazed look began to clear from his eyes, and he looked at Annie, first in confusion and then in recognition. She took him into her arms for the first time since he was a little boy. Not resisting her embrace, he lay against her, his head on her shoulder, his body limp. Later, they had put him to bed, having cleaned his hand as best they could and applied salve to the cuts.

Remembering, Martha sighed, and then called his name, awakening him so he could tend to the milking. "Matt, here's your coffee. It's time to get up. Breakfast is ready." She handed him the coffee, and then left the room.

Left alone, Matthew sipped the coffee, gratefully feeling its warmth spread through him. Feeling a movement under the covers, he grinned. Tippy, as usual, sneaked his way into bed. Remembering that all the women will be gone today gives him a feeling of relief. Thinking he might get a little hunting this morning, he glanced out the window. Still dark, must not be but about five o'clock. Daylight won't be showing for another hour. *'If I leave right away, I can be sitting by the creek come daylight. A perfect time to get a couple of squirrels, and then get back to milk.'* Finishing the coffee, he lay back on the pillow. Holding his right hand up, he examined it. Unbelievably, the ugly wounds he inflicted on himself healed fairly quickly. Flexing his fingers carefully, he winced. Continuing to bend first one, then another of his fingers, and then closing his hand slowly, several times, each time exerting more pressure, feeling the pulling and tightening of the skin over his knuckles, Matthew attempts to regain the flexibility of his hand.

Finally, throwing aside the covers, he got out of bed and dressed. Picking up his gun with his left hand, he turned back and gathered Tippy up under his arm. Reaching the hall, tiptoeing past the kitchen, he quietly opened the front door, setting the little dog down on the porch. Returning to the hall, he then entered the kitchen. "I'm going down by the creek. I might get a squirrel or two. I'll eat when I get back," he told Martha, ignoring Millie altogether.

Going quickly out the door, he loped down the trail toward the creek, heading for his favorite spot. Entering the woods, where the towering oaks and pines seem to dwarf him, he slows down, moving cautiously deeper into the trees. He has not brought his dog, for too many leaves remain on the trees. Hopefully, a good frost will send the remaining leaves to the ground, making it easy for him to detect the squirrels. Now, selecting a giant pine, he seats himself against the trunk and becomes so still that he seems a part of the forest. It is quiet, except for the sleepy twittering of birds and the sound of the creek running over the rocks. Under the trees, it is still dark, with just a little morning beginning to creep up on the night shadows. A barely discernible pinkness is showing in the sky, off to the East. Patiently, he waits, knowing just about the exact moment a squirrel will appear. Suddenly, Matthew's attention is riveted on the opposite bank of the creek.

Squinting, attempting to see more clearly, he can tell that a darker shadow has detached itself from the darkness under the trees. Unable to believe his eyes, he watched as a large buck paused with a lifted head, then walked to the edge of the water and began to drink. Sitting beside the tree, Matthew doesn't have a clear shot and would have to get up, at least to his knees, to draw a bead on the buck. Undecided, he sits still, watching. The deer raised his head, seeming to look directly at Matthew. He can see the spread of antlers rising from its head. Itching for a shot at the big buck, he very slowly shifted his position, attempting to get up on one knee. As the buck raised its head, water dripping from its mouth, Matthew drew a bead. Knowing he has only one chance, he fired. In one fluid motion, the beautiful animal whirled and plunged into the thicket of vines and undergrowth. He can hear him as he crashes through the woods, rushing headlong away from him.

Not knowing whether he had hit him or not, Matthew quickly followed, easily tracing the path of the big buck, for the vines are trampled and small bushes crushed by his flight. After following his path for almost a quarter of a mile through the woods, Matthew decided he must have missed him altogether. He has not seen any blood on the ground, indicating he had hit the deer.

Disappointed, he turned back, thinking he might still get a squirrel if he changed his location. Moving slightly down the creek bank, crossing over to the other side, he finds a likely spot and settles down again next to a fallen tree. Soon, he hears the loud fussing bark of a squirrel. Midway up a big hickory tree, he saw a bushy tail flicking up and down as a cat squirrel makes its way toward the ground to feed. Pausing, bright eyes looking rapidly all around, the squirrel suddenly senses danger. Too late, it turned to run, but Matthew fired rapidly. Running to pick up the fallen squirrel, he nodded in satisfaction, as he started for the house and his chores.

The day is still young when Matthew entered the kitchen once more, having already cleaned the squirrel. His appetite was whetted by the cool morning air and the excitement of seeing the big buck, so he went straight to the stove, looking for something to eat. Finding Aunt Martha has left his plate in the warming oven; he quickly retrieved it and sat down to eat his breakfast. Relishing the quiet of the house, he wonders where his uncle is this morning. As he eats, Matthew considers the changes that have come about in the last month.

Looking at his right hand, flexing his fingers, he regrets his foolish action, resulting in the injury to himself. Then, some good had come from that terrible day, he had to admit. Remembering the look on his Aunt Martha's face and Annie's kindness, plus the change in Uncle James's treatment of him, Matthew decided it was almost worth the pain of his injured hand. Realizing that Uncle James had convinced his Pa to leave him here so he could work for another year, Matthew had lost all sense of reason. He hardly remembered climbing on his horse, returning home that evening. His mind had gone blank, shut off, refusing to function. Waking up in his bed, his hand throbbing, feverish, he was the object of much attention by the family.

He was relieved of his chores for a week, while his hand healed. Matthew felt as though he was in a dream. Aunt Martha and Annie had tended the cows, milking morning and evening. Much to her dismay, Millie was told to bring in the firewood and water each day. Katherine, complaining loudly, had slopped the hogs and gathered the eggs, always on the lookout for a chicken snake around the hen house. The plowing and clearing of the pea patch still waited for Matthew's recovery. His brothers and Wiley had pitched in and gathered the corn, now stored in the crib, safe from rats for the winter feed. Unable to restrain himself, Matthew had to grin, remembering the sight of Katherine, her skirts hiked up around her knees, holding her nose, leaning over the fence, and feeding the hogs. And Millie! You would have thought it was the greatest insult possible for her to have to bring in wood for her mother to use to cook the food.

Matthew's grin widens at the pictures his thoughts have created in his mind. "Now they have a little taste of what's been put on me all my life," he muses. "Good!" Finishing the delicious biscuits and tomato gravy, he took the milking pails from the nail and went out the door to milk once more.

Chapter 3

The country church is full of family and friends. Unbelievably pretty in her wedding gown, her eyes sparkling with anticipation, Katherine walked slowly up the aisle, her daddy determined to perform his duty by her side. There had been much discussion about whether or not James could manage this feat, but Katherine, determined for everything to be done correctly, insisted. So, despite the pain involved, he completed the short walk, handing his daughter over to her smiling, nervous bridegroom. Seating himself beside Martha and Matthew, he gave a sigh of relief.

Millie is in her element. As radiant as the bride, she draws admiring looks from all the single young men. Matthew, watching her, grudgingly has to admit what an attractive picture she presents in the flowing rose gown, flowers pinned in her dark hair, swept atop her head in cascading curls. "What a put-on she is," he can't help thinking. Remembering all the fights they have had and her ugly displays of temper, he feels sorry for the man she captures with her sweet, innocent manner. She has been fluttering her eyelashes at the best man, Richard's brother, Joel, who seems to be taken with her.

Flexing his toes in his new shoes, Matthew is reminded of the circumstances of his acquiring them. Just a week before the wedding, Uncle James had announced that he and Matthew were going into town, alone. Mystified, Matthew had accompanied James in the buggy, giving him a smoother ride than the wagon. Wonder of wonders, his uncle had handed the reins to him without a word. Still in the dark as to the purpose of the outing, he had been very careful to keep a moderate pace into town. Very little conversation passed between them all the while they were on the road. Arriving in town, James directed him to tie up in front of the mercantile. Once inside, he gruffly told him to find himself a pair of shoes.

Before leaving the store, James purchased a piece of hard candy for himself and Matthew. Totally stupefied, Matthew remained in a state of unbelief all the way back to the house. The next day, Aunt Martha presented him with a new pair of pants and a shirt, which he was to wear to the wedding. Deep down, Matthew knew this kindness was actually due to Katherine's fear of being embarrassed by his appearance at her wedding. Richard's parents and brother, who would be his best man, had arrived a few days ahead of the ceremony in order to become acquainted with their future daughter-in-law. Katherine had warned Matthew, upon fear of death, that he better not do anything to cause her to appear ill-bred in the eyes of Richard's family.

Suddenly, Matthew realizes the ceremony is drawing to a close, for the minister is now pronouncing Katherine and Richard, man and wife.

"Whatsoever God has joined together, let no man put asunder," he concluded. "Now let us pray."

"Dear Lord, we thank you for your love that has brought Katherine and Richard together. We pray you be the center of their marriage and they always love one another as you love them. May their home be filled with your presence and the joy of knowing you take them through every day of their future lives together."

Richard and Katherine turned, smiling happily, then proceed down the aisle, accepting congratulations and well wishes. Many of the guests will follow the family back to the house, where refreshments have been prepared.

Matthew climbed into a wagon loaded with young men, driven by Billy Johnson, the blacksmith's son. Danny and Douglas Sampson, the red-headed twins whose parents run the mercantile, also jumped on the wagon. Then there's Jack Reilly, curly black hair and full of mischief; he's always ready for a good time. As the wagon rolled out of town, the boys are in high spirits; laughing, slapping each other around, joking.

Driving the wagon up in front of the house, the boys all jumped out, heading for the punch and cake.

Noticing a little cluster of young women seated on a quilt under a tree, sipping punch and eating cake, the boys gravitate toward them. Matthew lags behind the other boys, for he has no desire for feminine company. The others, though, approach the group, laughing and talking to each other, seemingly unaware of the girls' presence. Seating themselves a short distance from them, they continue to talk among themselves, ignoring the young women.

Matthew watched as one of the girls stood, shaking out her skirts and tossing her blonde ringlets, she said something to the others. They dissolved into giggles. She turned and went toward the table holding the punch, passing close to the group of boys. Returning shortly, a fresh cup of punch in each hand, she again walked by the group of boys, this time bestowing a dimpled smile upon them. After she passed, Jack grabbed himself across his chest and fell backward onto the ground, moaning in pretended agony. The others erupted into hilarious shouts and laughter, beating him on the back. "Generally making fools of themselves," Matthew thought. Looking around, he saw Duncan with his little boys on the other side of the yard and went to join them.

Before he can reach them, there is a little flurry of activity among all the young women as they rush to gather for the traditional tossing of the bridal bouquet. Katherine, her face flushed and excited, throws her wedding flowers high into the air, watching to see who will be the next young woman to become a bride. Standing to one side with Buddy Miller, Annie makes no effort to participate in the activity. Amazingly, the flowers sail over the reaching hands of all the other girls and fall straight into Buddy's outstretched hand. Smiling sweetly at Annie, he presents her with the bouquet. Accepting it from his hand, she returned his smile.

Millie's face showed disappointment as she turned away quickly and smiled at Joel Hayes, who has been glued to her since the wedding.

The guests began to disperse. Shaking hands with James and Martha, complimenting them on the cake and punch, they climbed into their wagons and buggies. Before leaving, the women helped clean up and for this, Martha is thankful, for this has been a long day. Realizing she has two more girls to get married brings a weary sigh from her. Anxious to sit down and rest her tired feet, she went to the porch, dropping thankfully into the rocking chair.

In the living room, Annie and Buddy, Katherine, and Richard gathered, having a cup of coffee and relaxing. Richard's parents, along with his brother, Joel, have returned to town and will spend the night at the boarding house, then return to their home in Atlanta on the next stage. Richard and Katherine have made plans to accompany them, staying with his parents for several weeks while enjoying the sights of Atlanta. Since the other alternative is a honeymoon spent at the boardinghouse, Katherine is anxious to finalize their plans.

"Why don't you and Richard stay in my room tonight, Katherine? I can sleep with Millie, and the two of you can get an early start for town. The stage won't arrive before nine or ten." Annie suggested to her sister.

"Richard? What do you think of Annie's suggestion?" Katherine asks her new husband.

"That sounds fine to me, Kate. If that's what you want to do, I'm in agreement. We'll probably be much more comfortable here, anyway. Mama said the boarding house is clean, but the mattress on the bed leaves much to be desired in comfort." Richard replied. "My sister and her husband are so anxious to meet you. They would have preferred that you and I stayed with them. She is anxious to get better acquainted with you. I'll have to watch her, or she'll have you so busy shopping you'll have no time for your husband." Richard grinned at Katherine jokingly.

"I think I'll check to see if Mama would like coffee," Annie said. Would you like to come along, Buddy?"

"Of course, Annie." he followed her onto the porch.

The evening air felt fresh and cool as they stepped out of the house. Martha, her head resting on the back of the chair, has her eyes closed. Annie put her finger to her lips, and then motioned to Buddy to follow her. Going down the steps and out the gate, holding hands, they walked slowly down the lane.

"Annie, you know I care for you very much. May I speak to your Father about us?" Buddy's question is only a formality, for Annie has known for quite some time how he feels. She has just waited for him to voice his feelings.

Smiling her answer, squeezing his hand, she shakes her head "Yes."`

As they turn back to the house, the sun is setting in a glorious display of color. Knowing he must be on his way before all the light has left the sky, Buddy reluctantly let go of Annie's hand. She watched as he climbed on his horse and galloped down the lane.

Coming from the barn, having finished the milking, Matthew heard Buddy's horse gallop off. *"Guess Annie will be marrying next. She's the only one that takes up for me. If I can just endure for the rest of this school term, I can be my own boss."* he thinks. *"But, where will I go when I leave here?"*

Chapter 4

As the days of fall passed in rapid succession, Matthew felt anticipation rise up in his heart. Each day brought him closer to freedom from Uncle James. He walked to the barn each morning before dawn through falling leaves, milking by lantern light, his breath blowing smoke-like into the frosty air of the milking stall. He welcomed the warmth emanating from the cows' bodies. Having built fires in all three fireplaces before going to milk, he returned to eat his breakfast in the kitchen's warmth. He would much rather ride his mare to school but is forced to take the wagon because of Millie. Arriving home in the evening, he again milks, tends the other animals, brings in wood for the night, and tries to hunt, bringing fresh meat home regularly.

By the end of November, the children are allowed to leave school earlier in the afternoon since some of them have so far to travel. Preparing for the Christmas celebrations, an air of festivity pervades the schoolhouse and a certain excitement takes hold of young and old alike.

Millie will portray Mary, the mother of Jesus, in the school play. The teacher asked Matt to play Joseph. Balking at first, not wanting to be the center of attention at anything, and certainly wary of being in such close proximity to Millie for any length of time, he finally relents and endeavors to learn his few lines by the night of the play. On many Saturdays, he recites his lines aloud while cutting wood, determined to avoid embarrassing himself by forgetting at the last minute.

The children set up a small tree in the school and decorated it with homemade decorations, holly berries strung together, and pinecones.

The Sunday before Christmas, a service will be held in the church. Candles are lit in all the windows in the small town, and out in the countryside, flickering lights can be seen, sending forth a friendly glow in the darkness.

Matthew has not seen his Pa, but once or twice since the day he questioned him about the angels. His heart is still sore from the happenings of that fateful week. He knows he cannot blame his Pa. It was Uncle James who put up such a pitiful story that his Pa could not bear to take him away and leave his brother in need. Becky, along with his brothers and Pa, had been at the wedding. She had looked really pretty in one of Annie's dresses, made over, with fresh trimming to brighten it up. In fact, she had caught the eye of a young man that day—a young man not at all suitable in Wiley's eyes.

Attempting to court Becky, he had met with solid opposition from her brothers and her daddy. In fact, he had bluntly been told to stay away from her. Wiley had caught his daughter trying to slip off to meet the young man against his wishes. Fearing the worst, Wiley and his sons had agreed never to leave her alone at the house until, hopefully, the man would grow discouraged and give up on her.

****

Tensions in the Carlisle house have somewhat lessened as Christmas drew near. James seems to be determined to hold on to his volatile temper and no more incidents have occurred between him and Matthew for some time now.

Realizing he has a term to serve, Matthew goes about his chores silently. Inside his heart, though, the resentment at his lot in life is eating away at his good intentions. He has not decided what he can do to shorten his time of unwilling service to his aunt and uncle.

The day of the Christmas festivities is only one week away, and he knows his lines perfectly. Normally, he does not want to draw attention to himself; he has a certain amount of dread when all eyes will be upon him as he recites his part in the play. A truce has been declared between him and Millie, which is shaky at best.

Matthew hunched down in front of the fireplace, feeding the feeble flame with small splinters of rich lighter pine gathered during the summer and stored in a dry place for such a morning as this. Light snow had fallen during the night and the morning air is crisp and cold. Each night, before going to bed, it was his job to bank the fire, preserving the coals.

This morning, shivering, his teeth chattering, Matt blew carefully on the glowing coals, coaxing them into life. Suddenly, the splinters caught, flaring up. Quickly, Matthew added more splinters, then bigger pieces of pine. As soon as the flames caught the bigger splinters, he began adding dry twigs, then small dry oak limbs, and finally oak logs. Standing gratefully in front of the blazing fire, he held his chilled hands close to the flames, feeling the warmth on his shivering skin. Then, he went quickly into the cold kitchen. Following the same procedure, first with small splinters, then dry twigs, and finally, short pieces of stove wood he had cut himself, he soon had a strong fire in the cook stove.

Bracing himself for the trek to the barn, he collected the milk buckets and opened the door to the biting wind. The snow is white and crunchy under his feet. No prints have as yet been made, marring its perfection. Seeing his breath hanging in the frosty air, his head down, he hurried into the barn, welcoming its shelter. Going through the ritual of feeding and milking the faithful old cows, which he could do with his eyes closed, Matt's thoughts are in a jumble.

A few days before, he had made a visit to his cave. For a reason he couldn't explain, he had felt a need to go there. It was one of those unexpected days that sometimes occur in the South, even in the middle of winter. The sun had been so warm; people shed their coats in the spring like air. Days such as this one caused many introspective souls to remember the warnings of the Good Book concerning the end of time.

Matthew avoids thoughts of the hereafter. He remembered as a small boy sitting with Aunt Martha and the girls in church each Sunday. The pastor preached of Heaven and of Hell and how to go to Heaven and avoid going to Hell. As he grew older and Uncle James and Aunt Martha became harsher in their discipline, he only went to church because he was forced by Uncle James. Fully aware of the requirements of God concerning salvation, thanks to Aunt Martha, he still has not made any kind of commitment of his own. He had been baptized, though, when he was twelve years old, at a big revival meeting held by a traveling preacher. Scared out of his wits by the picture of a roaring lake of fire, so vividly painted by the enthusiastic man of God, he went down into the river to wash his sins away.

When he returned from school that day, he quickly rushed through his chores, and then jumped on Firefly, Black Beauty on his heels. Galloping out of the barnyard, he raced against the early winter darkness. When he reached the cave, he went straight to his hiding place, retrieved the metal box, and reached inside. Feeling the smooth coldness of the white stone in his hand, he held it tightly for a moment, warming it in his palm. Then, replacing it, he withdrew the coin. Returning the box to its hiding place, he quickly exited the cave.

That night, searching his room for a hiding place, he chose one spot first and then another. Where could he put it so that Aunt Martha would not come across it while cleaning his room? Not sure just what he would eventually do with it, he just needed a secure hiding place. Finally, he had slipped the coin into the pocket of an old, worn-out pair of pants, which he had outgrown. Not really satisfied with his choice, he decided that it would have to do for now, anyway. That night, waiting for sleep to come, Tippy snuggled up under the covers. Matthew had felt a little prickle of excitement deep inside. For the first time since his daddy had agreed to leave him with Uncle James, he began to look forward to his future.

Matthew frowned, in thought, as he finished the milking and started back to the house through the cold. What perplexed him was that last night, checking on the security of his coin, as he had done every night since bringing it from the cave; he found it missing from its hiding place. At first, he thought that maybe he had moved it himself, and then forgot, but he quickly discarded that assumption since he had looked at it the night before. Someone had removed it between the night and the following evening when he returned from school. A hot flush of fear and anger had clouded his mind as he pictured someone going through his belongings. Why would Aunt Martha even bother with the old pants rolled up in the back of the ancient pine wardrobe that held his few clothes? He could come to no clear course of action but purposed to observe each family member, watching for any sign that one of them had possession of his coin.

The kitchen was warm and cozy when Matt returned from the barn. Breakfast is on the table and his stomach growls in response to the smell of the bacon and eggs aunt Martha has cooked. Anxious to get to the food, he paid no attention to Millie, who sat at the table, sleepy-eyed and tousle-headed. She wasn't too sleepy to give him a verbal jab though. Looking at him threateningly, she issued a warning.

"You better not embarrass me by acting a fool at the play. I don't know why Miss Bartlett gave you the part of Joseph anyway. Sam would have done a better job, I'm sure. He's very smart. Have you even learned your lines?" Raising his head, directing the full force of his dark eyes on her, Matthew spoke through tight lips, his words low, intense.

"That's none of your business, Miss high and mighty. You'll find out what I know when the time comes. I never wanted to be in the stupid play, especially with you. Some choice for the mother of Jesus, you are. Maybe the mother of the devil would suit you better." he finished scornfully.

Millie's face turned white. Furious with him, yet helpless to do anything about it, she would have struck him had she held a weapon. Just then, Annie came into the kitchen for her morning coffee. Feeling the tension, she looked from one of them to the other, sighed, then poured her coffee and sat down between them at the table.

"Good morning, Matthew, and Millie. It'll be Christmas soon. I'm really looking forward to the Christmas play, and seeing the two of you cooperating for a change. It always takes me back to the real reason for celebrating. It makes me count my blessings, too." She sipped her coffee, ignoring their angry faces.

"Good morning, Annie. Christmas doesn't do some people any good at all." Millie snapped, her eyes flashing with anger.

Matthew returned her greeting, and then gave Millie another black look before he finished his breakfast. Getting up to leave, he passed her chair, grabbed a handful of her long hair, and gave it such a vicious jerk that her head snapped back painfully. With a scream of fury, she swung her arm; fist balled up, and struck him a glancing blow. Laughing at her feeble strength, Matthew went out the door. Enraged, Millie jerked the door open and screamed at him.

"Wait until I tell Daddy on you, Matthew Carlisle. You won't be so smart, then." Stomping her foot in frustration, Millie returned to the kitchen. Red-faced, she saw Annie's restrained laughter.

"What's so funny about him pulling my hair almost off my head, Annie?"

"Millie, you bring it on yourself. Why don't you just keep your mouth off Matthew? You provoke him, and then run tattling to Mama. You never tell what you've done; only what he's done. Why don't you act your age, instead of like a spoiled brat, jealous and spiteful?" Annie scolded.

"Annie, you make me sick. Matthew is nothing but an orphan, living on our charity. Do you realize that Uncle Wiley has never given us anything to help feed and clothe him all these years?" Millie's voice rose in volume as she jerked her chair out and sat down again.

"And do you realize that he does the work of a man, even though he's only a boy? Do you realize that because of you, he has been beaten unmercifully, many times undeservedly? How would you feel if you were in his place, forced to live with people who make it plain they only tolerate him instead of giving him real love?" Annie spoke earnestly, trying to generate a little kindness for Matthew, for whom she has a genuine affection and concern. "Jesus told us to love others like we love ourselves," she added.

"I'll get even with him, regardless of what you say, Annie. Taking up for him won't change my mind in the least." Having said this, Millie left the kitchen to get ready to go to the schoolhouse. "Yes," she purposed, "you will be sorry, Matthew Carlisle, very sorry, for what you've done to me."

About an hour later, sitting beside Matt on the wagon seat, Millie is silent, still seething with anger. Forcing herself to wait for the opportune time to make him pay for the insults he had inflicted on her, she wished she had not had to depend on him to transport her to the schoolhouse. The last practice for the Christmas play is today; then school will be over until the first of the New Year.

Matthew chose to ignore the morning events and Millie's presence beside him. He seems oblivious to her ill humor, singing a Christmas carol in a surprisingly good baritone. Millie grudgingly admits he does have a pleasing voice, but she would cut her tongue out before she would ever give him a compliment of any kind.

As soon as they reached the school, she jumped down from the wagon and hurried into the schoolhouse ahead of him. Seeing Millie come in, Miss Bartlett smiled. "Good morning Millie." Thank you so much for being such a blessing to the Christmas play." She hugged Millie and beckoned to Matthew to join them.

"Now, Millie, and Matthew, I'm depending on the two of you to make this scene the most moving part of the play. Millie, the two of you will stand beside the manger. The angels will be in the background. Look lovingly at your husband and then fall down beside the manger. Lean over the baby, look at him tenderly, like a mother would look at her baby, and kiss him. Matt, you then kneel beside Millie. Put your arm around her shoulder. The two of you gaze at the baby while the angels begin to sing 'Silent Night'."

Miss Bartlett is excited and anxious that everything is just right. This is the culmination of her first year of teaching here, and she wants to impress the parents with her abilities. She has prepared certificates of achievement for those students who have excelled in their academics, certificates for those who have shown a marked improvement over the last year, and then graduate certificates for the ones who will not be returning for the fall term. The normal age limit for the school is usually sixteen, but many of the boys quit before they are fifteen, even some earlier than that, if not encouraged by their parents to continue.

"Children, children, let me have your attention, please." Clapping her hands, a signal for silence, Miss Bartlett rounds up the players for the first scene and soon everyone is caught up in the nervous excitement of preparation for the big event.

Millie and Matthew, though disliking every minute of their forced closeness during their scenes, try to please their teacher, as she has always treated them kindly and been patient with Matthew's escapades. Early on, she sensed that his antics were not originating from a mean spirit. Her tender heart longed to help him.

Matthew had been prepared to dislike the new school teacher. She was nothing like he had imagined she would be when the school year began. Miss Bartlett is pretty and young. She spoke to the children in a soft voice. Through the year, she had made attempts to win his confidence. He treated her respectfully because for some reason, he didn't want to hurt her feelings. She made him feel that he was capable of learning and achieving. She praised him when he did well. No one else in his life gave him the feeling that he was a worthwhile human being. The uppermost reason for him agreeing to be in the play was that Miss Bartlett made him feel as though no one else could do it as well as he could. He wanted to justify her faith in him. He wanted to show everyone that Matthew

Carlisle was someone who held their respect, not just an orphaned Indian boy.

Finally, Miss Bartlett is satisfied that she has done all she can do. The rest is up to the children. Being a teacher, she knows to expect some type of mishap but hopes it will be minor and not too embarrassing to her or the children. Sending them home with encouraging words and hugs all around, she gratefully sighed in relief.

The silence of the school room, warm from the big wood stove, is welcome after the last two hours. Seated at her desk, Miss Bartlett prayed for her students, their families, and finally, for herself, that she will be able to be the best teacher she can possibly be to all these children. Hearing a wagon outside, she gathered her coat and purse and closed the damper on the big stove. Reaching the door, she turned for one last look at the schoolroom. She and the children have done a good job on the decorations. With small trees in buckets and cedar boughs, they have created a passable manger scene. The Christmas tree, bright with homemade decorations and topped with a slightly crooked star, stands in the corner. Smiling in contentment, Miss Bartlett walked out the door, greeting Mr. Walker who is waiting for her.

The following Sunday, the church was full. The smell of cedar permeated the small building, for the ladies had made wreaths of the fragrant limbs and hung them around the sanctuary. Soon, all the pews were filled, and people were still coming, lining up around the walls and finally filling the porch. Astonished by the crowd, the minister is delighted to have such a congregation to hear his Christmas message. As the notes of "Oh, Little Town of Bethlehem" filled the church, then floated through the open windows and through the crisp air, to linger in the minds of all within the realm of the sound, even those stoic members of the crowd felt a burning within their soul. "What heart, the Pastor wondered, even those hardened, seemingly to stone, cannot but respond to such sweetness. Surely, for a space out of a lifetime, no matter how short, the spirit of man may soar to touch the edge of unutterable joy for which it was created."

As all who were blessed enough to have a seat sat down, the minister walked to the pulpit. Laying his Bible open before him, raising his hands in an attitude of blessing, he prayed. He is just a common man, this preacher. Having very little in earthly goods, he relied upon the generosity of others for the means to continue his ministry.

Standing before the people that day, something divine touched him. A fresh anointing poured over his soul. Afterward, he could not remember a word of his message. He only knew that he never looked at a note he had made to prompt him as he preached. The words poured from him with such power, eloquence, and love; there was no sound to be heard other than the roll and surge of his voice. He painted such vivid pictures of the lives played out two thousand years before that the listeners heard the beat of Roman feet, the cries of the Jewish slaves, felt the birth pangs of Mary and the fear of Joseph as he searched for a place for Jesus to be born.

His voice carried them to the heights of joy when the angel announced His birth, to the depths of fear as Joseph fled into Egypt, and then again to a shout of victory as all came to worship the King of Kings and Lord of Lords. His voice sank to earnest entreaty for all to bow their knees and worship Him, along with the shepherds and wise men from long ago. Many wept openly, unashamed of their tears; even grown men, never before known to shed a tear, wiped at their eyes, blinking back the unfamiliar wetness clouding their vision. Finally, as the words of the minister ceased, praying was heard as many repented, even asking forgiveness for wrongs committed against neighbors. Surely, the Savior had come down to earth this day. Could anyone ever be the same again?

Filing from the church, out into the pale winter sunshine, shaking hands, greeting friends and strangers alike, the settlers seemed reluctant to leave. They milled around on the church steps, out in the churchyard, and some even wandered through the graveyard, next to the church. Finally, family by family, by twos and threes, some solitary ones, they drifted out to their buggies and wagons. Calling "Merry Christmas" and "May God Bless You All," they departed for their homes

"Surely, this has been a Christmas service to be remembered for many years to come." Annie told herself.

Riding Firefly along the road out of town, Matthew felt tightness in his chest. He wished he could talk with someone who could explain what this feeling was inside of him. The same kind of feeling he remembered that day by the creek when the angel man smiled and touched him. "What is the reason I have such a feeling and what should I do about it?" He wondered. He cannot even explain what it was "like," for it was not "like" anything in his experience. Something inside of him, part of his insides, he guessed, seemed to want to just explode, as though there was not enough room on the inside of him. He felt a touch of excitement, a need to shout out loud, and then, he felt a little sadness, as though he needed to cry. As Firefly walked slowly along, Matthew is sunk in deep thought.

Suddenly, he stopped the mare, turned his head around quickly, and looked behind him, expecting to see the wagon carrying Aunt Martha and the girls. The road is empty. Wonder what is taking them so long. He thought they were close behind him. Oh, well, they would probably be along pretty soon. But he felt strange, realizing there was no one behind him. He knew he had heard his name called. Just as clear as day, someone called "Matthew." Kicking his heels against the mare's sides, he urged her into a trot, hastening on down the road toward home. His thoughts went right along with him. Is he losing his senses? Hearing voices when no one is around? Puzzling over these strange events he reached the barn, quickly unsaddled Firefly and gave her water and hay in the warmth of the barn. Realizing it is only four days to Christmas, a little prickle of anticipation touches him. Maybe he will soon be free.

That night, the weather turned nasty. The wind howled around the corners of the house, as though some wild legion of spirits were on the prowl. The snow was flung helter-skelter by the wind, swirling flakes that stung the skin of anyone who ventured out in it. When morning sought to assert itself against the darkness of the lowering sky, the result was semi-darkness, an eerie light. Finally, the wind died down, but the clouds rolled across the strangely colored sky as though possessed.

Matthew struggled to the barn to do the milking, his eyes going constantly to the strange sky overhead. This weather made him nervous and fearful. Suddenly, he was face to face with a force greater than anything he had ever known in his short life. He felt small, inconsequential beneath the huge expanse of roiling clouds piling up in threatening mountains of blackness. Hurrying through the milking, he secured Firefly in a stall, and then fed her. Trying to calm her, he talked comfortingly in a low voice, rubbing her nose and her sleek neck. Black Beauty, also seeking shelter in the barn, whined nervously. He retreated to the back corner of Firefly's stall, where he sat upright, his eyes watching Matthew's every move.

"It'll be all right, girl. You're safe in the barn. Just be calm, now. Nothing's going to hurt you while I'm around." Matthew's words to the horse brought a measure of comfort to himself as well. "Black Beauty, you watch out for Firefly, now."

Hearing his name, the big black dog barked sharply in response, then, as though reassured, curled up in the corner, his eyes still watchful.

Finally, Matthew slipped through the big barn door, securing the bar that held it shut. Then, feeling the wind begin to pick up again, he hurried quickly across the yard and into the house.

James, standing at the window, was observing the sky, his face concerned. Martha and the girls sat at the table, eating breakfast. They all jumped nervously when the door swung back with a bang, admitting Matthew, along with a gust of cold wind. Pushing hard to shut the door, he then went straight to the stove, holding out his hands to the warmth.

"What do you think, Uncle James?" he asked.

James turned from the window and returned to his place at the table before answering Matthew's question.

"Well, I don't know hardly what to think. I can't say if it's some kind of Northerner or just a bad winter storm that'll blow itself out without doing any damage. Did you shut the lot gate so the cows can't wander off in this?"

"Yes Sir. I did everything. I shut Firefly up in the stall. She might get scared and hurt herself outside." Matthew answered.

"Daddy, do you think we can still have the Christmas play?" Millie's voice quivered with nervousness.

"How would your daddy know that, Millie? We'll just have to wait and see what this weather does." Martha spoke rather sharply, jumping up and going to the window to look again at the sky.

"If it clears up tomorrow, maybe we can find a small tree to decorate. If Buddy happens to come, I know he'd be glad to help us." Annie spoke calmly, having noticed that everyone seemed to be on edge right now.

"That's a good idea, Annie. Let's see what we can find in Mama's scrap box. We can use some of the decorations we made last year. That angel was so beautiful that you made. If we can get some holly berries and pine cones, we can fix a really pretty tree." Millie's eyes lit up with excitement.

Annie looked at her sister in surprise. What has happened to her, she wonders. Millie is agreeing with her suggestion? Must be a Christmas miracle, she decided. She hoped the storm wouldn't last long so they could get a tree.

As soon as the breakfast remains were cleared away, Martha and the girls went off to search out the Christmas decorations. Matthew wandered into the front room, where the fire blazed cheerfully. James sat at the table, sipping on a cup of coffee, keeping an eye on the storm through the window.

As the morning wore on, the black clouds, pushed by the wind, rolled across the sky and the snow stopped falling. The North wind, which had been blowing all night and all morning, biting cold, began to lessen. One could see gray, overcast patches of sky. With the temperature below freezing, it seemed unlikely anyone would attempt to go anywhere for the rest of the day.

James sent Matthew out to check on the livestock early that afternoon, as soon as the weather cleared enough for him to make it out the door. He also made several trips to the big wood pile, stacking wood on the porch, close to the door, to fuel the fireplaces and stove through the night. Finally, he made sure there was plenty of kindling just in case the fires got too low during the night and had to be restarted.

Martha had been sewing all day, making tiny dolls for the tree, while Annie and Millie put the finishing touches, button eyes, and yarn for the hair. Matthew, retreating to his room, could hear them laughing and exclaiming over their creations.

With the lack of activity, he had time to think about the lost coin. With all the excitement of practice for the play and his chores, he had put the matter of the coin aside. Now, sitting alone in his room, he began to consider the problem again. No one seemed to be acting differently. He had not noticed any member of the family looking at him strangely, nor had anyone said anything that would make him suspect he or she could know about the coin. He promised himself that as soon as Christmas was over, he would begin earnestly to pursue the lost coin until he found out what had happened to it. Sooner or later, he would hear something from someone and then he would know who had gone into his room and took the coin.

Looking out the window for the hundredth time, Matthew decided he would venture out and try his luck at locating a small pine or cedar just to have something to do. Bundling up, he took his gun, just in case he got a shot at a rabbit, and slipped out the door.

Down near the creek would be a likely place to find a nice little cedar. A likely place to kill a squirrel or a fat rabbit, too, he figured. Amazingly, as he plodded through the snow, the sun suddenly broke through the overcast sky and shone brightly on the snow. Looking up, he could see patches of blue above the gray clouds. Involuntarily, he felt his face break into a grin.

He continued toward the creek. A sudden movement at the base of a tree brought him up short, his gun instinctively going to his shoulder. Before he could get off a shot, however, he almost stumbled in his excitement. There, not more than thirty-five steps away, standing in the shadow of the trees, was a huge buck deer. Steadying his gun against his shoulder, sighting down the barrel, straight into the deer's eyes, he lowered the barrel and pulled the trigger. The stillness of the afternoon was shattered. Snow drifted down from the trees from the explosion. Matthew realized he was holding his breath, knowing he could not have missed such a target; he looked at the spot where the deer had stood. The buck had died almost instantly. For a moment, Matthew felt sorrow as he looked at the magnificent animal. The blood ran from the gaping wound in his chest and dripped onto the white snow. The proud head was bowed, the beautiful eyes glazed by death. Pride at his accomplishment won out over the tinge of regret he felt as he hurried as fast as he could back to the house to seek help in transporting the deer home.

As he burst through the door, his face was transformed by the ear-to-ear grin he couldn't restrain.

"Uncle James, I killed a great big buck down by the creek! I don't know how I'll get him home, though, through the snow." Matthew's voice is loud in his excitement.

"Boy, don't be funning me with your tall tales." James looked up from his chair by the fire.

"I'm not funning you, Uncle James. I did kill a big buck. Come on and I'll show you." Matthew insisted.

"Well, why didn't you say so in the first place? We'll have to get the girls to help, too. Go hitch up the wagon. We may be able to use it since the snow is not very deep." James started to the back of the house to tell Millie and Annie to get bundled up so they could help with the deer.

Matthew took off like a shot for the wagon. Excitement lent wings to his feet and he forgot all about the cold, wet ground. As he jumped off the porch, sailing over the steps, his feet went out from under him and he sat down hard on his backside in the snow. Nothing could deter him, though, for he jumped up immediately and took off again.

Soon, the whole family was standing around the deer, marveling at his beauty and expressing astonishment that Matthew had brought down such a big buck with a single shot. James had decided that in order to transport the deer, they would go ahead and dress it out there, cutting it into smaller portions that they could handle. The rack they would dry would be hung on the porch.

Within a short time, the deer had been skinned, quartered, and loaded in the wagon. That night, Martha fried the back strap and made hot biscuits. Licking his fingers with relish, Matthew sighed with pleasure. The day had sure started bad, but it sure had ended up good, he thought. He would never forget Annie's words of praise as they walked back to the house, following the wagon with the deer carcass.

"Matt, you shoot as well as any man I've ever known," she said. Then, she had given him a little pat on his back.

Later, as they were hanging the deer up high from a tree limb, Uncle James said, "You did good, boy."

Matthew felt happy that night as he went to bed, though much was yet troubling him. He felt as though he had received a gift that day as he remembered James's words of approval: the greatest gift of all.

By morning, though the snow still lay in places and around the bases of the trees, it had melted to slush everywhere else. Matthew guided Firefly carefully along the trail, fearful that she might slip on the icy patches. He was on his way to enlist the help of Duncan so that the deer could be salted down and preserved before the weather turned warmer. The exertion of the day before had been almost too much for Uncle James. Riding along, Matthew felt the warmth of the winter sun on his face. It was amazing how good he felt. A sudden exuberance took hold of him, and he let out an Indian war whoop, startling his mare and causing her to jump sideways, almost unseating him on her bare back. Holding her steady, the reins taut, he reached down and patted her shiny neck.

"Sorry, girl, I'm just feeling good today. Guess I took you by surprise, hollering like that," he spoke reassuringly. Firefly's ears twitched as though she understood every word.

Reaching the path leading up to Duncan and May's house, she nickered a greeting to the old mare standing at the lot fence. Throwing the reins loosely around the porch post, Matthew cleared the steps in one jump and knocked loudly on the door.

After a few moments, the door opened and Duncan's sleepy face appeared. "Oh, how are you doing, Matt? Come on in. We're just getting up. Sammy kept us all awake till really late with a bad cough. May's making coffee now. Would you like some?" Duncan led the way into the kitchen, Matthew following.

"Hey, May, how you doing?" Matthew greeted his cousin and then turned to Duncan. "I've already had breakfast. Uncle James sent me to get you to come down and help us. I killed a buck yesterday and he's too big for me to handle by myself. Uncle James kind of overdid himself yesterday and we need to take care of the meat today." Matthew informed them quickly.

"I sure will, Matt. As soon as I get a bite to eat, I'll be right on down there. I sure would like to have a fresh mess of meat. How did you bring down a big buck all by yourself, anyway?" Duncan's face showed his amazement.

"I was down by the creek looking for a tree for Aunt Martha and the girls to decorate. I had my gun, 'cause I thought I might get a squirrel or a rabbit. Then, there he was, big horns and all, standing, just looking at me. I just aimed for his heart and pulled the trigger. Next thing I knew, he was on the ground. Wait till you see the antlers! Uncle James said I did good." Matthew added, his eyes shining at the thought of the praise he had received from his uncle over his accomplishment.

"Well, I'll say you did good. That meat will carry ya'll through the winter." Duncan added his approval, wishing he could be so lucky to bring down a big buck for his family. Not really concerned, though. He knew they would never go hungry as long as James and Martha were around.

Matthew left shortly after that, being assured that Duncan would be there right away to help him. Riding back, he suddenly remembered that the Christmas play was tomorrow afternoon. He had completely forgotten about it in the excitement of killing the deer and the bad storm. With a touch of fear at having to be up in front of everybody, he began to go over Miss Bartlett's instructions, trying to remember everything she had told him to do. By the time he got back to the house, he was plenty nervous about the next day's events.

True to his word, Duncan soon appeared, along with May and the boys. Upon hearing the hacking cough of little Sammy, Martha scolded her daughter sharply for bringing him out in the cold. Taking charge of him, she dosed him with her cold remedy, along with warm sassafras tea. His cough eased, and the little boy soon fell asleep, exhausted from the sleepless night he had endured.

While Duncan and Matthew tended to the deer meat, salting it down in the big wooden barrels, hanging some up to dry, Martha prepared a huge pot of venison stew, dropping dumplings into the rich broth as it bubbled on the stove.

Dinner time brought everyone from their respective duties to gather at the big table. James questioned Duncan and Matthew concerning the handling of the meat, promising to check on them after dinner.

"Looks like we're set for the rest of the winter, he told Matthew. If you kill a few rabbits, we'll make it all right. You need to get those traps out, so you don't have to go out looking for them."

"Yes sir. Uncle James," he replied quickly. "I got them all made already."

"Matthew, you know the play is tomorrow. Do you remember what Miss Bartlett told you to do for your part?" Millie reminded Matt.

"Yeah, Millie, I remember. I don't need you to remind me." Matt replied.

"Well, you be sure and don't do anything stupid. I don't plan on being embarrassed in front of everybody because of you." she shot back, with a frown in his direction.

"Can we go to the play, mama?" Jimmy asked May.

"Sure, honey, we're all going. Well, that is, if Sammy doesn't get worse," she told the little boy.

"If you'll keep giving him that cough syrup I fixed and tonight, put that poultice on his chest, he'll be all right," Martha told her daughter. "I don't understand why you don't take better care of these boys, May. You know I'll give you some of my remedies anytime if you just let me know what you need."

"Okay, boys, let's go check on that meat. See if ya'll are doing it right." James got up, having finished his dinner.

Matthew and Duncan, like two little boys, followed him out the door, waiting to see what he would have to say.

A little insulted by her mother's reprimand, May silently got up and went to check on Sammy, still sleeping in Annie's room.

Annie and Martha began to clear away the dishes, while Millie made herself scarce, as usual, when there was work to be done.

Returning from the bedroom, May took the boys into the front room to admire the tree Matthew had brought them. Holly berries, strung together in a chain, added a bright note of red against the dark green of the cedar branches. The little dolls Martha and the girls had made hung from the branches along with the angels made with bright buttons, yarn, and pieces of fabric. The little boys were fascinated and clamored to have a tree of their own. May suddenly realized that Christmas was fast approaching and her house did not have a sign of the coming event.

Coming into the room, carrying a tray with steaming coffee, Annie smiled at Jimmy and Johnny as they examined the little dolls. "Look, boys, Grandma made you some cookies. We have some more of those dolls and some gingerbread men, too, if you want to hang them on your tree."

"Really, Annie? Oh, mama, can we have a tree, too, please, mama." Jimmy begged his mother excitedly.

"Calm down, Jimmy. Of course, you can. We'll get one on the way home today. I have some little pine cones, too, that would make some decorations. Some red berries and we'll have a nice tree for Christmas," May reassured her boys.

"That coffee smells mighty good, Annie. As soon as Duncan finishes, we'll be going, so we can find a tree for the boys." May helped herself to a cookie.

"You know, Mama doesn't mean to be hurtful, May. That's just her way of speaking. She cares about the boys." Annie knew May had been offended by Martha's earlier remarks at the table.

"Oh, I know. It's just embarrassing when she talks to me as though I'm still a child," she replied, sipping the coffee.

"Mama loves her family. She's just not a person to show her feelings." Annie said.

Just then, Duncan appeared at the door. "May, you bout ready to head home?" he questioned his wife.

"Come have some coffee, and then we'll go. The boys want a tree, so we can probably find one on the way home." May answered.

"Your daddy gave us a mess of meat. That was sure a big deer. Can't get over Matthew getting off such a shot," Duncan continued to marvel at the big buck. Johnny climbed into his daddy's lap, wanting a sip of his coffee.

Martha came in, a package in her hand. "Boys, this is for all of you. Open it up when you get home. It's something to hang on your tree, and then you can eat it."

"Thank you, Grandma." Jimmy took the package with a smile and a hug for Martha.

"I'll go get Sammy and be out front in a minute. You take Jimmy and Johnny with you," May told Duncan. Setting her cup down, she left the room to get the baby.

The winter darkness closed in early. Duncan left with his family to cut a tree on their way home. After they left, Matthew brought in wood for all the fires after doing the milking. Tomorrow was the big event: That night, he went over and over Miss Bartlett's instructions, vowing to do it right.

Chapter 5

Millie sat in her bed, examining an object she held in her hand. Frowning slightly, she looked around the room, her eyes stopping here and there as she searched the area around her bed. Finally, standing up on the bed, she reached up high and slid the object into a crack above her bed. Then, smiling in satisfaction, she snuggled under the covers and soon fell asleep.

Early the following afternoon, everyone gathered at the schoolhouse for the Christmas play. Soon, the building would hold no more people, and so Miss Bartlett stepped out to greet everyone and thank them for coming. As the manger scene was played out and the angels sang, the shepherds knelt to pay homage to the Baby Jesus lying in the manger. Mary and Joseph, his loving parents, gazed on the baby adoringly and greeted the three Wise Men who had come from afar, led by the star.

Matthew, as Joseph, and Millie, as Mary, his sweet-faced wife, made an appealing picture, kneeling beside the manger. True to his promise to Miss Bartlett, Matt performed his part without a flaw, even being in such close proximity to Millie, which he dreaded. When everyone lifted their voices to sing at the finale, Miss Bartlett breathed a sigh of relief.

Then, she paid honor to the students, passing out awards and certificates of merit to those she felt deserved them. At the very end, she congratulated all those who would not be returning. Among them was Millie, now sixteen. The teacher praised them for attending school and passed out their graduation certificates. The parents applauded Miss Bartlett and praised the results they could see from all her labor of love with their children.

Matthew longed for the day he could leave school forever. It looked as though Annie and Buddy would soon marry and build on Uncle James's land, which he hoped would give him some relief from the burden of so much work, keeping everything going. He knew he did not want to be left in that house with Millie very much longer.

He experienced a touch of sadness at the thought. He had loved Millie when he was very young. Then, when he got older, it seemed there could be nothing but animosity between them. He never really understood what triggered the pattern of the past that seemed to set them perpetually at odds with each other. So, that night, lying in his bed, he dreamed of a future free of authority, a future where he would be the one in control of his own life.

*****

Matthew felt no excitement Christmas morning when he woke up. He remembered how disappointed he had been over and over when his birthdays came and went with no gifts. Feeling the sting of tears, he refused to give in to them. His childish innocence and faith that Uncle James and Aunt Martha loved him had been crushed within his heart long before now.

Throwing back the covers he vowed again to leave this place. He went from room to room starting the fires and then building a fire in the cook stove in the kitchen. Hurrying back under the covers, he waited for the house to lose its chill and for Aunt Martha to rise and make coffee.

He must have dozed back off, for he was awakened by the entrance of his aunt bringing him coffee.

"Matthew, I have something for you this morning. We'll be eating breakfast a little later, since it is Christmas. I expect May and the children for dinner, so I'll need quite a lot of firewood today. You may have to cut some more if the pile is low. Duncan can help when he comes." Martha left him alone with his coffee.

Despite himself, Matthew felt a touch of anticipation at Martha's words. She usually gave him a suit of clothes for Christmas, but he had not expected anything this year because of the new clothes he had received for Katherine's wedding. Enjoying the strong coffee and the peace of the moment, he dreaded having to cut more firewood in the cold. Maybe Buddy and Duncan would both help him.

Throwing back the covers, he shivered as he quickly dressed, then carried his boots and socks into the kitchen to put them on beside the stove. Millie and Annie were having their coffee in the front room beside the fire. Uncle James had not made an appearance yet, but Martha was making biscuits at the table. Sticking them into the oven, she poured herself a cup of coffee and joined Millie and Annie. It was not yet full day outside, so Matthew delayed going out into the cold to tend to the milking, staying by the fire as long as possible.

Hearing laughter, he walked into the front room. Millie and Annie had unwrapped gifts lying on their laps. Looking up at Matt, Martha handed him a bulky package. He tore into it quickly, anxious to see his gift. His eyes widened in pleased surprise at what he saw. A real cowhide jacket, just like cow hands wore. The inside was lined with soft fur and there was a pair of soft, warm gloves to go with it. He could not believe Aunt Martha had given him such a gift. Opening his mouth to exclaim his thanks to her, the words died on his tongue when she spoke quickly.

"Before you thank me, that didn't come from me. It came from Buck and Willie. They want you to come visit them this summer. I've been holding it for you since a month ago when they sent it over by one of their hired hands." her words were abrupt, as though she disapproved of the gift.

"Why would Uncle Buck give him such an expensive coat, Mama? They didn't give me anything for Christmas." Millie's voice was whiney and jealous.

"Millie, why don't you grow up," Annie exclaimed in disgust. "You have a mother and daddy to buy for you. You should be thankful for that instead of always being jealous of Matthew."

"Annie, that's enough about the matter," Martha said rather sharply. "Buck and Willie are free to buy for whoever they wish to buy for. Let that be the end of the matter. Millie? Am I understood?"

"Yes mama." Millie, for once, does not have anything more to say as Martha leaves to check on her biscuits. As soon as she was out of sight, though, Millie turned to Matthew. "Don't think I've forgotten what you did to me, Matthew. You've been buttering up Uncle Buck and Aunt Willie, but it won't do you a bit of good. You're going to pay for being mean to me." she made a face at him like a two-year-old instead of a young lady of sixteen.

Annie shook her head in despair. She doesn't care anymore what Matt does to her sister, she told herself. Soon, she will have her own home and be free of the tension and anger constantly permeating this house. Where is the kindness, gentleness and long suffering Christian believers are to show to others. How can her family say they love God when they don't show love to each other?

Matthew gathered up his fine coat and gloves and went to his room, his heart bursting with happiness in spite of Millie and her ugliness. What did he care about her? He would soon be going to visit Uncle Buck. In the privacy of his room, he slipped into the warm coat and pulled the gloves on his hands. Oh, what a coat! The fur lining was so soft and warm against his body. The gloves were softer than Firefly's sleek hair. Never in his short life had he experienced such a feeling of luxury. A sudden sense of being cared for overwhelmed him. The same feeling that came over him on the creek bank when he saw the angels. The feeling he had when he had sought refuge in his cave and held the white stone in his hand. That's the feeling he wanted. An unexplainable happiness mixed with sadness. He hugged himself in the warm coat, looking forward to once again escaping to Uncle Buck and Aunt Willie in the summer.

Chapter 6

That winter was the longest Matthew could remember, for he was so afraid Uncle James would change his mind about his going to Uncle Buck's house in the summer. Up to the very last, he lived with the ever-present certainty that something would happen to stop his leaving. Then, suddenly, he was on Firefly and on the trail that would eventually take him to the big white house of his favorite aunt and uncle.

He spent a month with Aunt Willie. It was the highlight of his life, the times he spent with her. That summer, the Macellwain family also paid a visit while he was there. They seemed like a happy family. There were three girls, but the one with red hair and freckles, Amelia, tagged along with him, talking and asking him a hundred questions about himself. He tried to evade her, not being much of a talker, but she seemed to appear wherever he happened to be. Although they were only there one day and night, he realized when they left that he liked how she looked up to him. He noticed her eyes filled with sympathetic tears when he told her his mother was dead. That was strange because she didn't even know him. Then, when they were eating, her mother had looked at him the same way.

His visit was over much too quickly, and he returned to finish the summer in his usual routine of chores and battling with Millie.

Having finished her education as far as the one-room school allowed, Millie was now allowed to receive suitors. She had thoroughly enjoyed the month that Matthew was gone. She had met Douglas Martin, a young man who was captivated by her pretty face. With James's permission, he had begun calling on Millie, sitting in the parlor or on the front porch in the long summer evenings.

It was on one such evening, after Matthew returned that Millie awaited the arrival of her young man. She was dressed and sitting in the swing on the front porch so as to see him when he came up the road. Matthew had finished the milking, deposited it in the kitchen, and then walked on through the house and out the front door. Seeing Millie sitting so prim in the swing, he laughed.

"Poor old Douglas," Matthew smirked, his voice dripping with sarcasm. "Is he ever in for a surprise if he gets you for a wife." he taunted her, for he loved to make her mad.

"Matthew, go away. I don't want you here when Douglas arrives. You act like an uneducated savage. You're always dirty and barefooted. Why don't you go clean up and put on some better clothes? You embarrass me." her eyes flashed angrily as she berated him, trying to get him to disappear before her suitor arrived.

"Let's see you make me, Miss high and mighty. Too bad Douglas hasn't seen you barefoot and dirty like I have." he laughed again, enjoying himself.

"If you don't leave me alone, Matthew Carlisle, I'll fix you really well with daddy. I know something about you. You're a thief; that's what you are." she was so anxious to get him to leave that she prematurely played her trump card against him.

She realized too late she had said too much. He was suddenly standing over her; his fist balled up, his eyes full of malice and suppressed rage.

"What are you talking about, calling me a thief? You better shut your mouth before I give you a black eye." he threatened.

Millie was spared whatever would have occurred by the sound of a horse galloping up the path leading to the house. Douglas had arrived, and Matthew turned away and went inside the house without saying another word.

*****

Only a few days later, Matthew found the perfect time to confront Millie with her own words. He had a sneaking suspicion that his coin was involved in her threats, and he intended to find out. He was cleaning the stalls in the barn and putting fresh hay down for the cows and horses. Millie was hanging clothes on the line, for it was a beautiful day and Aunt Martha was washing everything that needed washing. Early that morning, Matthew had built a fire and filled the big wash pot with water, starting it to boil, then adding the lye soap. He had to continually add wood to the blaze so the water would stay hot. Seeing Millie alone, he decided to find out why she had called him a thief. He checked the fire under the wash pot, and then walked down to the clothesline.

"It sure is good to see you working for a change, Millie. I'll bet it really makes you mad to have to hang up clothes. You know, you being so high and mighty." he grinned as he saw her eyes flash dangerously.

"I'm warning you, Matthew. Don't start anything. I've already told you I can get you in trouble any time I please. You better watch your step." she faced him, her hands on her hips.

"Just what are you talking about, anyway? I haven't stolen anything from anybody. You better watch your mouth, calling somebody a thief for no reason." his voice was calm and controlled.

"You know very well what I'm talking about. I found that coin, the one in your room. Who did you steal it from? Probably from Uncle Buck. You have never had any money in your whole life, Matthew." she finished with triumph at his look of surprise. "Yes, I know all about it. I have it put away. You'll never get it back, either. If you don't leave me alone, I'll tell daddy about your being a thief." Her expression changed as Matthew advanced on her, for she saw his intent too late.

Although she was a grown woman, he was strong, and before she realized it, he grabbed her and pinned her arms behind her back, giving them a vicious yank as he grinned at her discomfort.

"I think you will give me my coin, Millie. I didn't steal it, but I don't have to explain that to you. If you don't want me to break your arms, you better go get it right now."

Instead of complying, she administered a savage kick backward, catching him on the shin with her heavy boot. For a moment, he loosened his grip, and she whirled around and hit him as hard as she could with her fist balled up like a man. That was her mistake, for his anger overcame his sense of reality, and he hit her back, knocking her to the ground. Millie seemed beside herself with her desire to hurt him. Jumping to her feet, she came at him again, meaning to hit him, but she never did, for he slapped her again, sending her sprawling to the ground, tears of pain and frustration clouding her vision. Screaming like a mad woman, she came at him again, and it was all he could do to protect himself from her flailing arms and determined kicks. Finally, he pushed her as hard as he could and left her there in the dirt. He went to the barn, where he climbed up into the hayloft and remained there for the better part of the day.

Millie had gone into the house, crying and filthy; her face bruised and cut from the blows Matthew had given her. Martha's gasp of dismay had turned to anger against Matthew for what he had done to Millie. As soon as she had taken care of Millie's hurts, she went out to find Matthew.

He knew he was in trouble. He also knew that Millie had lied. She always lied. She never told what she had done; only what he did. 'Well,' he decided, 'I'm not taking a whipping for beating her up. She deserved what she got. She's stolen my coin. I've got to get it back.'

But Millie has told her story, and there is no escape for Matthew, for she has convinced her parents that he attacked her for no reason other than that she had found the coin and accused him of stealing it.

Now, he must face Uncle James, as he knew he would. James is very angry.

"You force me to this, boy. You know what to expect. Take your whipping like a man, for you know you deserve it." His voice was low and threatening. James motioned Matthew toward him.

Since he was a small boy, James had administered punishment in the same way. Putting Matthew's head between his legs, he would thrash his backside with his cane or strap. Submission always seemed to be the only recourse for a small boy. Today, it will be a different scene, for he has determined his uncle will not whip him ever again. He's no longer the little boy who had no defense. He's strong and muscled from hard work. Resentment at his treatment has become a seething anger toward everyone in this house. This is the first time he has felt strong enough to resist his punishment by Uncle James. James felt uncertainty and a flicker of fear as he faced Matthew and ordered him to take his whipping.

"No. You won't whip me today, or ever again. Millie stole that coin from me. I'm not a thief." His fists are clenched, his legs spread in a fighting stance, as he faces James.

"Are you calling Millie a liar? You're the liar and I'll whip it out of you." James raised the cane in a fury, striking out at Matthew.

Raising his arm to block the blow, Matthew stepped aside. James was unable to stop the forward lurch of his body and was knocked off balance, staggering on his bad leg. He caught himself against the table and turned furious eyes on Matthew.

"Either take your whipping, or you can't stay under my roof." He is breathing hard from the exertion and the pain in his leg.

"I'm gone." the words are final, as Matthew walked to the front door.

He had reached the porch when Martha hurried through the house, calling his name." Matthew, where are you going? You have no place to go, boy. Why didn't you take your whipping? You know you shouldn't hit Millie."

Matthew didn't stop until he reached the gate. Uncle James had come to stand beside Martha.

Turning, Matthew shook his fist at James, his face terrible in its fury. "Come on out here. I'll show you what kind of a man I am. I'll give you a whipping. Come on, Uncle James."

James remained on the porch as Matthew strode off down the trail, disappearing out of sight as they watched him.

Chapter 7

Matthew leaned against the corral, one foot propped up on the bottom rail. His hat hid his eyes and expression as he watched the horses mill around inside the enclosure.

"Is this all you have?" his question was directed at Mr. Reeves, an older man standing beside him, who looked at him in surprise.

"Is this all I have? What do you mean? These are fine horses. Look at that little bay mare there. She's a beauty."

Matthew's expression didn't change, for he couldn't allow Mr. Reeves to see his excitement. As soon as he approached the corral, his eyes had found the mare. He didn't know how much she cost, and he had very little money in his pocket.

"I've seen better. Supposing a man wanted to buy one of these horses. What would be the asking price, say, for that mare? Although, she's not much to look at in my book. I'm used to much better stock than what you have here, sir." he continued to watch the mare. His heart had begun to beat against his ribs; he was so anxious to have that mare. He had finally accumulated enough money to buy a horse for himself. Odd jobs and staying here and there had been his life since he left home. He was a fairly good carpenter and had found his skills were worth food and lodging at most ranches for a while. He needs a horse badly.

Mr. Reeves shot a shrewd look at the young boy, for he realized that he was just a kid trying to appear smarter than he really was.

"Well, let me consider some things for a moment. I could use a good hand right now. I've got a job opening for a bronco buster. I might consider trading out some of the price of one of these second-rate horses of mine. 'Course, you might not be interested, being an expert judge of horseflesh, as you say." Mr. Reeves grinned at Matthew. His thinning white hair blew in the wind, his friendly blue eyes watching the horses. He pretended not to see the tenseness in the young man standing beside him.

"Just what did you have in mind? You know, in case I am interested?" Matthew finally glanced his way, but the hat hid his eyes still.

"I've got a stallion that needs a knowing hand. None of my boys can do anything with him. I'll tell you what, Mr. Carlisle. If you would be interested in calming that bronco down for me, I'll trade your skill for that mare out there. 'Course, I would like you to stick around if you would. My wife has been mighty lonesome since our children grew up and moved away. She loves to cook, and she always tells me to be sure to invite any strangers to our place to stay for a good meal." Mr. Reeves waited patiently while Matt seemed to be considering his offer.

Actually, it was all Matthew could do to keep from letting out a whoop of gladness. He had way too much pride to ask for a meal, but it had been a while since he had eaten good cooking. His eyes were lit up like stars when he finally looked at Mr. Reeves, whose grin was infectious.

"I believe I'll take you up on that offer, Mr. Reeves. It sure is kind of you. Course, now, if you need some cash along with the Bronco breaking, I'll be glad to oblige you." he added.

"No, no, but wait until you see this stallion. You may want out of the deal." his face became serious again as he warned Matthew.

Together, they walked around the big barn to another corral, one with higher fences. Inside, his tail held high, his proud neck arched, was the most beautiful black stallion Matthew had ever seen. What a horse, he thought. Now, a man could feel proud, sitting astride such a horse as that. He watched the powerful hooves tear up the dirt as he raced around the perimeter of the enclosure. Then, rearing, pawing the air, he presented a magnificent picture of wild beauty, untamed by man. Free, Matthew thought. He's free. In his own mind, he's free. But not really. For the bars of man's making hold him prisoner. He thought he would be free, too, once he walked away from Uncle James's authority. Reality faced him quickly, however, and he soon realized he had no one he could depend on for food and clothing. In spite of his ill-treatment, he had always been well-fed and had a good, clean bed in which to sleep. As he watched the wild stallion, Matthew felt sudden empathy for him, for he would never be free again.

Mr. Reeves was looking at him curiously, wondering at his expression. He hoped he wouldn't back out, for he liked this young man, despite his bravado. He knew it was a defense against the world. A man had to appear tough. Life demanded it. He leaned his arms against the fence as they watched the black horse in silence.

Matthew began his conquest of the black stallion that very day. Entering the corral, he stood, waiting to see just how much malice there might be in the big black. If he was a man killer, he could never be tamed. If he had been mistreated up to this point, Mr. Reeves might as well let him go back to the wild herd. The stallion eyed the man, sizing him up, it seemed. Then, he raced around the corral, avoiding coming close to Matthew. With another show of dominance and challenge, the stallion reared, pawing the air, screaming in defiance of this enclosure that prohibited his flight. Matthew did not move nor advance. The horse seemed to calm down some. His running slowed to a walk, and his eyes became less wild. Matthew walked a few steps away from the fence. He held a hand out, talking in low, even tones.

"Yes, sir, boy, I know how you feel. It must be great out there, running free, feeling the wind blowing through your mane, the thundering of your mares behind you. This is sure a big comedown, I can tell you right now. I have all my feelings for you, but I need you to calm down now. Nobody is going to hurt you. Come on, I won't push you, but I want to be friendly. I'm giving you space and time to think about it." his voice went on and on as he walked toward the big black.

He was careful not to hem the horse into a corner but left him plenty of room to avoid him if he wanted. Finally, he stopped once more, standing still, his voice was soft, cajoling. The ears pricked forward, and the eyes watched him warily. As the horse made no move to try to escape, Matthew walked a little closer, carefully. Without warning, the big horse wheeled and took off, away from Matthew, racing around the corral again, and then coming to a sudden stop, his eyes watching the man. Matthew continued to advance until he stood within arm's reach of the proud head. Tentatively, Matthew took a slow step, then another, until the tips of his fingers were within an inch of the velvety lips. He began to back away, one step at a time, slowly, slowly. He grinned as he saw the beautiful eyes follow him, and then the stallion began to walk forward as Matthew walked backward. He continued talking the entire time, saying anything that came into his head but keeping his voice even and soft. When his back bumped against the corral, the black had followed him across the length of the corral and he touched the silky mane and rubbed the white diamond between his eyes. Reaching into his shirt, he offered the black something white on the palm of his hand and felt his velvety lips nibble up the sugar.

Mr. Reeves grinned delightedly. What a show! He liked this boy. He sure hoped he would stay on for a while.

"Mr. Carlisle, I do believe you have the touch. Most men would have fought with that horse, got him tied, saddled, climbed on, got thrown, climbed back on and gotten thrown again. You have too much sense for that, I can tell. I know you're going to stay and finish the job. I think Mama's about ready to put the biscuits on the table. Come along, now, that horse will be there tomorrow." he led the way toward the sprawling ranch house surrounded by beds and beds of flowers and shade trees that cast their cool shadow over the wide porch.

Mr. Reeves introduced him to Mrs. Reeves. He saw kindness in her dark eyes and instantly felt welcomed.

Matthew was shown where to wash up. Ushered to the table by Mr. Reeves, he sat down.

"Thank you Lord, for this food you have provided and bless Matthew Lord, on his journey." Mr. Reeves grinned at his wife as he finished. "Now Matthew, you eat all you can hold, because Mama doesn't know how to cook a little bit of food."

"Pay no attention to him, Matthew. Mr. Reeves is a soft-hearted old coot. That's why I love him. Never turn a stranger away lest you feed him. That's his motto." she smiled fondly. Her eyes twinkled with mischief as she watched Matthew eat.

"How is it you don't have yourself a good wife to cook for you, Matthew? A handsome man like you should not be alone." She hoped he would tell them something about himself.

"I haven't thought about that, Mrs. Reeves. I'm just trying to take care of myself right now. I left home a couple of years ago. I haven't had a real home since. I will someday, though. I'll have my own place, my own land. These are mighty good biscuits, Mam. I appreciate you asking me to stay. I'll have that black riding by the end of the day tomorrow. I promise you that, Mr. Reeves." Matthew looked from one of them to the other as he talked and ate.

That night, Matthew moved into the bunk house, where he inspired curiosity from the other men, mostly older and more experienced than himself. He didn't invite conversation, although he felt they expected him to explain his presence among them. They did wonder why Mr. Reeves had hired him, seeing as how he already had a full crew.

The next morning, after breakfast, Matthew returned to the corral, anxious to make progress with the big black stallion. True to his word, that afternoon, he opened the gate and rode the horse out and across the pasture, much to the amazement of the men working there. His pride in his accomplishment lifted his shoulders and put a satisfied smile on his face. After showing off his expertise, he returned to the house, meeting Mr. Reeves at the corral.

"Matthew, I must say, I had my doubts, you being so young and all, but you have kept your word. Yes, sir, you can take your place with any man in my book." he slapped Matthew on the back, congratulating him for breaking the big horse.

He noticed the sudden tensing of the muscles in the boy's face at the unexpected contact and wondered at his reaction. Indian blood in him, for sure, he decided thoughtfully. What lay beneath the dark skin and darker eyes of this young boy? He carried a chip on his shoulder. That is apparent. Acts kind of like a whipped dog that suddenly turns on the ones who have kicked him around. Mr. Reeves was a pretty good judge of men, and he felt a need in this boy in spite of his show of confidence.

"I guess I'll hang around for a while, Mr. Reeves. Now that I've got me a horse, I plan to move on, but I'll work for you a few months, anyway." he consented.

"I've been thinking, Matthew. I don't know what your plans are for your future, but you might consider buying the black. Imagine what a colt you would have with your mare and this stallion. Give you a good start when you get your own place." he waited anxiously, wanting

Matthew to stay with him and Mama. He didn't fully understand his own reasoning; he just felt a need in this boy for kindness.

"I'll think about that, Mr. Reeves. Depends on how much you ask for the black. Maybe I can just pay you to breed the mare. Would you be agreeable to that?"

"I sure will, Matthew. If that's what you want, I'm agreeable." Mr. Reeves shook his hand to bind their word.

Matthew found life on the ranch was very pleasant. Now that he was no longer afoot, he felt confident of his future plans, which included going to Buck and Willie's as soon as possible. He had left no trail behind when he walked away from home that day, so as far as Wiley and the rest were concerned, he had just dropped out of sight.

He had gone to a friend's house that first night and stayed until the boy's daddy decided he had enough children of his own without taking on Matthew. He had then gone to Wiley, thinking of staying there permanently. Problems immediately arose, when Wiley after many years of being alone, remarried. A widow woman with a half-grown son, she had taken advantage of Wiley's lonely life and insinuated herself into his affections. Once her position was secure as his wife, she became dominating and overbearing. She resented Matthew's presence and constantly berated him over every small incident. Finally, he left, almost striking her in his anger at her constant browbeating of his daddy and himself. After that, he had gone from one job to another, just trying to eat. So, he had arrived at Mr. Reeves' ranch.

Several months later, with money in his pocket and a good horse beneath him, Matthew rode away from the

Reeves ranch, leaving the black behind. He felt a longing to see Aunt Willie and Uncle Buck. In spite of Mama and Mr. Reeves' pleading, he could no longer delay his departure.

His saddlebags were full of food, and his bay mare was full of the foal belonging to the big black. He felt happy that day, and the future looked bright ahead. His thoughts were far from the cave behind James's house and the box's contents beneath the leaves and sticks. The loss of the coin along with leaving Tippy and Firefly behind was just another source of pain he pushed down inside.

Remembering the incident that had marred the otherwise good feeling of his stay at the ranch, he put it out of his mind. He did not want to lose control like that again, he determined.

Buck and Willie welcomed his arrival with joy. Buck pumped his hand and exclaimed over the change in him since he had last seen him. Willie cried and immediately ushered him into the kitchen, where she plied him with food. She could not believe he had been eating right, roaming the country, alone. They insisted he stay with them, helping Buck, until he decides what he will do with his life in the future.

When his mare gave birth to a chestnut filly, his heart seemed to come to life with joy. Buck and Willie witnessed his happiness with thankful hearts to God, for they had been praying many years for Matthew. He found himself smiling continually with pride in his eyes. His joy in the little filly, with her long, graceful legs and dainty head, was healing salve to the wound of Firefly's loss. Buck shared in his pride and offered to let him breed her to one of his fine horses when the time came.

He was surprised when Ian Macellwain paid them a visit. "Well, hello, Matthew, Ian reached out his hand to Matthew. It's been a long time, hasn't it?"

He shook hands with Ian, with a grin. "I'm surprised you remember me, seeing as how I was such a skinny kid back then." Ian laughed as they walked to the stables. "Yeah, you've really filled out. What have you been doing since then?"

"I'll tell you about it later," Matthew replied. "I bought a mare and I'm now the proud owner of a little filly. Uncle Buck is going to let me breed her to one of his stallions. I hope to have my own horse stables some day."

"It looks like we have the same goals in mind, Matthew. When I got the first foal from Mr. Buck's stallion, I didn't have any place of my own. But that Christmas, my daddy gave me a piece of land, and we began clearing and building a barn. That was the beginning. Someday, I hope to have a big house and more stables. Right now, I have a cabin." Ian's eyes shone with enthusiasm at the success of his life's dream being realized.

"I sure would like to have my own place. What you're doing sounds like something I would be interested in for myself. Would it be alright if I rode back with you sometime and saw what you've got going? You know, someday, I may be able to get me a piece of land." his heart leaped when Ian nodded his agreement.

"Sure, Matt. In fact, you can come back today if you want. You can spend the night with me in the cabin. My Mama is a good cook. You can see my set-up and get some ideas for yourself." he added.

Matthew could not remember experiencing such peace in his heart as he anticipated going back home with Ian. As he and Ian rode down the trail that afternoon, they talked and talked. Matthew did not know how long it had been since he had met anyone as easy to talk with as Ian. He revealed more about himself than he realized in that ride. Ian told him all about his family. His oldest sister was planning to be a teacher, and Amelia, the second sister, would probably become a famous author, as she had shared her dreams with him.

Matthew wondered at Ian's expression when he spoke of Amelia, whom he remembered as having red hair and lots of freckles. He could not imagine what she would be like now, for she must be about sixteen, he figured. Oh, well, he really wasn't interested in girls. His past involvement with women had left a bitter taste in his mouth. He had no intention of getting mixed up with any girl.

WHO TO FOLLOW

Hark, who goes there, I heard a voice call

This way is fraught with dangers.

This road is filled with snares.

The path is strewed with pitfalls.

Things are not as they appear.

Evil wears a mask of love.

From faces of beauty, demons leer.

So beware, when the voice of the siren calls,

Haunting the air.

Shine your light upon my face.

I have walked this way before you.

See my footprints there, upon the ground.

I have grace that is sufficient.

I'll lead you safely through.

Take my hand. I'll never leave you,

For I gave my life for you.

PART 2

AMELIA

I sought Him as a child when night shadows made me cry.

Closing my eyes so tight, I trembled and shook with fright.

Who can understand the mind of a child? Can we travel back in time? Experience childish fears again?

Hold fast to someone else's hand? The mystery of eternity is there.

There inside the child that we were. For faith and trust are born in all But sometime lost before we're old.

Be not afraid to reach out, though you be assailed by doubt

He is always there, never fear. Your urgent call He will hear. The crooked paths He'll make straight. The mountains He'll bring low.

To heights of glory He'll carry you, because He loves you so.

Chapter 8

Introduction

School is out for the summer and the five Macellwain children follow the well-worn path through the woods that lead to their home. Ian, the oldest at fifteen, has four year old Victoria, on his shoulders as he gallops ahead of the others. Six-year-old Caleb runs to keep up while fourteen-year-old Belle and twelve-year-old Amelia trail behind, talking continually.

Entering the kitchen through the wide back door, the tantalizing aroma of supper causes the children's noses to wrinkle expectantly. Turning from the fire with a smile of greeting for her brood, Constance MaceIlwain pulled out a chair and sank into it with a thankful sigh.

"Well, my darlings tell me everything," she said, reaching for Victoria. Climbing onto her mother's lap, she placed a moist kiss on her mother's face. Hugging the chubby little girl, Constance beckoned to her shy son, Caleb. He rushed into the circle of her arm and laid his head on her shoulder.

"O, Mama, you should have been there," Belle's clear voice rang with excitement. "Amy beat the whole school in the race."

"Yes, Amelia chimed in, "even the boys."

"Not Ian," Caleb protests.

With a wrinkle of her freckled nose, Amelia grinned. Her eyes sparkled with mischief as she teasingly answered her little brother. "I could, though, little brother, if I tried."

"No, No Amy, not beat Ian," Victoria's sweet soprano chimed in defense of her revered older brother.

The kitchen resounded with laughter as the door opened to admit Papa. His eyes took in the scene and lingered on Constance. Victoria screamed in excitement. "Papa! Papa!"

Climbing quickly from her mother's lap, she ran to be caught up and swung into the air by strong arms. She dissolved into helpless giggles as he rubbed his beard against her face. The others smiled delightedly at their Papa's horseplay. Though not a large man physically, William MaceIlwain has an immense spirit. His sense of humor and love for his wife has won his children's adoration. Seeing Caleb looking left out, William beckoned to his small son.

"Come see Papa, son. Now that you have been promoted to your second term at school let me see how big you are. William ran his hands along Caleb's arms, then with an   amazed look, he exclaimed.

"Why, I do believe you can help Ian and me get in the hay this year." Caleb's eyes lit up with joy as he went into the circle of his Papa's arm.

They all gathered around the big table, bowing their heads. William prayed for a blessing on the food. A smile curved Constance's lips, and tears of thanksgiving filled her eyes. She looked around the table at her children, hungrily finishing off her chicken and dumplings. The joy of the Lord welled up within her heart, as she remembered: "Surely the goodness of the Lord has followed me all the days of my life."

Chapter 9

Two years later

"Now faith is the substance of things hoped for, the evidence of things unseen. When you pray, believe that your Heavenly Father hears and cares that your prayers be answered. When you have real faith in God, you can believe in those things that cannot be seen through the eyes of a man. Only real faith can see through the eyes of the Spirit and continue to believe for the answer you are seeking. Real faith in God never gives up praying or believing. God is the rewarder of those who diligently seek after Him."   Pastor Haney concluded his earnest sermon.

Seated beside her mother, Amelia felt God had heard her prayers and was giving her the answer through the Pastor's message. Her heart's desire to use her gifts to give glory to God was the uppermost goal of her life. Now with one more year of school, she must make decisions for her future.

"Please, Jesus. Help me make the right choices for my future" She prayed, feeling tears dripping down her face.

She felt her Mother's arm around her shoulders. "Amelia, Jesus hears you. He sees your tears, my darling. They are precious in His eyes." She whispered.

"Oh, Mama, I so want to give my all to Jesus, as he gave his all for me." Constance smiled as she tipped Amelia's face up and looked into her eyes. "You are filled with God's Spirit, Amelia. Just let His Word be your guide and you will please the Lord. He will lead you in His will, for He has thoughts to bless you and He knows your thoughts are to please him."

Rising, Constance pulled Amelia to her feet. "Let's go home, now. The Lord never turns anyone away who seeks His will. You remember that Amelia.

*****

"Belle, we're home," Constance called as soon as she entered the house. Removing her bonnet and smoothing her dark hair, she continued into the kitchen. Belle had set the table and the food was ready for them to eat. "Thank you, sweetheart," she hugged Belle and kissed her cheek.

William arrived as the rest of the children gathered around the table. Seeing Ian's place empty, William looked inquiringly at Belle.

"Where is Ian, Belle?" he asked her.

"Oh, I forgot to tell you. He's brought Philip home for dinner. They went down to the pasture to see the colt. I told them we would be eating as soon as all of you arrived. They should be back by now." She had hardly finished speaking when the door opened and Ian and Phillip came in, offering apologies for being late.

"Hello, Mr. and Mrs.Macellwain." Phillip greeted them as he and Ian sat down at the table. "Thank you for having me to dinner."

"You're quite welcome, Phillip," William replied. "Let's have prayer," he adds, bowing his head.

"Amen!" in unison heralds the end of the blessing.

"Please, somebody, help my plate. I'm most nearly starved." Victoria immediately pleads.

Laughter filled the room as Constance satisfies her youngest daughter and then began passing the fragrant bowls around the table to the others.

Phillip and Ian, seated at one end of the long table are deep in conversation, planning their deer hunting. Ian notices his friend's glance frequently going to Belle, seated at the other end of the table. Suddenly suspicious of Phillip's motive for inviting himself to dinner, Ian kicked him under the table to get his attention. Phillip blushed, and looked back at Ian with a grin.

At the head of the table, William noticed the little exchange and the admiring looks Phillip is giving Belle. Constance, seated on his right, shakes with suppressed laughter.

Grinning at her, he thinks, "Well, they're growing up. It's too soon, though, too soon to think about losing any of them." It's remarkable the changes that just one year have brought in each of his children. His glance rested on Amelia. For all the outward exuberance of this child of his, William senses an introspective quality, a sensitive spirit, delicately balanced on the threshold of maturity. "How can I protect her from her own nature?" He shuddered, as he felt a touch of dread, a shadow of things to come.

Wanting to rid himself of such thoughts, William looked down the table at Ian and Phillip. Where Amelia shares her daddy's auburn hair and fairness, Ian's hair is darker, his skin prone to tan rather than freckle. From the time he could toddle about, William has kept him by his side. Deep in his thoughts, William suddenly realizes his wife has spoken to him.

"Darling, I said, would you like to have coffee and dessert on the front porch," she asked.

"Oh, I sure do. I'm sorry, dear. I'm wandering. You know how I am." Smiling into her eyes, he stood. "Well, children, your mother and I are headed for the front porch. I know all of you will help clear things away and join us for dessert and coffee."

The wide front porch, stretching across the front of the house, is a favorite spot for Constance and William.

"Come, me fetching beauty. Sit on me knee here, before yon brood of young'uns invade our peaceful retreat." William used his best Irish brogue as he pulled Constance onto his lap, kissing her lingeringly.

Laughingly returning his embrace and his kiss, she rested her head against his shoulder as they waited for the children.

"William, how could life be any better?" Constance waved her hand towards the view lying before them. "God has surely weighed us down with blessings. Do you think Phillip is falling for Belle?" she suddenly changed the topic, catching William by surprise.

"Well, I wouldn't blame him if he did. Our daughter is very beautiful. But, dear wife, even though he is falling for her, does she favor him as a suitor." William grins boyishly. "Of course, with such a beautiful mother as you, our girls are sure to attract many admirers. It'll be up to me to weed them out, you know." he ends on a more serious note.

"William, whatever will we do, when all our babies begin to leave us, one by one?" Her smile is teasing as she looks at her husband.

"Well, me blushing bride, perhaps we can find some pastime to keep us occupied, such as swinging and kissing and hugging." William executes each action in sequence, smacking Constance loudly just as the children erupt onto the porch. Falling upon the two of them, Victoria caught them both around the neck.

"I want a kiss, too," she cried, giggling, as William tickled her ribs.

Just then, Belle arrived with the fragrant coffee and chocolate pie on a tray. Constance passed the cups around. Even Victoria was served coffee milk. Phillip accepted the cup of coffee and pie, and then sat on the porch steps, his back against the post. Ian, on the opposite side of the steps, sighed in contentment.

"Mama, this pie is mighty fine. I may never leave home," he teased, "Cause, where would I find a girl that could cook like you?"

"I have you to know, big brother, I made that pie," Belle informed him proudly.

"Unh Oh, Ian, you messed up." Phillip laughed, and then turned to Belle. "Miss Belle, you are a fine cook. I don't think I've ever eaten better. Course, don't be telling my Mama that, Ms. Constance," he adds.

"I understand perfectly, Phillip," Constance replied, her eyes twinkling in good humor.

"Thank you, Phillip. At least someone appreciates my efforts." Belle bestowed a sweet smile on him, causing his face to redden in pleasure.

"Pa, if I can drag Phillip away, we want to ride over to the Rougeou farm. Mr. Rougeou has a fine stallion I want to see."

"Sure, son. Go on. I wouldn't mind taking a look at him, myself. Let me see, now. Could we make it there and back before dark?" William looked across the fields toward the sun, noting the time must be about two o'clock. "I guess not," he decided, "Night would catch us, I'm afraid."

"William, are you forgetting that the days are longer now, that summer is here. We could take the wagon and all the children could go. It's been a while since we visited the Rougeous. I have an extra pie I could take along. There's no school tomorrow, so it wouldn't hurt for the children to stay up later than usual." Constance seemed eager to persuade William.

"Well, Ian, it looks like you and Phillip will have the whole clan trailing along, if that suits the two of you." William looked questioningly at the two boys.

"Sure, Mr. MaceIlwain," Phillip quickly agreed, anxious to spend all the time he could with Belle.

"That's fine with me Pa. Phillip and I may ride ahead, though. Warn them ahead of time that all of you are coming." Ian grinned mischievously at his parents.

Chapter 10

Two hours later, the little group turned into the tree-lined drive leading to the large white, plantation-style home of Wilhelmina and Buck Rougeou. He and his wife, Willie, as she is called by all who know her well, are generous and hospitable. With a family comprised of seven boys and one girl, they manage their holdings without using slave labor. Buck came out the door as soon as the wagon drew up to the entrance of the imposing home.

"William, my friend, what a pleasure it is to see you and Constance. Ya'll get down, come on in." Buck, a tall, robust man in his prime, laughed with pleasure as he shook William's hand. Ushering them into the large entrance hall, he called loudly for Willie.

Willie came hurrying in from the kitchen, her plump face exuding warmth and friendliness. Her dark hair is shot through with gray and there's a lively light in her eyes as she enveloped Constance in a motherly embrace. Turning to Belle, hugging her and Amelia in turn, she dropped down to Caleb and Victoria, enfolding them both to her ample person,

"You precious children. My, how you are growing." She exclaimed. Come along. Bertha has something I think you will really like."

Motioning to Belle and Amelia, and then winking at Constance, she beckoned to her to follow as she led the children toward the back of the house and down a covered walkway. Following Willie, the children and Constance entered the delicious-smelling abode of Bertha, the sweet-faced black woman who is the resident cook. She is married to Buck's trusted blacksmith, Isaac. Mr. Buck has given them a parcel of land where they have built a home for themselves and their three children.

"Ms. Constance, how in the world are you? And these babies of yours. My, oh, my. Such fine children. Climb right up here by Bertha. I know ya'll little things are hungry. All little children are always hungry." Bertha's merry laugh filled the kitchen, and the children smiled in return.

Their eyes sparkled at the sight of every kind of sweet-tart imaginable. Cookies and pastries oozing fruit, hot and smelling so delicious are spread out on the table. A pitcher full of lemonade to wash it all down sat beside the tray.

"Bertha, you mind Caleb and Victoria get enough to eat, now. Constance and I will have our lemonade on the side porch in the shade.

Willie linked her arm through Constance's as they walked back through the house to the porch. Seating themselves, the two women are silent for a moment, taking in the colorful scene before them. Roses, opulent in their summer bloom, climb trellises, and spill over the low wall enclosing the garden, filling the air with fragrance. Bees, drunk on so much nectar in one place, furiously buzz from one flower to another. Butterflies, floating clouds of luminous beauty, bright blues, greens, and yellows look like flower petals in flight. Finally, drawing her eyes away from the lovely sight, Constance turned to her hostess.

"Willie, what have we ever done to deserve so much goodness from the Lord?" Her voice is soft and reverent.

"Honey, we have done nothing, that's what we've done. Nothing but made a lot of mistakes that He has to fix. Buck and I are trying to do what we can for others, while we are still in charge of things. You never know what will happen after you're gone, you know. Hopefully, we can train our children and grandchildren so that they will feel the same." Willie replied. "Now, tell me how all of you have been doing. Belle and Amelia are beautiful girls, you know. Won't be long some young fella will be willing to take them off your hands."

"I know, I know, but I dread that day, Willie. I realize that's life, but somehow, I just want to preserve things as they are. Every day seems like a treasure, a jewel, to be stored and saved for another season in our lives. We never know how long such happiness can last, but we know there are bad times mixed in with the good." Constance fell silent, her eyes again going to the beautiful garden lying serenely in the afternoon sunlight.

"Mama, Amelia, and I want to sit with you and Ms. Willie," Belle said from the doorway as she and Amelia walked onto the porch. "Bertha has taken Caleb and Victoria to visit Ms. Willie's grandchildren."

"Why sure, honey, ya'll come on out here with us. Constance replied.

"Oh, Ms. Willie, look at the flowers!" Amelia walked straight to the edge of the porch; her eyes luminous with pleasure. She continued down the steps, drinking in the beauty that lay before her. From flower to flower, she went. Burying her nose in a rose and cupping a lily in her hand, she felt overwhelmed by the fragrance and color all about her. "If I had a place like this, I could write beautiful words of poetry. I could spend my days sitting under this tree, smelling the flowers, and watching the butterflies." The need to put pen to paper filled her heart with joyful pain.

Belle saw how the sunlight turned Amelia's hair to a halo of golden red as she stood spellbound in the garden. Her pale skin, sprinkled with freckles, had a luminous quality; "I wonder why Amy cannot see how pretty she is, she wondered. She has a quality I cannot name."

Amelia turned back to the porch, and then climbed the steps. "Belle, could we ever have a garden like this, you think?" She turned back to look at the flowers again, longing in her voice.

"I don't know, Amy. It takes a lot of work, you know. Mr. Buck has a lot of people around here to take care of all of this." Seeing the disappointment beginning to gather in Amelia's eyes, Belle quickly added, "But, you know what? We could make a little place, you know, maybe around a tree, plant some flowers, small, so we could take care of it. I know Mama would help us. We probably can't do it now, though, because the summer's too far along. Next spring, though, we'll get started early. Get some cuttings from Miss Willie, maybe."

"Yes! Oh Yes! I'm so excited. I can hardly wait. It's a long time, though, Belle, until next spring. I don't see how I can possibly wait that long."

"Amelia, what are you so excited about, my dear?" Willie turned her attention to the girls, hearing the last of their conversation.

"Oh, Ms. Willie, would it be hard to make a garden like yours? It is such a heavenly place. I could stay here forever." Amelia's face again took on the dreamy, longing look of moments before.

"Mr. Buck's Mama started the garden years ago when this house was built. Now, to answer your question, I'll be glad to give you some cuttings and all the advice you need, if you would like to try your hand at gardening." Willie finished, moved by the longing she sensed in the young girl.

"That would be so generous of you, Willie," Constance spoke for her daughter, who seemed to be speechless at the prospect of such an offer. "I've always loved flowers, but have never attempted such an undertaking as you have here. It would surely require the cooperation of the whole family since we have no hired hands, other than at harvest time."

"Well, early next spring, you send Ian for the cuttings. I'll root them for you beforehand, and then all you do is stick them down, baby them until they get started, and wait for the roses to bloom at your house." Willie smiled as she witnessed their delight at her offer.

Hearing the sound of voices, they all turned to see Caleb and Victoria, followed by Bertha.

"Ms. Willie, we done went down to see Cherry and Henry. I'm fixing to lay out the supper in the dining room." Bertha spoke pleasantly as she turned to go back into the house.

"Thank you, Bertha. As soon as the men return from the stables, we'll be ready to eat." Willie replied. "Constance, ya'll may as well spend the night with us. We get to see all of you so seldom. I'm going to check on the supper preparations, so you just enjoy yourself."

Mr. Buck sat down at the head of the table and with a smile, bowed his head. "We thank you Lord for the blessing of wonderful friends to share our meal today. We know all good and perfect gifts come down from you, Father, who is the Father of lights. We ask you to bless this food and my wife, who has prepared it. In Jesus Name we pray. Amen"

Amelia felt the sweet presence of God as Mr. Buck prayed. The image of the garden filled her with such joy; she could hardly remain silent and eat the delicious food. Imagining the garden she would have possessed her thoughts. Anticipating walking through her own rose garden caused a rush of joy to her heart as a smile spread across her face. She could hardly wait to get back home and get started preparing the place for the planting of her own roses.

Everyone rose from the table, after eating the dessert of apple pie with cream. The men, along with Ian, and Phillip, went into the library with their coffee. The boys stared in awe at the magnificent array of fine books, many leather-bound, filling the walls of the room. The shelves rose as high as the ceiling. They had never seen so many books in one place.

Noticing their expressions, Buck chuckled. "Well, boys, what do you think of my daddy's library? Quite a sight, isn't it?"

"My gosh, Mr. Buck. How did your daddy ever buy so many books? He must have spent a fortune," Ian blurted out, then quickly added, "I'm sorry, sir. I spoke out of turn."

"No need to apologize, my boy," Buck assured him. "Most of these books were inherited from my daddy's father, a wealthy man in England who owned a castle with a moat. My daddy was adventurous. When he and my mother fell in love, they decided to come to America, despite my grandpa's objections. They never saw England or their parents again until my grandpa died, and then Mama and Daddy returned. I was young, and my little sister was born years later, so she never knew her grandparents. When she was five years old, she slipped out to the stable one day and we think, tried to get on her pony, fell and died from the fall. Her name was Cristobel and my mom went into a terrible time of such grief we feared for her sanity.

I remember a huge, cold house with pictures on the walls, heavy draperies, and many servants. We stayed about three months. Grandma was glad to see us, but she was afraid to travel back with us. I wrote her letters for years, until we received word from my aunt that she had passed away. My daddy and aunt divided Grandpa's belongings as his will directed. These fine books are part of that inheritance. Willie showed them in the Book of Acts, where the Holy Ghost was given on the Day of Pentecost. She told them that in order to be reunited with Cristobel, they must obey the gospel plan of salvation. That's all they needed to motivate them to pray and seek God, until they were filled with the Holy Spirit, speaking in an unknown tongue. It's a miracle how she ever convinced my English, stiff-necked parents, to humble themselves that much. She did, though. That Willie, she's some kind of a good woman."

"Why, thank you, Buck, honey, for that compliment." Willie came into the library, seating herself beside Constance.   Wouldn't it be wonderful if we could "see the beauty" and think no evil?" Willie's words are quiet but powerful.

Chapter 11

Amelia could not remember a hotter day as she left the house mid-morning, hoping to find relief from the scorching sun. Not a leaf stirred, and not a breeze arose to dry the perspiration clinging to her body. Her hair felt limp, and her long dress wrapped her legs in smothering folds as she walked deeper into the trees.

At the base of the big oak, she let her head fall backward, squinting against the sun as she debated whether to climb to her favorite perch. Suddenly deciding, she turned and struck off through the woods, holding her skirt high. Emerging from the underbrush, she heard the trickle of water and felt a change in the air. Coolness brushed her face as the damp air moved upward from the spring, causing the ferns to sway. Breathing in the moist air, Amelia stripped off her shoes and stockings, wriggling her toes in the damp sand. Looking around, as if expecting someone, she began unbuttoning her dress. Soon, clad in her undergarments, she walked into the ice-cold water, holding her breath as it inched up her legs like icy fingers, sending shivers through her body. Feeling energized, she followed the creek as it wound between damp banks.

The water gradually became deeper, and the banks farther apart. The trees reached across the creek, forming a canopy of cool shade. This was a different world from the sunlit fields. Here, in the stillness, her imagination could run unfettered.

So many of the poems she had written had been inspired while sitting high in the oak tree or wandering in the woods, She realized. "Oh, I so love to be alone with you, Jesus" she whispered. Remembering the portion of scripture she read earlier that morning, she looked up into the towering trees. "Cause me to know the way in which I should walk, for I lift up my soul to thee. "Dear Lord, I so need to hear your voice. I'm finishing school soon and I want to be a teacher. I want to know your will for my life so I can make the right choices" She turned around and waded back to retrieve her shoes and dress.

Walking home through the woods, her thoughts went back to the day at Ms. Willie's house. Her longing to have a flower garden of her own filled her mind daily. She needed to decide where such a place could be created. She determined to ask Ian and her dad to prepare the ground, so as soon as she received the cuttings Ms. Willie had promised, she could have her own special place of such peace and beauty. She is suddenly struck with the thought of how soon she could be going away from home to further her education. Belle has her plans all made and will be leaving too. She seems so focused on pursuing her dreams without distractions.

"Why can't I make up my mind? I can't stay at home and go away too. Only a few months and I will be finished with school here at home," she reminds herself. Deep in thought, she climbed the steps to the porch. Constance looked up from her seat in the porch swing, and then raised an eyebrow as she saw Amelia's expression.

"Do you need to talk?" She patted the place beside her.

"Mother, please pray that I can know what to do. Belle is going to school in the spring and I so want to go with her"

Amelia felt her eyes sting with unshed tears. "I don't want to leave my flowers and you and Daddy. I've realized how limited my future will be if I don't go to school with Belle."

Constance looked searchingly into her tear filled eyes. "What do you want your life to be, Amelia. What do you know that you can do that will give glory to God and how you can be a blessing to others? That should be the motivation that gives you the answer as to your next season of life. If you settle now, you will never know what plans the Lord had for you. It isn't as though you are going away forever. What gives you peace in your heart when you consider your options? She asked.

"I want to be a teacher and share all that God gives me in my times in prayer and studying His word. It gives me joy and I get excited when I read my Bible and wonderful thoughts just seem to flow into my mind." Her eyes lit up with excitement. Constance laughed and hugged her. "There's your answer, sweet girl. Now, let's go have some lemonade and cool off."

Chapter 12

Down by the creek, where Amelia waded, was part of Ian's dream. With the scent of fall in the air, Amelia found it easy to share her dreams with her brother as they walked through the woods to his land. They formed a bond of understanding and trust in that unforgettable summer. Ian admired her poetry and encouraged her desire to become a published writer, affirming her dreams with sincerity.

"You can do it, Amy. You have a gift. Don't ever give up, no matter what. Hold on to your confidence in yourself. If you believe in yourself and trust in God, you can do anything." Ian impulsively hugged his little sister, then, laughing excitedly, they ran like children through the woods, their hearts bursting with emotion.

******

On the day of the Harvest picnic, William and Constance, along with Amelia, Caleb and Victoria rode to the festival in the wagon. Phillip had arrived in his paw's buggy to take Belle. Her parents, watching from the door, shook with laughter as Phillip offered his arm to Belle and escorted her to the buggy. Amelia felt a little nudge of longing, seeing her sister receiving the attention of such a sweet and handsome young man. "Will I ever have someone who loves me like that?" she wondered.

Later, enjoying all the wonderful food and fellowship of friends, she watched Ian coming through the crowd toward them. Smiling a greeting, he seated himself next to Victoria.

"Little princess, what have you been doing today?" He asked his little sister, placing a kiss on her cheek.

"Well, I've been chasing the boys, Ian. Danny is my boyfriend, but he runs away from me." Victoria's tone is exasperated.

Ian's mouth moved strangely and his eyes danced with amusement as he attempted to answer Victoria. He is spared an answer when Amelia jumped up suddenly.

"There's Belle and Phillip coming this way! Who is that with them?" She exclaimed.

Walking with Belle and Phillip is a young lady about Belle's age. She is dark where Belle is fair and her thick brown hair is drawn up high on her head, with curls framing her face. Smiling shyly at the family seated on the ground, she waited for Belle to introduce her.

"Mama, Daddy, everybody, this is Penelope Harris. Penelope, meet my mother and Dad, Ian, my brother, Amelia and Victoria, my sisters. Belle finished the introductions and then dropped to the ground beside her mother.

"I'm pleased to meet all of you." Penelope greeted everyone in a soft voice.

"Sit beside me, Penny, I'm tired." Belle patted the ground beside her. Phillip seated himself next to Victoria, greeted her, and then engaged Ian in conversation.

"Penny's dad is trying to get a bank started. So many settlers have come here from all over the country, from back east. He has connections with businessmen who are interested in establishing a bank in our community." Belle said to her parents.

"That sounds great!" William spoke enthusiastically at the news. "I would love to see more businessmen set up here."

"That's what my dad said, Mr. MaceIlwain. Penny replied.

Their conversation is interrupted by the arrival of Nathan, Ian's friend. He dropped down beside Ian, nodding to the others. When his eyes reached Penny, they lingered before he turned to Ian, talking in a low voice the others could not hear.

"Will you introduce me to that beautiful girl over there?" He nodded toward Penny.

"Oh, I'm sorry, my friend." Ian jumped to his feet, causing all eyes to turn in his direction. "Miss Penelope Harris, may I introduce my lifelong friend and companion in crime, Nathan Sanders." Ian turned to Nathan, who had also gotten to his feet, his face brick red. "Nathan, this is Miss Penelope Harris, who has graced us with her company today. I know the two of you will become friends." With a flourish of his hand in Nathan's direction, Ian completed his introduction and sat back down.

Catching Amelia's puzzled glance, he winked slyly, causing her to smile at his comedy. Penny, somewhat taken aback, not knowing Ian's sense of humor, nevertheless smiled graciously at Nathan.

"I'm very pleased to meet you, Nathan." She said. Nathan vowed he would choke Ian when they got away from there. "Nice to meet you, too, Miss Penny." He managed the words with difficulty, feeling like a fool, as Penny turned back to William, who had watched the whole scene with amusement.

Standing awkwardly, Nathan saw nothing to do but turn away and reseat himself beside Ian who was shaking with mirth at his embarrassment. Grinning in spite of himself, Nathan whispered, "I'll get you, Ian, you just watch for it."

"Okay, my friend. But, I might be able to put in a good word for you through Belle, you know. You better treat me nice, if you want to become better acquainted with Miss Penelope Harris." At Ian's words, Nathan's eyes lit up with anticipation.

"Would you do that, buddy? She's the prettiest girl I've seen in a long time." Nathan's eyes are once again on Penny, deep in conversation with William.

"Why sure. What are friends for, anyway?" Ian can see his friend is besotted by the young woman. He also admits that Nathan is not alone in his condition. What a predicament he is in now. Ruefully, Ian passed his hand across his face in perplexity.

Noticing the gathering was beginning to break up, William and Constance excused themselves and took Victoria with them, to begin packing up for the ride home. Belle and Penny, too, stood, shaking out their skirts.

"Miss Penelope" Nathan asked quickly, "Will you permit me to escort you back to your family?"

"That is very sweet of you, Nathan. I'll introduce you to my parents." Bidding the others goodbye, Penelope took Nathan's offered arm and they strolled off.

Amelia watched them go, and then turned to her brother, starting to say something but falling silent. Ian, too, was focused on his friend and Penny. Unaware of Amelia's gaze, his expression was unguarded, revealing a fleeting look that, if she didn't know him so well, she might have mistaken for jealousy. But the look vanished as he turned to meet Amelia's eyes, where he saw understanding and sympathy. Smiling ruefully at himself, he turned away toward his horse. Amelia's heart ached for her brother. He had never shown interest in any girl before. Now his best friend had fallen for the one girl who caught his attention. Love! Maybe a girl would be better off without getting tangled up with boys. She wondered what it would be like to have a man like Ian look at her that way. Her heart gave an unexpected flutter as she walked slowly toward the wagon.

Chapter 13

Amelia stared at her reflection in the mirror. Why was she born with so many freckles? How could three sisters look so different and be born to the same parents? Belle is blonde and beautiful. Victoria is dark-haired and cute. Amelia is redheaded and freckles cover every inch of her skin. Wishing she could somehow scrape every brown spot from her face, revealing what she really looks like, Amelia draped her hair across her forehead, seeing if she could hide some of the obnoxious little speckles. With a sigh, feeling it was no use, she decided there was no way any boy would ever look at her the way Ian looked at Penelope. Surely God would not let some people suffer while others are happy, would he? "Maybe if Mama makes me a beautiful green dress for Christmas, no one will notice my freckles," She said to her reflection in the mirror. Turning away from the mirror, a scripture from the Bible came to her mind. "Charm is deceitful and beauty is passing, but a woman who fears the Lord shall be praised."

"Oh, Jesus, she whispered, forgive me these selfish thoughts and help me trust you for my future. Thank you for coming to save us from our sins." She wiped the tears from her eyes with a lighter heart, turned and smiled into the mirror.

****

William and Constance gathered all the children together in the parlor two days before Christmas. The big tree, giving off the pungent smell of pine, the crackling fire, and the lamplight created an atmosphere of peace and thankfulness. The girls' faces were animated and lovely in the glow of the lamps as they tried to contain their excitement, eagerly awaiting their mother's appearance with their dresses. The real Christmas gifts would be exchanged on Christmas morning.

"I hope my dress is green." Amelia voiced her desire to Belle as they sat together on the sofa.

"I hope mine is royal blue," Belle replied.

"I hope my dress is purple," Victoria chimed in, not to be outdone by her older sisters.

"Why, Victoria, do you hope it's purple?" Belle asked, smiling at the four-year-old.

"Because, because purple is my most favorite color. It matches my eyes, too." She added.

"Victoria, your eyes are not purple," Belle replied. "They're blue."

"Oh, yes, they are too purple," Victoria declared. "Danny told me."

"Oh, so Danny told you that did he?" William joined the conversation from his chair beside the fireplace. Cracking a peanut in his hand, he looked at his little daughter with a stern expression. "What else did Danny tell you, little miss?"

"Danny told me that as soon as he can get a job, we'll get married and I can come live with him in his room. He likes me." Victoria looked as smug as a little cat with this last statement.

"You tell Danny that before he marries you, he must come and talk to me," William said, still sounding very stern.

"Victoria! You are way too young to be talking about marrying anyone." Amelia looked at her baby sister, aghast.

"Now Amelia, we have nothing to fear on that point. Danny must first get a job, and then he must come and talk with me." William's mouth is twitching mysteriously, as he solemnly admonishes Amelia.

"That's right, Papa. I already told you Danny would get a job first. I have to have new dresses and he must have a job to buy them." Victoria seriously reassures her family about her future marriage plans.

Immediately, they all erupted with laughter. Belle gasped and choked, trying to hold herself under control. Ian chuckled, and then laughed out loud as William joined in. Caleb looked from one family member to another, puzzled by what was so funny about Victoria wanting to get married. He didn't find it amusing at all. In his opinion, that little Danny was nothing but a mean opportunist. He ran away from Victoria unless she had something he wanted, and then acted friendly just long enough to get her candy before disappearing again. No sir, he saw nothing to laugh about in the situation. Determined to keep a close watch on Danny, Caleb resolved not to let the likes of him steal his little sister. His fists clenched at the thought of punching Danny right in the nose.

"Okay, everyone, close your eyes," Constance called from outside the parlor.

"One…two……three…..Yes, you may look now." Mama cried triumphantly.

Amelia stared, speechless. Her eyes filled with tears as she laughed with happiness. The dress was green—not just any ordinary green, but green silk, soft and delicate, trimmed with dainty white lace that spilled down the front and flowed from the sleeves. The sight of the beautiful dress would transform her from an ugly duckling into a beautiful swan, if only for one night, she thought.

Constance held the dress, her heart swelling with joy at the look on the girls' faces as they admired their dresses. Over by the fire, William smiled in satisfaction. Bless Mrs. Willie's kind heart; she was the one who had gifted the green silk to Amelia. Her heart had gone out to the little red-haired girl, recognizing in her a mutual love for flowers and all things beautiful in nature. She sensed Amelia's seeking spirit, for she had once been a seeking spirit too. Willie understood what a pretty dress could do to bolster a young girl's self-confidence.

Victoria's eyes were big blue orbs of wonder as she beheld the dress held up in front of her mother. She would be a fairy princess, for the deep purple of the dress filled her eyes with sparkling lights of deep purple. Danny was right, William thought. Victoria's eyes are too purple. Across the room, Caleb's face reflected his protective love for his little sister. His smile was just as big as Victoria's. He vowed to take care of Danny if he bothered Victoria ever again.

"Belle, once Phillip sees you in that dress, his fate is sealed." Ian grinned at his sister.

"Well, Phillip should not take too much for granted," Belle replied. A mysterious little smile curved her full lips and her eyes shone in the lamplight.

Looking up in surprise, William thought. "Uh Oh, what's going on that I don't know about?" He looked at his wife questioningly, but she was absorbed with Victoria and her new dress. Ian, too, looked a little taken aback by his sister's curious look. He didn't know of any other young man in Belle's life, other than his friend, Phillip. Maybe he should be more attentive in the future. He didn't want just anyone courting Belle. He considered his friend a suitable match for his sister, but there were plenty of young men interested in her that he certainly frowned on.

"Well, girls, now that all of you are fixed up so grandly, what about our boys? Will they be able to accompany you fine young ladies, or will they be too shabby?" William winked at Ian as he teased the girls.

Constance turned around with an excited cry. "Oh, William, I'm glad you said something to remind me. Wait just one minute. I'll be right back." She rushed from the room, her skirts swirling. Almost immediately, she was back, something held against her chest, wrapped in a white sheet. "Ian, this is for you. Caleb, I made yours just like Ian's, because you are getting to be a big boy." Proudly, she presented the boys with the shirts, her eyes sparkling.

The shirts were of fine, soft fabric, tucked across the front. They were surely the fanciest shirts the boys had ever owned. Ian smiled in appreciation while Caleb held his shirt up to himself, trying to see how he would look in it.

"Thanks, Mama. I might be able to attract some young lady at the Christmas festivities." Ian winked at Constance teasingly.

Caleb looked at his brother with a sudden worried expression. There goes Ian, now, thinking about girls. Belles' courting, Victoria is already talking about marrying, and now Ian. Caleb could see his family falling apart right before his eyes. His small face looked so perplexed that William wondered what was going through his little son's mind at that moment.

"Caleb? What do you think about that fine shirt?" his papa asked kindly.

"It's really nice, Papa. I sure do like it." He smiled his pleasure at his new garment. "Thank you, Mama." He turned to Constance, who stooped to the floor, putting her arms around her little son.

"You are so welcome, darling. Don't you worry about anyone marrying for a long time, Caleb. But, someday, you'll want to marry too," she whispered into his ear, so the others could not hear. Hugging his mother gratefully, Caleb's fears were relieved for the moment.

Constance clapped her hands excitedly. "Now, let's all gather around the piano and sing and have our prayer together before we go to bed. Tomorrow will be a very active day and I need some rest." Seating herself at the piano, she began softly playing, "Silent Night, Holy Night." Her family gathered around her and soon the sound of their voices rose sweetly, in the beautiful Christmas carol sung through the years by so many other families at this most special time of the year.

Later, lying in bed, Amelia envisioned herself in the gorgeous green silk dress, making an entrance not in the wooden schoolhouse but in a splendid ballroom, with crystal chandeliers like those she had read about in Mr. Buck's library. She imagined floating across the floor on the arm of a handsome prince, all conversation halting as everyone stared, wondering who the beautiful lady could be. Her face would be pale, without a single freckle, and she would wear long white gloves, her hand resting on her escort's arm. Her hair would be piled atop her head in cascading curls, falling over her shoulders in shiny ripples. She would be the envy of all the other women.

A pleased smile curved her lips as the glistening color of the green silk caught the moon's glow through the window. The sight of the dress illuminated by moonlight was the last thing she saw before her eyes closed in sleep.

Chapter 14

Christmas Eve morning came too soon for Constance, who had labored long hours to finish all the sewing for her children. There was still the Christmas feast to prepare and the church service to attend before Christmas Day. Rising early, William had the kitchen warm and cozy for her. The two of them sat at the big old table, sipping their coffee and enjoying the peace of being alone. Reaching for her hand, William planted a kiss on her palm.

"Mrs.Macellwain, does your husband know what a lucky man he is, do you think?" He teased her, his twinkling eyes full of love.

"Why, Mr. MaceIlwain, I cannot tell for sure. Suppose you inform him what a blessed woman his wife thinks herself to be." Constance touched his bristly cheek with a soft caress.

"You're a special kind of woman, Mrs. MaceIlwain. Your children surely shall rise up and call you blessed and the heart of your husband does always trust in you." William quoted softly from the book of Proverbs.

"Thank you, William, for always being a seeker after the heart of God. I am so happy being your wife and the mother of your children." Constance moved to seat herself on William's lap, wrapping her arms around his neck. So, they were when Ian came into the kitchen, tousled-headed and sleepy-eyed, heading for the coffee pot.

"Mama, don't you know that's a married man you're messing with?" Ian's grin was a copy of William's as he raised an eyebrow at his mother.

"Oh, you! Always teasing. You Irish men, always teasing" Constance laughed at her son as he seated himself across from his parents, inhaling the fragrant smell of the hot coffee.

Later that morning, the kitchen became the source of all kinds of good smells. With the fire creating a warm ambiance, Amelia once again wondered how she would be able to leave her home, for it represented all that was safe and secure. She relished this time with her mother and Belle, as they worked together, talking quietly, and laughing frequently in the fragrant room.

Working beside Amelia, Belle felt the tension in her sister and thought it was the excitement of the day and all that was in store for them. Giving her a reassuring smile, Belle reshaped a cookie that Amelia had just laid out on the cookie sheet. Instead of smiling in return, Amelia shot a look of resentment at her sister, then turned and left the room abruptly. Staring after her in astonishment, Belle wondered what on earth was wrong with Amelia.

"Are you girls finished with the cookies yet?" Constance turned from the stove as she asked the question. Seeing Belle alone, she looked inquiringly at her.

Shrugging her shoulders, Belle replied. "Amelia just got up and walked away. She seemed upset about something. She gave me an angry look. I can't imagine what made her mad at me." Belle looked confused.

Constance frowned slightly. That's all she needed today; with all she had to accomplish. Amelia getting temperamental just when she needs their help irritates her. Deciding to ignore Amelia for the time being, she put the pan of cookies in the oven. With all her loving ways, her second daughter sometimes displayed her Irish temper. Amelia seemed to have a need, to always be the best at everything. She could not deal with coming up short, inferior, she thought, to anyone else. Constance did not understand why Amelia should not have confidence in herself, for she is blessed with much that the other children do not have. Her sense of being a failure when she failed at a task continually plunged her into anger at herself.

"Whatever is bothering her, she'll get over it. Let's get started on the pie crusts." She dismissed Amelia from her mind and began clearing the table for the pie-making, now that the cookies were finished.

Amelia stood by the window in her room, staring out across the yard. The trees had lost their leaves and the landscape was looking rather dreary. Immediately upon leaving the kitchen, she had wanted to return, to take back the ugly look she had directed at Belle. Now, with her display of bad temper, how could she go back in there? The whole spirit of the morning had changed for her. The good feeling with which she had awakened had been replaced by darkness in her mind. She hated the bad feeling. Victoria had awakened and was watching her as two big tears of self-pity oozed from her eyes and ran slowly down her face.

"Amy? Why are you crying, Amy? Why are you sad on Christmas Eve?" Victoria's soft voice startled Amelia out of her reverie and she turned quickly, wanting to hide her tears. She felt even worse when she saw Victoria's teary eyes.

"I'm not sad, baby. Let's get you dressed, and then we'll go to the kitchen and fix you some breakfast." Thankful for an excuse to return to the kitchen, Amelia went quickly to gather Victoria's clothes. Then, with Victoria talking excitedly about Christmas, Amelia followed her into the kitchen. She felt embarrassed by her previous behavior and bustled about, fixing Victoria's breakfast to hide her reason for leaving in the first place. Constance and Belle said nothing, just exchanged glances.

"Well, good morning princess. Are you all ready for Christmas?" Constance planted a kiss on her baby daughter's silky dark head.

"Yes mam, Mama. I dreamed I was chasing Danny in my purple dress and fell down and tore a big hole in it. I'm glad that was just a dream. I must be very careful not to fall down in my beautiful dress you made me." Victoria's eyes grow larger as she relates her dream.

"You're right, Victoria. That would be a terrible thing to happen to your dress. You must be a little lady when you wear it." Belle kissed Victoria's soft cheek.

"Let's all have a bite of breakfast. Ian and William will be back shortly, I'm sure." Constance sank into a chair as she spoke. Amelia carried the breakfast dishes of ham and eggs and biscuits to the big table, trying to make up for her ugly action earlier. She was rewarded by a smile of approval from her mother. Amelia smiled in return, brushing away fresh tears that welled up in her eyes.

*****

That evening, with the girls bundled up in coats and robes against the cold air, the Macellwain family arrived at the Christmas Eve service. Handing each of them down, William's heart swelled with pride as each of his girls clasped his hand as she stepped from the buggy. Attired in their new dresses, their hair curled and shining, they were all beautiful in his eyes. Finally, he bowed formally, offered his arm to Constance and they led the way into the candle-lit sanctuary. Ian and Caleb, looking very handsome also, brought up the rear of the little procession as they mounted the steps.

The church was full for the service. As the congregation rose for the reading of the sermon text, Ian craned his neck, looking for a certain young lady. Finally spying her up near the front on the other side of the church, he felt relief at noting she sat beside her mother and there was no young man with her. Vowing to beat Nathan to her side as soon as the service was over, Ian waited impatiently for the minister to finish.

"The way that you know real love is when you are willing to sacrifice yourself for the happiness and well being of another. Jesus gave himself so we could live with Him for eternity. The pain and suffering he endured on the cross was for each of us to know joy and peace in Him on earth, in spite of the world's lack of peace. Jesus told his disciples that the world would know that we are his people by the way that we love each other. Love is gentle and kind, willing to sacrifice for the good of those we live with and that God brings into our lives. God so loved mankind that He clothed Himself in a body of flesh and came to save us. He proved His love. He said if we love Him, we will obey Him. The proof of our love is obeying God's Word.

Jesus tells us to love Him with all our heart and soul and mind and strength and our neighbor as ourselves. We must always make choices considering how our actions will affect others. Only with the love of God being shed abroad in our hearts can we love as Jesus loves." The words of the minister lodged in Amelia's mind as he concluded his message.

As everyone milled around, Amelia heard her name spoken. Turning around, she was face to face with Levi Nichols. Her eyes widened as she took in the sight of this Levi, whom she had never known existed. His hair was cut and neatly combed. He wore pants that were actually long enough, covering his skinny ankles. His coat was dark blue and he wore a white shirt with a narrow tie that matched his dark pants. He also wore shiny new shoes. His face was scrubbed and as shiny as his shoes as he stood awkwardly, shifting from one foot to the other before Amelia.

Levi chewed on his lip, swallowed, and gulped, finally managing to speak in a strange, stilted voice. "Amelia, I-I-I want to ask you to be my friend. I know you have no reason to want to be, but I'm asking you to think about it. You don't have to answer me right now, but you can let me know later on." he finished, his face red from the effort.

Amelia was so taken aback by the sight of Levi and then the things he was saying shocked her even more that she was speechless, not really knowing what to say in reply. Her face turned as red as his as they stared at each other for endless moments, it seemed.

"I'll think about what you've said, Levi. I surely will." She said, just as her friend Holly arrived by her side. Thankfully, Levi used the opportunity to slip away.

"Amelia, you are perfectly gorgeous!" Holly exclaimed; her hands drawn to the silk of Amelia's dress. "Where did you get such a fantastic dress? It must have cost a fortune."

"Holly, you are gorgeous, too. I love your dress. It's unbelievable!" She exclaimed. Animated with happiness, she feels beautiful on this Christmas Eve night.

As soon as the last notes of the last carol faded, Ian exited the pew and made his way straight to the place where Penelope and her parents were seated. Introducing himself to Mr. Harris, he asked permission to speak with Penelope. As her father stepped aside for her to pass, Penelope smiled a welcome to Ian, taking his offered arm. Walking slowly down the center aisle, and making their way through the crowd, they reached the door and stepped out onto the stoop in front of the church. For a moment, they were silent, for the stars filled the heavens with a million points of light. The winter moon, white and pristine, shone on them as Ian reached for Penelope's hand. Her hand was small and warm as it rested in his. Ian wanted to prolong this moment as long as possible. He hoped no one else came out of the church for a long time. This was not to be, for someone slapped him on the shoulder and suddenly Nathan was joining them. Ian hated the look his friend gave him, his eyes going from him to Penelope, fastening on her hand in his. "So that's the way it is," Nathan thought. Ian's moving me out." His mouth smiled, but his eyes were hurt and disappointed. Ian felt like a traitor, even though he knew Penelope would not be with him if she did not want to be. He grinned at his friend.

"Nathan, what have you been up to lately?" he tried to ease the tension coming from Nathan.

"Oh, nothing much, Ian." Nathan said, avoiding Ian's eyes. He turned to Penelope with a smile. "How are you, Miss Penelope?"

"I'm quite well, Nathan. It's good to see you again. My father enjoyed your visit. He enjoys talking with young men since he has no sons." her tone held a touch of wistfulness as she spoke.

"Any man should be proud to have you for a daughter, Miss Penelope," Nathan reassured her kindly.

"Perhaps someone should remind my father of that fact." Penelope's voice held a note of resentment as she spoke.

"If you will allow me to call on you again, I'll be glad to stand up for you." Nathan's voice was almost pleading. Ian felt embarrassed at his friend's lack of pride. He would never beg any girl for her favors, he decided, and appear foolish to his friends.

"I'll send you an invitation to my New Year's Eve party, Nathan. You're invited too, Ian. It'll be a really gala affair. My mother is spending quite a sum on the decorations and the food will be quite elegant." Penelope smiled at each of the boys in turn as she spoke.

"I sure will be there, Miss Penny," Nathan tipped his hat to her, and then walked away without a glance at Ian.

Just then, the bulk of the crowd inside began to exit the church and the young people were forced to move away from the door and on out into the church yard.

"Hope to see you soon," Penelope whispered with a smile to Ian. His eyes followed her as she walked away.

"Ian? We're about to start for home, son. Are you ready to leave?" William inquired.

"Oh! Sure, Pa, I'm ready."

When they reached home, Ian saw Caleb into bed, and then slipped out to sit on the porch, though the night was cold. He didn't seem to notice, for his thoughts were in turmoil. He could still see the look on Nathan's face as they stood on the church steps. Should he just back off and not pursue Penelope? Could he and Nathan still be friends, regardless of who won her affections? He wondered how Nathan would treat him if Penelope chose him, Ian over Nathan. How would I feel, Ian thought, if she chose Nathan? So, his thoughts ran around, like a mouse caught in a maze, never finding a solution to the dilemma. Finally, with one last look at the cold white of the glowing moon, he went inside, sliding into bed beside Caleb, deeply sleeping. Lying on his back, his head pillowed on his arms, Ian prayed for a solution to his problem. He valued his friendship with Nathan, but what about his future?

Constance and William sat by the fire in the parlor, sharing a snack before going to bed. William finished the last of his ham sandwich, and then got to his feet. Constance started to get up too, but he reached into his pocket and pulled out a small box, then presented it to her with a grin. He bowed from the waist, and then went down on his knee before her. His eyes twinkled as he raised her hand to his lips and placed a kiss on it. Her eyes widened in amazement when she opened the box and saw a beautiful diamond ring.

"Miss Constance, will you pay me the honor of becoming my wife?"

"Mr.Macellwain, sir I would be most delighted to become your wife." She replied, as her eyes danced with mischief.

As he placed the ring on his wife's finger, next to the plain gold band she had been wearing for so many years, he felt an overpowering sense of joy, for they had come full circle and their lives are complete. They have built their house upon the sure foundation of Jesus Christ, the chief cornerstone and rock of their salvation. He pulled her to her feet, wrapped his arms tightly around her. "I will love you always and forever, Constance." he promised.

Even though it was Christmas morning, Amelia still felt the need to be outside that morning, early, before anyone else. She put her coat and slippers on before slipping quietly out of her room, then through the silent house, to the front porch, where she curled up in the big old chair that had been there as long as she could remember. Her breath hung in the cold, still air and there was a hushed quality about the morning. Amelia is overwhelmed by a thirst in her spirit, an almost painful emotion, as her eyes took in the misty fields and pink-tinged sky. Tiny wings fluttered within her soul as the beauty before her nourished her spirit. Words began to pour into her mind, lines of poetry that are the expression of the unexplainable yearning she felt so often.

It's early in the morning, and the freshness of the day,

Spreads itself across my senses, as the night flees away.

And the love of the Father falls fresh on those he loves,

I am filled with His spirit; I am one with the Lord.

Oh, look upon His beauty; just bask in His love,

Open, little heart bud, for your time has come,

To give off that sweet aroma that is special just to you.

Open up to the father, be filled with the dew.

Amelia watched as the sun began to move upward, above the treetops. A wonderful sense of well-being filled her heart. The bulk of the house behind her gave stability to her world. Her sleeping family made her a part of a whole. Tears welled up in her eyes from the painful joy within, but her lips were smiling even as the tears coursed down her face. "Thank you, Lord Jesus," she whispered reverently. "Thank you for letting me see your beautiful world." Hugging herself, beginning to feel the warmth of the sun breaking through the chill air, she jumped to her feet. With one last lingering look at the morning outside, she joined her family to celebrate Christmas.

Chapter 15

Amelia hurried down the street, holding her skirts with one hand and trying to keep her hat from blowing away with the other. Spring winds whipped around the corners of the buildings, stirred up the dust in the wide street and played havoc with the ladies' skirts.

She had gone to the home of her friend Holly, and now rushing along, she saw a young man approaching from the opposite direction. Something about him seemed familiar. As they drew closer, his dark eyes met hers for a fraction of time. But he quickly looked past her, as he moved on down the street. She reached the mercantile just as Ian and Caleb rode up to the hitching rail.

"Dad's on his way with the wagon, Amelia. He'll be here to load up all the purchases." Ian grinned. I know all our women are buying out the store." He held the door open for her and Caleb. Trying to adjust to the dim interior of the mercantile, they looked for Constance and the girls.

Amelia followed the sound of Victoria's piping soprano toward the back of the store where the bolts of fabric and sewing notions were displayed.

Caleb went immediately to the large jars of candy displayed on the counter.

Ian browsed up and down the aisles, examining the bright new tools hanging from the walls. Since becoming a landowner, his focus had suddenly shifted to the acquiring of implements that would aid him in developing his property. Curving his hand around the handle of a heavy hammer, he was startled by a voice close to him.

"Are you about to become a carpenter, Ian? That seems like awfully hard work to me," her eyes were big and innocent, but her voice held a touch of condescension as Penelope stood next to him.

"Hello, Penelope. Yes, I am thinking of doing quite a lot of building. Since our Lord was a carpenter, I see no shame in that occupation." Ian spoke with a hard edge to his words.

He had seen very little of Penelope since the fateful New Year's Eve party. He had been so eager to develop his relationship with her; he had failed to see her true character until he realized how she was playing him and Nathan one against the other, enjoying causing friction between the two friends. Both of them had felt very out of place, amidst the glitter and extravagance of the Harris event. There had been friends of Mr. Harris, banking associates and their wives, elaborately gowned and adorned with expensive jewelry. Ian had assumed the gathering was for Penelope's acquaintances, other young people in their age group. Upon arriving, he found that he and Nathan were the only local young men invited. Their clothes were in stark contrast to the suave appearance of the polished associates of Penelope's parents. Several single men, aspiring for positions in Mr. Harris's various business endeavors, were also aspiring to become his son-in-law. Their flattering remarks and open courting of Penelope sickened Ian, especially when he saw how she enjoyed all the attention. Before the affair was half over, Ian and Nathan had slipped out the back way, not even telling Penelope they were leaving. He had avoided her since then, for he still found her attractive and was determined not to let his feelings be known.

"Why are you so angry, Ian?" she sounded hurt. "You've been avoiding me. Why?"

"I've been busy." He absently slapped the hammer against his hand, hoping his sisters would interrupt them.

"Too busy to see me? I looked for you at the party. Daddy expects me to be nice to his young men as he calls them. I hate it. They care nothing for me, only hoping to further their careers by marrying me." Penelope spoke bitterly, her full lips twisted in scorn.

"You're a very good actress, Penelope. I could have sworn you enjoyed the attention."

Ian wished immediately he had not let her see that it mattered, for her face softened at his words.

"Why, Ian, you sound very close to being jealous. I had plans for us, you and I, after the party, but you left before I could get rid of the others." Her tone was confidential.

"Oh? Is that so? What about Nathan? Had you plans for him, too? Or have you told him the same thing?" Ian would not let her arouse his sympathy.

"I was never interested in Nathan, merely avoiding hurting his feelings. He asked me before you did, Ian. Please don't be angry. You don't understand my situation." Her eyes begged for understanding.

"I'm not angry, Penelope. You're not the girl I thought you to be that first day we met. I guess disappointed would be a better description of my feelings toward you." He spoke a little sadly, finally meeting her eyes.

"Please, Ian, give me time to explain myself. Meet me somewhere we can be alone. I need you to be my friend. Please." her words were desperate, her voice pleading as she held his eyes captive with her own.

Ian could not believe he was hearing Penelope right. Gone was the poised young lady, seemingly so confident, sure of herself. Gone, too, was the flirtatious, worldly-wise person he had watched at the party. The sincerity of her plea touched his heart and he believed her. Forgetting the agreement he had made with Nathan, that they would both avoid Penelope, he decided to meet her and get to the bottom of this puzzle.

"Where do you want to meet me?" His voice was suddenly gentle.

"I'll go home and change clothes. I'll meet you in the woods outside town in an hour. Will you be there, Ian?" She touched his arm, her eyes pleading with him.

"I'll be there, Penelope. There's a trail that turns off the main road. Take that trail and you'll come to a little spring. Wait for me there." Ian promised, his heart once again filled with hope that he had not been wrong about her.

Penelope quickly approached the counter, paid for her purchases and left the store, giving Ian a little wave as she hurried out the door. He stared after her, the hammer still held in his hand.

"Ian, are you planning on buying that hammer, or are you just going to wear it out beforehand?" Mr. Tobias, the owner of the mercantile chuckled as Ian, startled by his words, jumped nervously. "Mighty pretty little girl, that Miss Harris. She seems kind of shy, though. I guess her daddy watches her pretty closely, her being his only child and all. I hear she's due to inherit quite a large sum of money when she reaches twenty-one. A lot of men wouldn't care how a woman looked. Money has a way of beautifying the ugly." Toby chuckled again as he gave Ian all this information.

"I think I will take this hammer, Mr. Toby. It seems to fit my hand just right." Ian led the way to the counter, where Constance and the girls had finally gathered, their selections filling the top of the counter. "Mama, we'll need two wagons to haul all that loot home." he teased.

"That's what I have you for, son. Those strong arms come in mighty handy at times like this." Constance smiled as she saw him.

Just then, William came to join them and Victoria saw her opportunity to get some candy for Caleb and herself. William grinned as he saw all the stuff his women folk had piled on the counter. "My goodness, are you preparing for a long siege? That looks like enough supplies for the army."

"Papa, you know it's been a long time since we've been shopping." Amelia looked worried as she defended her mother.

"Now, Amy, your papa is only joking. You should know that. He doesn't mind what we buy." Constance reassured Amelia, who looked relieved at her words.

"Well, let's get this stuff loaded up, Ian, Caleb. I'm ready to dive into that picnic lunch your mother packed us this morning." William added a handful of assorted hard candy to the purchases Toby was adding up. "No candy until after our lunch." He directed Victoria and Caleb.

Victoria's face fell in disappointment, but Caleb whispered something in her ear and she suddenly smiled, skipping out to the wagon ahead of the others.

Soon, the wagon was loaded and everyone was on board. Ian and Caleb brought up the rear as they left the store, waving to Mr. Toby where he stood at the door. Just outside town, William pulled the wagon over to a sheltering ok with spreading branches and unloaded the big picnic hamper. Constance and Belle spread a cloth on the grass and soon they were having fried chicken, potato salad and homemade bread. The dessert was Belle's peach pie. Victoria and Caleb finally indulged themselves with the store-bought candy, lying back on the grass, sleepy and replete.

Amelia walked away from her family, lost in her own thoughts as seemed to be her usual state of mind lately, she told herself. Somehow, she determined that she would be able to make the right decisions for her future. Everyone else seemed to know exactly what they wanted to do with their lives. Why am I so torn, she asked herself. Belle is so confident that she is doing what is best for her happiness and Ian is carrying out his plans already. With a sigh, she turned back to help gather up the remains of the picnic.

Chapter 16

As spring moved into summer, the days grew longer. Amelia once again walked the trail to her favorite place in the woods, now accompanied by her mom and dad, as they joined Ian in building his cabin and stables. By the end of the summer, a barn, with stables for six horses had joined the cabin on the land by the creek.

Amelia felt her world shifting and changing and it gave her an insecure feeling. Ian had become withdrawn, though excited about his land and all that had been accomplished in one short year. She wondered about the day of the picnic. Why had Ian left them without an explanation? She thought her Papa knew, but she could never ask him about Ian. So, she watched her brother and waited for the closeness they used to have on their walks. Several times, she had allowed him to confide in her, but he never did. He never mentioned Penelope and Amelia almost knew that the change in him concerned her. They saw the Harris family at church and sometimes when they went into town, but Ian seemed to avoid Penelope, which seemed strange to Amelia. She saw Penelope's eyes following Ian when she didn't know anyone was watching. Amelia could see that she liked Ian; just by the way she looked at him. She didn't understand why they didn't just talk to each other. It made no sense.

All through the summer, Amelia had watered and weeded her beautiful flower garden. She never would forget the day that Mrs. Willie, driven by Isaac, arrived at the house, early in the morning. By the end of the first day, the chosen site had been transformed as though by magic. The beds had been laid out, seeds and seedlings planted and rose cuttings carefully put into the bed prepared especially for them by Isaac. The next day, borders had been laid out, determining the shape of the entire garden. Right in the center, surrounded by clematis and wisteria, honeysuckle vines, and morning glories, was a small gazebo, just big enough for a small table and chairs. Outside the gazebo, was a stone bench, which Mrs. Willie had brought all the way from her house to set in Amelia's garden. She said it was so she would have a place to sit when she came to visit, but everyone knew it was only her generous heart that prompted the gift. For weeks, as soon as she could see just a little morning outside, Amelia walked barefoot through the dew-wet grass to sit in the gazebo, gazing with unbelieving eyes on all that was hers to enjoy.

Then the long, wonderful days of summer drew to a close. The hay was cut, crops were harvested, and corn was stored for the winter's feed. Fall came and the woods were full of yellow, orange and red leaves, floating, and sailing, spinning upon her, as she spun through the days, filled with the joy of knowing she is loved by her Heavenly Father and He will direct her path and make her know His will. She watched the leaves being swept to the ground by the gusting wind, filling the air with bold colors. "They will rise to be born again in another form," her heart reminded her. She wished she could hold on to each season a little longer, for it seemed none was really quite long enough. Another year of school was almost over. She could hardly believe how fast everything around her was changing. She felt a change within herself and sometimes it was frightening, sometimes exhilarating. Rather like a worm inside the cocoon, gradually becoming a butterfly. No one could see the changes until suddenly, a new creature emerged. She wondered if the inward changes she felt were visible to others.

Just when she had begun to relish the cool, peaceful days of fall, winter moved in on them and work on Ian's land had to stop. He had begun to spend the night frequently in the snug little cabin. He now had two colts and a broodmare for his stable. He consulted with Mr. Buck, frequently riding to his place. He would leave before daybreak and return at dusk.

Amelia went there to the little cabin during the short winter days, preparing food for Ian, finding she could cook fairly well when there was no one watching her. She helped him tend the horses, too, falling in love with the gentle mare and the frisky colts. By spring, another colt would be added to the stable. She shared Ian's deep satisfaction in all that he had accomplished.

She did not share Belle's decision with joy, for she had decided to postpone her commitment to Phillip and go away to school near Aunt Faith in Maryland in the spring.

 "Belle, why do you have to go so far? When will we see you? Are you sure you need to do this? What about Phillip? I thought you and he would get married and live close so I could visit you. Now, you'll be miles and miles away. I'm sorry, Belle, I'm not glad to see you go, but hurry and come back as soon as you learn enough." Amelia could not understand her brother and sister.

Ian had changed, imperceptibly, but surely. Now, Belle was going away. Her safe, secure world gave another lurch and she felt unbalanced, almost afraid to see what would happen next.

"Amelia, when you get a little older, you'll understand. I don't love Phillip enough to spend the rest of my life with him. I have to know for sure before I marry anyone that it will last, like Mother and Daddy. I don't feel that way right now. Maybe, once I'm away from him, I'll feel differently, but this is something I've always dreamed about. You know how you dreamed about having a garden? Well, that's the way I dream about going to school, to a seminary. I want to learn more about the Bible, about the world. I want to be a teacher." Belle's beautiful face shone with enthusiasm and her eyes sparkled with joy as she tried to explain to Amelia her feelings. Amelia understood how it felt to dream and wanted to see your dream become reality. So, she said no more to try to discourage Belle.

Christmas morning found them all gathered around the breakfast table, the stove aglow, filling the room with warmth. William let his gaze rest on each one in turn, before bowing his head to pray. He didn't know how many more times he would be able to look at each of their faces altogether before they began to leave. Belle would leave in the spring, spending the remaining months getting her clothes together and deciding exactly which school would best suit her needs. He had not told anyone yet, but he planned for the whole family to travel with her, doing some sightseeing on the way, giving all of them a chance to see the world outside their limited horizons.

After breakfast, they all gathered in the parlor, where the brightly wrapped gifts absorbed everyone's attention.

"Oh, how heavenly," Amelia exclaimed, as she unwrapped a soft fur muff. Immediately, she slipped her hands inside, closing her eyes in rapture before hugging and kissing her parents.

Each of the girls unwrapped similar fur muffs, their eyes round in wonder, at this extravagant gift. Then, when William presented Constance with a new wool cape, lined and edged in soft fur, they were silent in astonishment. What had prompted such luxury for all of them, Amelia wondered, running her hands over the soft fabric of her mother's cape. Ian and Caleb were sporting fur caps and William a black felt fedora, looking like a stranger with the Eastern style headgear placed atop his red hair. Belle looked at her Papa thoughtfully and then a light seemed to come on in her head, for she smiled delightedly as their eyes met. Realizing she was on to him, William winked, putting a finger to his lips, cautioning her to silence.

An air of conspiracy pervaded the household throughout the remainder of Christmas day and even into the cold wet days of January. Amelia celebrated her birthday at the end of that month with her friend Holly. She even condescended to have the new Levi Nichols at the affair, considering how nice he had treated her for the last two years. She had surprised a strange look on his face several times, during the months following their conversation at the church. It made her feel odd, that look. She wasn't sure she didn't prefer the old Levi, for at least she had known what to expect. She didn't quite know how to react to his new way of treating her.

She had suddenly grown taller and slimmer. Her beautiful green dress had been altered and the hem let down to compensate for the changes in her figure. As she blew out the candles on her birthday cake on that exciting day, she made a wish. Across the burnt candles, her eyes met Levi's intent gaze. For the first time, Amelia noticed what a change had taken place in his appearance over the last couple of years. His face had filled out and some of his awkward movements had become surer. Funny, she had never realized what really nice eyes he had. Clear hazel with flecks of brown, they were fixed on her face. She felt herself flush and quickly looked away, embarrassed by the look on his face. Clapping her hands with excitement, she began to remove the candles so the cake could be cut.

That night, just before she went to sleep, Amelia stood once more at the window, staring into the night sky. What a wonderful birthday it had been. Holly had given her a diary, with a key for all her secret thoughts. Her parents had presented her with a valise, which she had never owned, never having gone anywhere to need one before. Wondering why they had chosen now for such a gift, she nevertheless accepted it with delight. It added to her feeling of entering the adult world where she would be the master of her own destiny. She would be unhindered by the expectations or demands of others. The gift from Levi, though, had been totally shocking. He had waited until the very last, just before everyone was preparing to leave. Then, coming up beside Amelia, he had whispered to her, taking her arm, drawing her into the kitchen away from the others. Mystified, she had gone without protest.

"Amelia, I have something for you." He seemed nervous, for his hands shook as he pulled a small box from inside his coat. His face turned a deep red up to the roots of his sandy-colored hair as he held the box out to her.

Amelia had taken the box with a puzzled smile, feeling sorry for him in spite of herself.

"Thank you, Levi, that's very nice of you." She began to tear away the paper, and then opened the box, suddenly realizing her hands were shaking. When she saw what lay in the box, Amelia raised unbelieving eyes to his face. His clear gaze revealed his feelings, openly and candidly, for her eyes to see.

"Oh, Levi, this is so lovely, but it is too much. You shouldn't have given me such a gift." Her words came in a rush, for she could not respond to the message in his eyes. She fumbled to remove the gift, almost dropping the whole thing. His hand brushed hers as he quickly caught the box, holding it so she could remove the dainty little locket. Then, he stood there, again at a loss for words, waiting for her next move. Amelia seemed mesmerized by the sight of the locket. A tiny catch allowed it to open. Inside was a space for a picture. Feeling Levi expected a response from her, she felt inadequate. Impulsively, without thought, Amelia placed a quick peck of a kiss on his cheek, surprising herself as much as him. Then, flustered even more by what she had done, she spoke in a rush.

"It's too lovely, Levi. I'll cherish it always. Thank you." her reaction is more than he could ever have believed. Then, with a swirl of green silk, Amelia hurried away, leaving him alone in the kitchen, the locket held tightly in her hand. He watched her go, and then, as the red faded from his face, he followed her. Levi went home with a satisfied mind. He was anxious to tell his mama how successful her advice had proven to be.

As she climbed into bed, Amelia took one last look at the lovely locket and marveled that such a gift had come from Levi. She remembered Ian's words from the day of the Harvest festival about Levi liking her. Could it be true? She didn't know if she felt good or not about such a situation.

She'd have to think about that, she thought, as she drifted off to sleep.

In her dream, she stood again with Levi, who offered the locket to her. As she reached to take it, she lifted her eyes to his face. Instead of the face of her friend that was so familiar, she looked into the eyes of a stranger. But she realized she had seen those eyes before. When she awoke, she retained a sense of something on the periphery of her mind, barely remembered.

When William revealed his plans for the trip to take Belle to school, Amelia was in a state of euphoria. She was filled with thoughts of seeing new places, dressing up and meeting her cousins. Fear of meeting strangers mixed with all the preparations was so exciting she could hardly sleep at night. It was worse than waiting for Christmas, she decided. She wondered if her cousins would like her and how it would be when Belle was no longer with her. She had never been on a train and could only imagine how thrilling it would be to ride through the country in such comfort. Letters had flown back and forth; plans had developed over the months. Faith and Felicity, whom the children had never visited, with the exception of Ian, were anxious to entertain Constance and her family. Their excitement was equal to hers at the thought of all the families being reunited. The small girl's school Belle had elected to attend was in Maryland, near the town in which Aunt Faith and her family lived.

Phillip was devastated by the news of Belle's imminent departure for more education. His stricken face touched her heart, but she knew if he really cared for her, he would care when she returned. There was another world out there that she must see, knowledge waiting for her hungry mind to absorb. She had to go.

At first, Ian received the news with mixed emotions. He had told no one what had transpired that day he went to meet Penelope. His pride had received another blow, for he had waited and waited at the appointed place, but she never came. After that, he kept his distance. Several times, she had made attempts to talk to him, but he brushed her aside, his eyes cold and hard when they met hers.

Finally, she began to turn her head away when they were in the same room or glimpsed each other in town. Once, Belle had invited her to go riding but Ian had been down at his cabin, so was spared the sight of her. Surprisingly, Belle had said nothing on Penelope's behalf. Later, Ian realized that he had hoped for an explanation from Belle about that day and once again his hopes were dashed by her silence. He could not bring himself to ask about her, for that would reveal his feelings, so he kept silent.

He was thrilled about the birth of another colt, a little filly. His stable was growing and so was his sense of accomplishment. Amelia had convinced him he needed a flower garden and gazebo and together they had begun to make plans for this project. For some reason he couldn't explain, he had an urge to plan to enlarge his cabin, using the existing structure as the kitchen, adding a large room at the front and two bedrooms, one on each side. A long porch across the front would complete the house. He would work on it through the summer and into the fall, after the trip; for he finally decided he would go with the family.

"What if they don't like me?" What if I embarrass myself because I don't know how to act with my friends? Amelia worried and tried to imagine what Aunt Faith's house would be like and if her husband was a nice person. She knew he was a banker, like her Grandpa Tilley had been because her mother had told her all about her distant relatives.

Caught up in the final flurry of preparation, she was swept along by the momentum her mother created, pushing them all to be ready on time. The tickets had been purchased, arrangements had been made for the care of their animals and farm and suddenly, there was nothing else to be done, except load up and meet the train. Their family being so large, William had made certain to get their train tickets well in advance. He hired a large carriage to take them to the train station. He and Ian sat outside in the driver's seat, while Constance and the girls, along with Caleb, rode comfortably inside.

Constance breathed a sigh of relief when the carriage rolled onto the road that would take them to the train depot. She was looking forward to being reunited with her sisters after such a long separation. She was anxious to show off her family, to see their children and just to talk the talk that is such a source of strength and joy to a woman's spirit. She smiled at the sight of all of her children in varying stages of expectation and excitement. This would possibly be the greatest adventure of their lives up to this point. They would have many tales to tell to their friends when they returned. She felt such tender gratitude toward William for his thoughtful planning of this trip. He knew what a wrenching time it would be for Belle to go, so knew how welcome the news had been that they would all go with her. Closing her eyes, Constance prayed for their protection and safe journey. Victoria and Caleb soon fell asleep once the train left the station. Belle smiled at Amelia, sitting beside their mother.

"Amy, just think, it won't be long before you will be able to join me at school. Belle waited for Amelia to reply, seeing her hesitate before turning toward her.

I've been thinking a lot about that, Belle. Sometimes, I want to go to school, but then at other times, I don't want to leave home. Is that the way you feel?" She sighed and turned to look out the window.

"Oh, yes, Amy. It's a big step, going from childhood to being an adult. It's so important to pray before making choices that will affect our lives. You have a great talent and God has given you gifts that everyone does not have. You owe it to yourself to seek the right way to use those gifts so as to give glory to the Lord. If you don't pursue your calling, you will always wonder what you could have done.

Amelia was silent, thinking about what Belle had said. She knew her sister was right, but sometimes she just lacked the courage to let go of where she was to know what it would be like where she wanted to go. To leave the familiar and safe world of her family and those who love her and live among strangers, who did not know her filled her with dread.

Chapter 17

After the exciting trip back East, life at home had seemed a little dull. Back in the familiar circle of her childhood friends, Amelia was suddenly the object of much conversation and attention. Belle had persuaded her to attend the same girl's school where she had found such a wonderful group of young women with the same dreams and goals she held. She had also met a young man, introduced to her by Uncle Robert, Aunt Faith's husband. "What about Phillip?" Amelia wondered, with concern. Phillip was patiently waiting for Belle to come back to him. She urged Amelia to join her as soon as possible so that they could be there together. Her letters painted such a glowing picture of the life she had found, that Amelia was persuaded she would go. William and Constance decided that only she would accompany Amelia this time, for he could not be away right at spring planting time. Amelia argued that she could very well go alone, but her mother would not hear of it. So, they began making their preparations for her to leave in April, for the term beginning in May.

Amelia looked around her room Easter morning, storing the memories it held as she dressed for the Sunday service at church. "Jesus, I'm about to enter a new season in my life and I need you now more than ever." Her heart felt the sweet response of the still small voice in her spirit. *"I am with you, child wherever you go."* She closed her eyes and stood silently as the comforting words calmed her anxious heart. Smiling delightedly at her reflection in the mirror, she placed her new hat atop her upswept curls.

Thankfully, her freckles had faded and there were no teasing boys in her life anymore. Looking forward to the Easter celebration, she remembered that Ian had gone once again to Mr. Buck's ranch and she had not seen him come back.

*****

Matthew had thought he would ride on back to Uncle Buck's house that Sunday morning.

He had not really wanted to go to church with Ian. He felt everyone staring at him, a stranger when he walked in and he was very uncomfortable. He kept his eyes straight ahead during the whole service, feeling that he stuck out like a sore thumb, anxious to escape as soon as possible. Against his will, he heard the words of the preacher.

"Jesus is the friend that sticks closer than a brother. When your father and mother forsake you and everyone turns against you, Jesus is always there. He never treats you the way people treat you, sometimes mean and ugly. His love is the kind you can depend on, the kind of love that no man can really understand. The mind of God is high above our mind, his thoughts as high above our thoughts as the heavens are above the earth. There is no greater love than when a man lays down his life for another. Jesus laid down his life for all of us before we were born. Because He was

God in a robe of flesh, he bled and died in agony, was buried in a borrowed tomb and rose out of the tomb to ascend back to Heaven. Today, each of us can live free of sin and be born again when we repent of our sins, are baptized in His Name and are filled with His Spirit. We too, one day can ascend to Heaven where we can live in joy with Him. Let us make our decision today to turn our faces toward Jesus and rise up from the grave of our past sins to live in victory. What will it profit a man if he gains the whole world and all the money he can get, but does not make sure his soul is prepared to meet the Lord when He returns? Let us pray."

The words were sincere. Emotion-filled, the eyes of the preacher seemed to look right into Matthew's heart. He seems to know what has happened to him. For a few moments, he believed the words, for surely the man was talking directly to him. There is no one else, surely, in this congregation to whom they would apply. Is he sinning for wanting to make money and have the respect of others?

Finally, the sermon drew to a close and Matthew shook his head, as though waking from a dream. Looking around, he realized people are beginning to move out of their pews, shaking hands, and greeting neighbors. He quickly stood and moved with Ian to the door, where the preacher stood, greeting everyone.

******

Amelia's heart was in her throat as she made her way toward the door where Ian and the strange young man were speaking with Pastor Haney. Is this handsome man Matthew Carlisle? Where has he been and how did Ian meet him after all these years? Her questions mounted up as she heard Ian introduce him to the Pastor.

"We're glad to have you today, son. Do you live around here?" Pastor Haney smiled as he shook Matthew's hand.

"Uh, no, I'm just visiting Ian. I'll be going back home today." Matthew replied.

"Well, if you happen to visit Ian again, we'd love to have you visit our little church again." Pastor Haney's eyes met Matthew's and his words were sincere as he issued the invitation.

"He'll be back, Rev. Haney. He loves my horses as much as I do." Ian grinned at Matt as he interrupted.

Grateful to be released, Matt smiled at the minister, and then turned away, as others moved out the door, trying to shake hands with him.

Amelia could hardly take her eyes off Matthew. Ian introduced him to William and Constance, who insisted he join them for dinner. All the way home, she was so nervous, that she felt as though she would be sick as she watched Ian and Matthew race down the trail ahead of their buggy. She suddenly remembered the handsome young man she had passed on the street long ago. His eyes were the eyes she had seen in her dream. What is it about him that she imagines being loved by him?

All through the time spent at the dinner table, Matthew never looked at her but focused on talking with Ian and William. He felt her eyes on him and was anxious to get away from her constant scrutiny. He felt accepted by Ian's family and after the delicious meal, extended his thanks. "I sure appreciate you inviting me today, Mrs.Macellwain. It sure was delicious." He smiled at her, and then shook William's hand. "Thank you, Sir. You have a nice place here and I appreciate Ian bringing me to visit."

"Matthew, you are welcome," Constance replied with a smile. "You come back anytime."

"I second that," William said, with a grin.

Matthew e followed Ian outside and down to the barn to get his horse.

"You sure are lucky, Ian, to have such good parents and all this." Matthew waved his arm toward the pastures and outbuildings.

"Not luck, Matt. God is the one who has made all this possible for us. My Mom and Dad love the Lord and have taught all of us to put Him first in our hearts. When we love the Lord and put Him first, He blesses us with good things." Ian replied.

Matthew mounted his horse, gave Ian a final salute and a grin. "See you," he called as he rode away. All the way back to Uncle Buck's he mulled over the words of the preacher, the feelings he had while with Ian's family and then what Ian had said about putting God first. For a fleeting moment, an image of a pair of loving eyes and a host of angels flashed through his mind. He looked up into the blue heavens above him. "Is it possible to know that kind of love?" he asked. "Do I love anybody like that? Ian's family seems to be the kind of people who really love each other. . How would it be to have a family like that?"

Matthew felt peace in his heart, anticipating returning to the company of Uncle Buck and Aunt Willie. Years before, when he had come here as a little kid, they had always treated him so kindly, that he had found it difficult to return to Uncle James and Aunt Martha when his visit was over.

When he rode up to the house later that evening, two strange horses were tied to the hitching rail.

Wondering who the visitors were, he entered the house to find Annie and Buddy, who had married before he left home, sitting with Buck and Willie. Annie rushed up to him, throwing her arms around him.

"Matt, it's good to see you again. Aunt Willie has told us how well you're doing. I'm glad for you. You surely deserve some good luck." She spoke rapidly, for Matthew had drawn back at her unexpected presence and was staring at her like a stranger.

"How are you, Matthew?" Buddy extended his hand.

"I'm okay, Buddy." Matt shook hands with him, and then looked from one to the other, wondering what had brought them.

"Would you sit down for a minute, Matt? I need to talk to you about something very serious." Annie seated herself, her tone pleading.

"What is it?" He seated himself, waiting for her reply.

"Daddy is pretty bad. Well, he's dying. He's been asking about you. Wanting to know where you are. He wants to see you, Matthew. We hope you'll go back with us. Mama wants to see you, too." Annie clasped and unclasped her hands as she talked. Her eyes never left his face.

He didn't reply. He couldn't. Uncle James is dying. All the years he had spent planning how to escape him and now he's dying. He remembered the beatings, the feeling of helpless rage, a little boy's pain that went on and on. Uncle James is dying. He could have killed him, there at the last. He had thought about it. He was strong enough then. Uncle James was old and clumsy, overweight. Now, he's dying. I had nothing to do with it. I didn't kill him. Why didn't he love me? What will I feel when he dies? Do I care? His face was unreadable, his hands clenched into fists, a vacant look in his eyes.

"Matt? Did you understand me? Daddy is dying. He wants to see you. Will you go back with us? Please." Annie looked at Buddy helplessly, as Matt still did not answer.

"Matthew, I hope you understand that you don't have to go back. This is your choice to make.

You are on your own. No one can make you do anything. They know that, too. If you go, it will be on your terms, as a man, no longer a boy." Aunt Willie spoke from the doorway, where she had heard Annie's last words and understood Matthew's feelings about returning.

At the sound of her voice, Matthew came back from where he had gone in his thoughts and looked at her gratefully.

"I'll go." His words were reluctant, but he knew he never really had a choice. He had always felt, since that day, that someday he would go back, for it was never finished. Now, it would be. He could be free at last.

"I've had Bertha fix a basket of food for you to take with you. You'll be hungry before you get there. I will be praying for you and the family, Matthew. Whatever happens, remember you have a home here with us. We love you." He felt the impact of her words against the lonely place inside his soul. The ties are broken. He's free to make a choice and no one will punish him for the choice.

Soon, they are on their way back and Matthew felt a touch of dread. In spite of his eighteen years, the closer they got to Uncle James, the more he wishes he could have refused to come. For, suddenly, at the familiar landmarks, he is again that confused, angry fifteen-year-old boy, homeless and alone. He had meant never to return. That day is forever burned into his mind. He remembered every word, every look, and every gesture. He could still hear Aunt Martha's voice, calling him to come back, as he finally walked out of hearing distance and there was only the sound of the bees droning in the honeysuckle vines alongside the road.

He had walked away from his childhood that day. He left Tippy behind. He had left Firefly, his beloved mare. He had gone back to get her. His Pa had gone with him, but Uncle James had refused to let them take her off the place. They had come away angry and frustrated at his stubbornness but without the mare. Matthew's heart burned in fresh anguish, as though it had been yesterday, instead of three years. As the miles stretched out behind them, Matt's thoughts stretched back into the past and he was silent most of the way as they rode together, he, Annie and Buddy.

At noon, they stopped to rest and eat the food Aunt Willie had prepared. They had reached the river by then and found a grassy spot to let the horses graze while they ate and rested a few minutes before continuing.

They rode up the familiar trail just before dark. Martha had been watching for them, going back and forth from the sick man's side to the window. She suddenly was taken back in time to that other day she had watched out the window for Matthew. He had not returned that day. She prayed he would come today. She remembered the way the mare had reacted to his absence. Martha had seen the mare standing at the gate and had gone out to give her a little feed. Firefly had heard the door open and her ears had pricked forward expectantly. Seeing Martha, she had nickered softly, and then took off in a wild gallop around the corral, showing her disappointment. Then, coming to a fast stop, she had snorted, blowing through her nose at Martha, who had come through the gate. She remembered talking softly to the distraught little mare.

"Sorry, girl, Matt's not here. You'll have to put up with me. Come on, now, behave yourself. Get in the barn before you get struck by lightning."

She had watched as the mare turned back toward the house, nickering loudly, insistently, and calling for Matt. Then she took off in another circle around the corral. Finally, she lowered her head and started to eat the feed Martha had put in her trough. After only a moment, she had suddenly raised her head, and with a loud, shrill, almost human cry, she had raced back toward the house, tail held high, ears pricked forward. When she reached the gate, she called Matt again in that almost human sound. Martha shivered now, as she had shivered then, remembering how helpless she had felt to deal with the animal in her pain.

The sound of horses brought her back to the present and her heart began to pound. Annie came in first, followed by Buddy. Then, Martha watched as a handsome man mounted the steps and paused at the door.

"Matthew?" Her voice betrayed her surprise at his appearance after three years. She didn't approach him, but waited, wondering how he would greet her.

"Hello, Aunt Martha." He waited, too, for her next words. He made no move to embrace her, for he could not ever remember being hugged by her.

Annie seemed to understand the awkwardness they felt. "Mama, could we have some coffee? It's been a long hard ride. We're awfully tired."

Given something to do, Martha went into the kitchen, relieved to have time to gather her thoughts. The other three followed her, sitting at the familiar old table where they had gathered so many times through the years. Annie looked at Matthew and remembered the scene at this same table the day she discovered he had walked out. She saw her Daddy's stony face, Matthew's empty chair. She felt the same anger now as she had then at Millie's gloating expression. Then, when the truth had finally come out, James's anger was directed at Millie over what she had caused him to do. The coin had been the reason for it all. The coin had been removed from its hiding place in Matthew's room. He had searched for it for over a year.

Then, just when he had given up on ever finding it, he and Millie had gotten into an argument and she had taunted him that she had something belonging to him, but she would never give it back. Matthew had caught her out in the barn and tried to force her to tell. Millie was a grown girl and strong by then. It had gotten out of hand and Matthew had lost his temper. He had slapped her repeatedly, bruising her face. She, naturally, had failed to relate the incident truthfully to Martha, who in turn had gone to James. This had led to Matthew's departure. The wrong had never been made right. Millie married a local boy and they now lived near his parents in a small settlement about fifty miles away. Annie determined that she would let Matthew know that the truth had been made known to her mother and daddy before he left this time.

Martha poured the coffee into the same cups Matthew remembered. She placed a platter of cookies on the table, and then seated herself, her eyes on the three of them.

"How is Daddy?" Annie spoke quietly in the silence.

"Not good, I'm afraid. He had a bad smothering spell. He can hardly breathe at times.

I've been praying that God will spare him like He did before. You remember, Matthew, you were there with me that night." Martha suddenly appeared vulnerable, afraid. Her hand trembled as she raised her coffee to her lips, sipping it slowly.

Up to now, Matthew had said nothing. He had felt overwhelmed with conflicting feelings and emotions as soon as he entered this house. He felt the burden of these people who had raised him suddenly fall upon him and he didn't want to feel sorry for them. He wanted to keep on being angry at them for all the wrongs he had suffered at their hands. His soul was forever scarred. These people had filled him with a darkness that threatened to overwhelm him. How could he feel compassion now, even though it seemed to be expected of him?

"What happened to Firefly?" He didn't know why the words formed in his mind and came out of his mouth. He had not intended to say them. This was not the time. He should be concerned about Uncle James. Another mistake, another breach of good manners, he thought.

They all looked at him in surprise; as though he had said there was a bear at the door. Same looks he had seen all his life.

"Matt, I'm sorry, but she died a year after you left. We couldn't figure out why. Duncan used to bring his boys and they would ride her. You know how they loved to ride. Then, she sickened and was gone in a day." Buddy's voice was soft, consoling, his eyes caring, as he told Matt the news.

The nausea rose up in him then. He tasted the bitterness in his mouth as he fought for control. His fingers turned white as he gripped the coffee cup. He kept his eyes down, lest they see the rage and pain causing him to tremble. The kitchen was filled with tension, the air still and hushed, waiting. Matthew got up, walked slowly to the door and went out onto the back porch, closing the door softly behind him.

The three at the table, realizing they had been holding their breath, exhaled slowly. Annie suddenly realized that an unpredictable force ruled Matthew. Something frightening and uncontrollable lived inside him. She had glimpsed it that day with May and she had been frightened then. She wished she had not gone after him. She should have left him alone in his new life. She realized no matter what she said now, the past could never be changed in his mind.

Out on the porch, Matthew stared across the yard to the barn and the empty pasture. For a moment, he saw a proud little mare, her coat shiny and sleek standing there, waiting for him, love in her eyes. Hot, angry tears coursed down his face and he tasted the salty taste of them on his lips as the image faded. He repressed a groan that rose up from his guts and threatened to escape his lips in agony. He dropped down to the steps, where he used to sit so often, not being allowed to remain in the house with the grown-ups and hear their talk. A big, dark head appeared from under the porch, weak old eyes peered at him and then the tail began to wag in recognition. Black Beauty, old and still ugly, laid his head on Matt's lap just like always. As he rubbed the grizzled head, Matt relived the day he had trailed the mountain lion and been rescued by this old dog. He buried his hands in the thick rough around Black Beauty's neck and found comfort in the welcome of his old friend.

James Carlisle didn't die that day. He lived six more months. Matthew stayed a month. He never intended to stay one day longer than he had to. In fact, he had made up his mind he would leave that next morning. Then, Annie told him something that had changed his mind. He had gone in to see his uncle and was unprepared for the sight that met his eyes. Uncle James was weak and hardly able to talk without gasping for breath. He was propped up on several pillows, which helped him breathe. He asked Matthew to forget the past and stay awhile to help Martha. He never asked for forgiveness, nor said he was sorry about anything, but his manner was no longer authoritative. He was no longer in charge. Matthew saw vulnerability in his face and knew that his uncle would soon be gone. In spite of himself, he agreed to stay awhile.

Later that night, sitting on the front porch, watching the moon come up over the trees, as they had done countless times before, Annie and Matthew talked. She revealed all that occurred after he left. She told him that Martha and James now knew the truth about the coin. When she finished speaking, she had held out her hand, palm up. Tentatively, he reached out and took the object lying there in her hand. His lost coin. A little smile touched his lips for the first time that day and she smiled in return. He told her where he had gone and what had happened to him as he sought a place to live. He told about meeting the MaceIlwains that summer when he was fourteen and had gone to Buck and Willie. Then he grinned as he explained how he had met them again recently. He spoke of Ian and his horses and the friendship he had found.

"I met a man who had offered me a job herding cows. Then, I found out he worked for a big rancher and was trying to steal some of his cattle, taking them, changing the brands and then carrying them to sell as his own. I almost went in with him. I had met him at a little town on the other side of the river, near the Macellwains. Just before I agreed to go to work for him, one of the young men who worked on the ranch warned me about what was going on. The rancher caught on to the plan and there was a shootout and the man was killed. I would have been right in the middle of flying bullets." Matthew shook his head in disbelief at the thought of his brush with death. "I sure was fooled that time. After I left there, I knocked about, barely making enough to eat, sleeping in people's barns, or wherever I could find a place when night came. Then I met Mr. Reeves." Matthew's eyes softened.

"He was a tough old coot. I made a deal with him to break a wild bronco as part of the payment on a mare he had. He didn't think I could do it. Annie, it was the funniest thing. I walked into that pen with that stallion and some instinct I didn't know I had seemed to guide my movements. I rubbed my hands on another horse and then rubbed the scent on myself. That horse was mighty wild acting. He reared and pawed the ground, raced around the corral and acted like he would just run right over me. I just stood there, still. Finally, curiosity won out and he came closer and closer, until he was eating out of my hand. After a couple of days, I was riding him. Mr. Reeves was tickled, for some reason. His wife fed me so much, that I could hardly walk and he put me to work. I slept in the bunkhouse with the other hands. I stayed there almost two years, then, I went to Uncle Buck and Aunt Willie for a visit. He told me I could go to work for him and make their home my home." Matthew fell silent.

This was the longest conversation Annie could ever remember having with Matt. She was amazed at how resourceful he had proven to be when forced out on his own. She was glad to hear the confidence in his voice.

"Thank you for coming back with us, Matt. Daddy regretted a lot, but he will never be able to voice that to you. Mama, too, has said she would do things differently if she could turn back the clock. Your mother's prayers are up there, you know. They're stored in God's storehouse. He is watching out for you. I know you don't think about it that way, but it's true. She hated to leave you, but she was a Godly woman. You can rest assured that she is with the Lord. I know she prayed for you to live the right kind of life so that you and she could meet in heaven someday. I hope you don't disappoint her."

Annie spoke earnestly, gently, hoping Matthew would not become angry at her words.

She felt so strongly that Matthew needed spiritual guidance. The rage she sensed in him would destroy him and everyone around him if he didn't forgive those who had wounded him. By now, the moon shone down onto the porch, even though it was only a half-moon that night. For some reason, Matthew felt moved to relate to Annie the experience he had down by the creek. Speaking thoughtfully, with awe in his voice, he told her about the angels and the subsequent visit to his daddy. When he finished, Annie remained silent. His story had overwhelmed her. She felt gladness fill her heart for his sake.

"I'm so glad you're telling me, Matt. All these years, my heart has hurt for you. I never approved of all that has been done. I've been terribly angry with Millie and Kate. You've been hurt, I know. If you are to have a life for yourself, you must not let what has happened affect you now. Ask God to take the anger out of you, so it will not rule your life in the future. Jesus was hurt by the people he came to give his life to save from Hell. He so loved all of us that no matter what people did to him, he forgave them and those who repented and were filled with his loving spirit, became his sons and daughters. Please forgive those who have wounded you and let God heal your heart and give you peace so you can be the kind of man God means you to be. Jesus even loved those who drove the nails into his hands." Annie's voice trailed away as she felt tears fill her eyes.

Matthew's face is half in shadow, half in the light. Annie watched anxiously as he seemed to be digesting her words. Which half would win out? The light or the darkness? It would be up to Matthew, she knew. He didn't reply but stood and stared up at the moon, his back to her. He had not told Annie everything that had happened in the last three years. He had held back the part about the fights he had and the man he had almost beaten to death. He could not tell her.

"I think I'll turn in, Annie. Do I sleep in my old room?" He asked. He wanted to be alone so he could think about what Annie has told him. At least, Uncle James and Aunt Martha know he was telling the truth about Millie. He felt a moment of satisfaction that her lies had been revealed. Deep inside, he is aware of a force that he must keep under control, for he has seen the violence he is capable of when he gives in to it.

"I'm sure that'll be fine, Matt. I'm tired, myself. I'll see you tomorrow." Annie went into the house to her old room where Buddy already was fast asleep.

Memories assaulted his mind the moment he opened the door of his old room. He wanted to turn and leave the room and this house, for he remembered the peace and love he had experienced at Uncle Buck's and Mr. Reeve's. He once again saw the love and compassion in Mrs. Macellwain's eyes and felt the acceptance of Ian, the only real friend he felt he could trust. A pair of blue eyes full of love and the touch of a loving hand filled his mind. *It is I, your father. I am with you and I will never forsake you for I loved you before you were born and I love you now.* The words seemed to float through his mind and he froze as something gentle enveloped him. It was the same presence he remembered from the day at the creek. Uneasily, Matthew backed out of the room, closed the door softly and walked through the house to the porch. He sat down in the rocking chair and stared into the star studded sky.

Chapter 18

Amelia scanned the churchyard quickly, and then felt her heart sink in disappointment. She did not see Matthew's horse anywhere. She had been looking for over a month, now. Every Sunday, she had hoped he would come back, but each time, she had gone away with her hope dashed. After that first Sunday, he had not returned. She had thought and thought of how she could see him again. Other than striking out for Mrs. Willie's house alone, there seemed to be no way they would ever meet again. Of course, he had totally ignored her. He probably thought her too young to be noticed. Finally, she decided to approach her brother.

Ian's face showed his astonishment. He stared at Amelia in disbelief. She couldn't be serious!

"Amelia, surely you don't expect me to take you to visit Matt. Why, that would be very inappropriate for a young lady to do. What kind of a girl would he think you to be, running after him like that? Besides, he's not interested in girls. They scare him. He was raised in a house full of women, he told me. He ran away because he couldn't stand them anymore." Ian was full of information about Matthew, Amelia found. He was no help to her at all.

April was fast approaching and Amelia felt she would die if she had to go away for two whole years. She knew Matthew would surely marry someone while she was gone. Finally, William persuaded her to go on to school for the spring term, which began in May. He promised her she could return at Christmas. If by then she did not want to go back, he wouldn't push her. She would be almost seventeen by then and she could make up her mind as to her future. She went with trepidation, however, praying that Matthew would remain unmarried until she returned. Somehow, she would figure out a way to get him to notice her as a woman and not a little girl.

Amelia had hardly left when Matthew paid Ian a surprise visit. He had been away; he said but was now at Buck and Willie's. He shared some exciting news with Ian. A group of settlers was working on getting a wagon train together to go to Texas. There was land for the taking. All a man had to do was stake his claim and build a shelter and it would be his. As much as he could manage to claim and work could be his. They talked far into the night, dreaming their dreams and making their plans.

Ian had finished his house and barn. He had pasture for his horses and plenty of fresh water close to his house. He had been waiting for something, he couldn't quite name. The last news he had of Penelope was that she was engaged to some Easterner who had come into town to help her Daddy in the new bank. He avoided her when he could. He felt like pulling up stakes and joining the wagon train, going to new territory, starting over. He wanted to forget her, but every glimpse of her brought a stab of pain to his heart. Nathan was courting someone else, seemingly none the worse for his brief infatuation with Penelope. Ian could not seem to get interested in anyone else.

By the end of that night, Ian had invited Matthew to move in with him and the two of them would work his place. With Matthew's help, he could get more pasture fenced and enlarge his stables. His stock of brood mares had grown, thanks to Buck's wise advice and he needed to expand. Buck's contacts had also brought sales for his fillies and stallions. Ian agreed to pay Matthew a substantial amount and furnish him with room and board. Now that Amelia was gone, Ian had to cook for himself. Constance had scolded him because he didn't take all of his meals with the family, but sometimes, he was just too involved to go to the house to eat. He had been forced to learn the basics of cooking plain food. Matthew agreed to the suggested amount and they parted in good spirits, excited about their future. Matthew promised Ian he.would return in a couple of weeks, bringing his belongings with him

* * * * * * * * * *

Away at school, Amelia and Belle spent a delightful time with Aunt Faith. She took them shopping, carriage riding through the countryside, and gave parties in their honor. Amelia met some of the young men who were friends with her cousins. Some of them were really nice, paying her compliments, and admiring her hair, which was totally new to her experience. She had always looked at her hair as a liability. Suddenly, it had become an asset. Aunt Faith was vivacious and young and loved to dress the girls up and go places, showing off her nieces. They visited the homes of the wealthy socialites and were wide-eyed at the maids and butlers who attended them.

When they returned to school for the remaining months before Christmas, it seemed the time flew by on wings. Then, they were boarding the train; going home, their bags packed with beautiful gowns and fancy slippers, elaborate hats and long gloves. They talked all the way, as the miles disappeared behind them. They were anxious to see Constance and William, Caleb and Victoria and Ian. It seemed they had been away for years instead of months.

Then, they were home and falling into the arms of their family. Everything was different, yet everything was the same. It was amazing, the family thought, to see the change in Belle and Amelia. Suddenly, they were confident and graceful young ladies, no longer children. The exposure had been good for them, William decided. He hoped Amelia would return to school for the next term. He prayed that she would get over her infatuation with Matthew Carlisle and choose to pursue a future away from him.

After getting settled and unpacked, the first thing Amelia did was walk over to Ian's to see the horses. She was surprised to see all that he and Matthew had accomplished in six months. He had new colts to show off, his pride apparent to her. She felt pride in her brother's hard work and was generous in her praise of him.

"Ian, I'm so proud of you. I remember what this place was like when you and I used to walk down here. I remember our time together and all the encouragement you gave me." They walked through the stables with Ian's arm over her shoulders, her hair a bright halo next to his dark head.

Matthew heard their laughter from outside where he was working. He didn't understand the relationship Ian had with his sisters. They seemed so close. They seldom disagreed. When they did, they usually ended up laughing together, as though it didn't really matter, after all. He watched them, without appearing to. Amelia seemed to have changed; in some way he couldn't put his finger on. He noticed how slim and graceful her figure was in her modest gown. She used her hands as she talked animatedly to Ian, her eyes sparkling enthusiastically. Funny, he didn't notice her freckles. He heard her infectious laugh and suddenly, he had a crazy desire to share in her laughter. She had bright hair and bright eyes. Something in him reached out to that brightness, longed to be a part of the laughter, the cheerfulness, the closeness. He just didn't know how to obtain it for himself. Then, they were walking toward him and he knew he would have to face her and he didn't know what he would say.

"Hello, Matt. It looks as though my brother has met his match when it comes to hard work. He's been telling me all about you." Her words were ordinary, but when he raised his head and met her eyes, he saw such feeling in their depths, that he was unable to believe what he saw.

"I hope he hasn't told you all the bad things yet." Matt met her gaze head-on, dark eyes looking into blue. It was only a fraction of a moment, but it seemed like forever they looked at each other. Ian felt it. 'Uh oh' he thought. 'He's noticed her. Yes, sir, he has sure noticed her.'. "Well, Matthew, if you wash up, we'll have supper with the family tonight, celebrating the girls coming home," Ian spoke into the silence, breaking the tension.

"Sure, sounds good to me. Our cooking leaves much to be desired." Matthew gathered up his tools and went into the house. Amelia and Ian followed close behind.

"I see you need a woman's touch in this place, Ian. I'll be down to get you straight. I'll cook you some biscuits, too. I learned how, you know." Amelia walked around the house, exclaiming over the new parts, critically eyeing the dust. Well, she would take care of that. She had plenty of time.

Ian and Matthew cleaned up and changed their clothes and went to join Amelia. She linked her arm through Ian's and then through Matthew's.

"My, oh my, wouldn't my classmates at school envy me now? I'm walking with two handsome men at once." She exclaimed, laughing.

She felt the knotted muscles under her hand as she held Matthew's arm lightly. He didn't pull away from her. In fact, it felt good. Her small hand resting on his arm aroused a protective urge he had never felt. He was confused by the emotion it brought to his heart. He hoped she didn't act this way with anyone else other than he and Ian. Some men might misunderstand her friendliness. He grinned down at her, suddenly looking forward to spending time with her and the family.

Amelia did not return to school after Christmas, for by then the feeling she had for Matthew possessed her every thought. She lay awake at night, planning ways to be near him. Her heart beat faster at the sight of him, even from afar. All her dreams and plans for her own future slipped from her mind as though she was under some spell. William watched with anxious eyes, the change in his daughter. Belle, too, became concerned.

William tried to draw Matthew into conversation at every opportunity. He hoped the man would reveal something of himself, his goals for his life, and the kind of person he really was inside. Matthew was courteous, polite, and seemingly confident in his plans for his future. He told William something of his experiences of the last three years.

"When I worked for Mr. Reeves, one of the men was a real bully. He ordered me around like I was a dog or a slave. When I left home, I swore nobody would tell me what to do, ever again. One day, we were building fences. He began bragging about what a bull he was. He told me no one had ever gotten the best of him. Well, I was only sixteen, then, but I've worked hard all my life. I'm pretty strong. I didn't say anything to him, but then he started poking fun, betting I couldn't pin him. Told me he would rub my face in the dirt before I knew what was happening. I ignored him, because I appreciated Mr. Reeves giving me a job and didn't want to cause any trouble. Then, he grabbed me by the arm, told me not to ignore him. Well, I can't stand for anybody to touch me. I've been beaten all my life. I just can't take anybody touching me. I guess I lost my mind for a while."

Matthew's eyes became furiously dark as he related the incident to William. His hands clenched into fists; his face changed unpleasantly. William felt a chill. He could see the intensity of Matthew's anger.

"I had him down on the ground and was beating his face into a pulp when the other men pulled me off him. He never did bother me again." Matthew said with satisfaction. "I guess I would have killed him if they had not stopped me. All I could see was a haze before my eyes." He looked off into the distance, as though he didn't understand his own actions.

William was silent, his thoughts more troubled than before. Dear God, what can Amelia know of the darkness, the pent-up rage that only needs a slight provocation to erupt into violence? If she makes a wrong move in his eyes, that fury could be directed at her. He shuddered at the thought. William vowed that day to do all he could to discourage Matthew in his courtship of Amelia.

The very next day, William had an opportunity to speak with Amelia about Matthew. She was in her favorite place, the gazebo, even though there was still a chill in the air. She looked up in surprise from her book, as her papa approached and sat down beside her.

"Why, Papa, I do believe this is the first time you have come to my hideaway." she smiled, placing a kiss on his cheek.

"I know, baby. I haven't spent as much time with you as I should have. I've been caught up in so many details around the place." He smiled and took her hand in his.. "I feel I need to talk with you concerning your feelings for Matthew" William saw her resistance at his words, for her smile faded and fear filled her eyes. "What do you want to know, Papa?" she asked..

"Amelia, what, really, do you know about Matthew? You know he's a nephew of Buck and Willie. You know nothing of the people who raised him. Evidently, there have been some terrible things done to him throughout his childhood. Matthew has anger and violence inside him. He has told me of fighting, almost killing a man, losing his temper to that point. I don't mind telling you, I fear you becoming involved with him. I feel so strongly about this, that I want to send you back to school, away from here. You will get over your infatuation with him with time and distance separating you. He has not indicated that he returns your feelings. Leave him alone, Amelia. For your own sake, please let him go his way." William now held her hands in his, gripping them so hard in his appeal that she winced. Loosening his grip, he held her eyes with his own, pleading with her to see his concern and love for her.

Tears formed in her eyes and her face crumpled as she threw herself into her papa's arms. "Please don't ask me to give him up. Please, please, Papa. I love him. When I think of never seeing him again, I get sick to my stomach. I would die if you sent me away. I love you. You've been good to me. I want your love and approval, but I want Matthew to love me, too. He doesn't love me yet. I'm not beautiful like Belle and Victoria, Papa. No other boy has ever made me feel this way." She sobbed on his chest.

William held her, his own heart hurting for her,, wishing a thousand times that she had never laid eyes on Matthew Carlisle. "Amelia, I fear for your future if you persist in your pursuit of this man. You're throwing away all your own plans. You don't see what is happening to you. You've become a different girl. Your natural gaiety and fun-loving spirit are being affected by his outlook. You're blind to his effect on you, but all of us who love you can see it. He could injure or even kill you if he became angry enough." William held her by her shoulders, forcing her to look at him, as he spoke the truth of his feelings. Amelia, you are a beautiful woman with a heart of love and you must not think you can change Matthew because you love him. Only God can make a new man out of him. You are not his savior. You don't even know him except what you see when he is with us. What you feel for him cannot be of God, Amelia. Matthew is not filled with God's spirit of love. He has deep hurts that are manifested in anger."

"I'm sorry, Papa. I can't give him up. Please don't be mad at me. I love you and Mama so much" Amelia is pitiful in her entreaty, the tears coursing down her face.

"Then, may God help us all, baby. May God help us all." He sighed in sorrow and fear.

A couple of weeks went by and William noticed that Amelia had not frequented Ian's house and stables in quite some time. Hoping that she had heeded his advice after all, he felt a lightening of his heavy burden for her. Deep inside her soul, Amelia knew that all her papa said was for her own good. She also knew his words were true. She could not tell him that she too had glimpsed the darkness in Matthew. She believed that God would change him, take away the anger and pain of his childhood. She refused to think about his anger being unleashed on her. Sometimes his manner scared her, for he talked about fighting a lot and seemed to feel that physical violence was the only way to solve differences between people. She thought of how she had been spanked many times as she was growing up, for at times, she had disobeyed her parents, just as any child does. But Matthew had not been spanked nor disciplined by a loving parent, but beat cruelly, by someone who evidently did not love him like Amelia's parents loved her. In spite of all of the evidence of Matthew's character, she cannot resist what she feels for him.

She had been troubled by Matthew's talk of joining a wagon train that would be going to Texas. What if he decided to leave before he had feelings for her? She would lose him forever. He had not mentioned asking William for permission to call on her, much less proposed marriage. Amelia knew that Ian did not approve of her open adoration of Matthew, either. He felt she was degrading herself. So, for a while, she forced herself to stay away from Matthew.

Matthew noticed Amelia's absence and waited for Ian to explain. He had not had much experience with girls at all. He had noticed the looks that women sent his way. Not realizing the effect his looks had on the opposite sex, nor even seeing himself as a handsome man, Matthew stayed away from them altogether. Once, when working for Mr. Reeves, he had accompanied the men into town and into a saloon. He had never been to such a place in his life. There was a woman there, what age, he couldn't tell. She had looked him up and down in a bold manner that made him blush, causing all the men to whoop in glee. She wore a low-cut gown and her face was painted up like the Jezebel in the Bible must have been. She wore a strong scent that smelled like roses. Making fun of his youth, she had grabbed him, surprised him, kissed him full on the lips, and then laughed with all the men at his embarrassment. He never did go back into that saloon again. He knew she was not a nice woman. He had seen the winks and sly grins of the cowhands, as they had followed her with their eyes. He hated the feeling of being the brunt of their joke. That kind of woman was as different from Amelia as night and day he now realized. In spite of himself, he missed her presence around the house. She was always cooking something delicious for them. She seemed to enjoy serving them, waiting on them. Well, that was what a woman was supposed to do, Matthew thought, remembering how Aunt Martha had served Uncle James and the rest of them all his life. Someday, he supposed, he would have a wife that waited on him like that.

One evening, after finishing their work, Ian suggested they have supper with the family. They had sorely missed the woman's touch that Amelia had offered with the cooking. Matthew felt a touch of anticipation and hurriedly cleaned up in the creek. The icy water made his skin tingle as he washed away the grime of the day. He and Ian discussed the satisfaction they felt at the way the place was coming together. Barely twenty-one, Ian now had a home he could be proud of for the rest of his life. He had a thriving trade in horses and his future seemed settled here. Matthew talked frequently of the wagon train going to Texas, but Ian had lost his enthusiasm as he saw his stable of brood mares increasing and as his reputation had grown for producing fine horses.

Belle and Amelia had been setting the table, as usual, when they heard voices. Belle saw Amelia's eyes widen in excitement and she almost dropped the stack of plates she was carrying to the table. Phillip had begun calling on Belle again, once she had returned home. He had been sitting in the parlor with William, waiting for supper. She smiled at Amelia in understanding.

"Amelia, don't act too glad to see him. Don't make it too easy for him. That's the only way you'll know if his feelings are as strong as yours" she cautioned her sister wisely.

Nodding in agreement, Amelia forced herself not to run into the room to greet Ian and Matthew. They finished putting the food on the table. Smoothing her hair, hating her everyday dress, Amelia walked sedately to the front room to announce supper. At the sight of Matthew, his hair glistening in the lamplight, his eyes dark and mysterious, she felt her feelings leap into her eyes. He had been talking to Phillip but turned as she announced supper. He saw her blush at his scrutiny and wondered why. He saw the gladness on her face and in the clear blue depths of her honest gaze. She could not hide her feelings. They were screaming at him with every beat of her innocent heart. His eyes were guarded, not revealing his own feelings. He didn't speak directly to her, just nodded at her greeting, and then followed the others into the dining room.

After supper, the young people moved out onto the porch, for the evening was warm. The lightning bugs could be seen as the darkness gathered. Here, there, a flash of light, cheerful, bright, tiny pinpoints of illumination all through the blackness. Amelia seemed entranced by the sight, though she had seen it many times before.

Matthew sat on the steps with Ian, his face silhouetted against the night sky. Amelia sat in the rocker, her eyes seeming to go to him of their own accord. Would he ever look at her with love in his eyes? She wished herself sitting beside him instead of Ian. She could not be so bold as to approach him without an invitation. She had not been close to him since the first day she had come back from school. What is wrong with her is that she wants so desperately to see inside this man, to know his thoughts, to have him share himself with her. His mind is a closed sanctum. His words do not reveal his soul. They are superficial, ordinary. Would he ever open his heart and let her in, she wondered, as she studied his every feature, though he seemed unaware of her gaze.

"My Pa said there's talk of a wagon train heading for Texas soon. Maybe by next summer." Phillip spoke from his place beside Belle on the swing.

"I've been hearing' that for over a year, now," Ian replied. "Who do you think would be going from around here?"

I've been thinking about it pretty strong," Matthew suddenly spoke up. "Seems like that would be the place a man could make a fortune if he's smart and tough enough. I figure I'm tough enough." he added with an engaging grin.

Ian laughed at his friend. "Yeah, Matt, you sure are tough, alright. You can turn out some work, that's for sure. Phillip, you never saw anybody as strong as old Matt, here. Why, he can do the work of two or three men like me and you." he slapped Matthew playfully on the back as he bragged about his work.

"Well, Matt, if you ever get tired of old Ian, we could sure use you over at our place. In fact, if I could get Belle to marry me, you could help me build us a house." Phillip spoke jokingly, but his eyes were serious as he looked at Belle.

She smiled but didn't give him the answer he longed to hear.

"Phillip, you need to come down and see the stallion I bought from Mr. Buck. Talk about some fine little colts, I've got them." Ian spoke confidently. "You might want to buy one for your wife, uh, sweetheart." his eyes twinkled just like his pa's as he teased Belle.

"If I could get a wife, Ian, I sure would buy her anything her heart desired." Phillip joined in the jesting, winking at his friend. "Belle, would you like to go down and look at Ian's fine horses?"

"Yes, I guess I can do that, Phillip." Belle suddenly stood up. "We can go now if you want." she surprised them all by saying.

"Sure. Let's get a lantern from William. Look, I believe the moon is coming up. We'll have enough light." Phillip was quick to take the initiative, seeing that Belle was agreeable to the idea.

"Amelia, are you going?" Ian looked at her, wondering at her silence all evening. It wasn't like her.

"I suppose so." She stood and started for the steps, where Matthew still sat.

He got up, moving over so she could descend the steps. He didn't offer his hand to her and she wondered at his lack of manners. He seemed not to know what was expected of a gentleman where ladies were concerned. Did anyone teach him anything, she wondered. She struck off down the path ahead of the others, aggravated at Matthew's lack of interest in her. Maybe he is just an ignorant, unread, ill-mannered person. Maybe she should just forget him and go back to pursuing her dreams and goals. Who needs him anyway? She thought of Levi and how he had visited her, inviting her to go riding with him. She felt the little locket inside her dress. Maybe she should encourage Levi instead of wasting her time on Matthew. She vowed that the next time Levi invited her to go somewhere with him, she would accept.

She suddenly realized that she was far ahead of the others and the trees were making the path hard to see. She didn't care, because she could walk this path in the pitch dark, it was so familiar to her feet. She heard the murmur of their voices behind her somewhere but didn't really want company right now. Suddenly, a dark figure appeared out of the trees and she screamed in fright. It grabbed her and she kicked hard, feeling her shoe contact with a shin. Then, she swung her arm wildly, as the figure grabbed her arm in midair.

"Amelia, it's me. Calm down" Matthew's voice, Matthew's hands holding her shoulders hard, so she couldn't hit him again. "I was just going to scare you. I'm sorry." He said.

She couldn't help herself. She felt her knees buckle and started to fall. He held her up with one hand and wrapped his other arm around her waist as she sagged against his chest. Her chin barely reached his chest. She's so small, he thought. A little girl. He shouldn't have scared her like that. He guessed she had fainted from the fright. His arms were under her arms, supporting her, for she had gone limp for a moment or two. Then, he felt her arms around his waist and her head lifted from his chest. She looked up at him, but he couldn't see her eyes in the dark.

"Matthew, I love you." her words were so unexpected, so out of the context of his life, they really didn't register with him. He stared at her in astonishment. He didn't know what to say. He didn't love her. At least he didn't think he did. He had loved Firefly, but something told him that this was not the same. He didn't remember saying those words to anyone except his sister Becky as far back as his memory went. Suddenly, he didn't want to disappoint her. He did feel some emotion inside, with her arms around him and her expression so sweet. What could he do?

"I like you too, Amelia." Then, he lowered his head and touched her lips lightly with his own. Why, he could not say. It just seemed like the thing to do at the moment. Then, he let her go so suddenly, that she almost fell. He had seen the lantern light as the others approached.

"Amelia, did you get a scare when Matthew jumped out at you?" Ian was laughing as he came up to them. "I told him about Levi and you down at the creek. Matthew cut through the woods and came out ahead of you, so he could scare you."

"I scared her alright. I have a bruise on my shin and she almost clobbered me upside my head. You didn't tell me what a wild cat your sister is, Ian." Matthew laughed, his eyes on Amelia.

She heard his laughter and suddenly, her spirits lifted. He didn't say he loved her. He said he liked her. He kissed her. He actually kissed her. He must like her more than just a regular friend kind of like. Maybe he didn't know how to act around girls.

"I think I scared him more than he scared me," Amelia laughed, too.

They went on down the path to Ian's house. Holding the lantern high to light their way, Ian went ahead. They went first to the stable, where he led them up and down, showing them his fine horses. His eyes shone with pride as they exclaimed over his accomplishments. Beautiful, sleek heads appeared at each stall and big, luminous eyes watched them curiously. Reaching the far end of the barn, his house came into view. The long back porch, where a lone horse stood, tied to the hitching post. Ian noticed the horse immediately. It didn't belong to him. It wasn't there when he and Matthew left earlier.

Then, he noticed something else. There was a glimmer of light, such as a candle would make, inside the house. He had not left any lamps lit, either. Someone is in his house!

Turning to the others, he quietly made them aware of the situation. Leaving the girls in the barn, he, Phillip and Matthew quietly approached the house. Ian crept up to the back, while Phillip and Matthew went around to the front. Ian had left the lamp with the girls. Now, he cautiously peered through a window into the kitchen area. His eyes widened in astonishment. A woman sat at the table. Her head is covered by a shawl and resting on her folded arms. She seemed to be asleep, for she was motionless. Going quickly to the door, he quietly opened it and stepped inside. He must have made a sound, for suddenly, she jumped up with a little cry, her shawl falling to the floor. He saw her face then.

"Penelope! What are you doing here?" He exclaimed in astonishment..

She faced him in the flickering light. The shadows created grotesque shapes on the ceiling and walls. Her face was swollen from crying, her eyes bloodshot from lack of sleep. She clasped her hands together and tears formed again as she replied..

"I have no place to go, Ian. I asked you once to be my friend. I let you down so many times. I have no right to even ask you for anything. I had planned to meet you that day. I was ready to leave, but one of the hands told Daddy.

He stopped me. I had no way of letting you know." Her eyes begged him to believe her.

He put a finger to his lips, and then went quickly through the house to let Matthew and Phillip in. He told them who was in the house and Matthew went to fetch Belle and Amelia from the barn. Soon, they were all seated in the kitchen. Ian built up the fire and soon the smell of coffee filled the room. Amelia was rummaging through the cupboards, trying to find something to offer Penelope to eat. Amelia had always felt that food was needed in any crisis. She found part of a loaf of her mother's bread and sliced it, toasting it in the iron skillet with some butter. Soon, she served up the coffee with the toasted bread, as they listened to Penelope's story.

"My grandfather, Mama's daddy, came over to America from Germany. He was a businessman with connections to the best families in Europe. He had great wealth in Germany. He established a jewelry business and continued amassing a fortune throughout the remainder of his life. My daddy's prosperity is due entirely to the start given to him by my grandfather. My mother was the sole heir. My daddy came into control of Mama's wealth because that's the way it's always been. When I was born, he felt that the next child would be a boy. Then, as time after time, Mama failed to be able to carry a child to term, he changed. One little baby boy lived for three months, but he, too, died." Penelope paused, took a bite of her bread, and a sip of coffee, before continuing.

My grandfather loved me and doted on me. He set up a special inheritance for me. At twenty-one, I would have my money and I would be the one to control it. He did not want me to be under the control of any man, who might steal my money and mistreat me. My daddy has been trying to get me married to the man he has chosen before I reach twenty-one. He knows that if I am not married by then, I will no longer be under his control. I would have enough money to live and go wherever I pleased, and marry whomever I pleased. When he saw my interest in you, Ian, he became frantic. He knew you to be an honest, Godly man. He knew you would never side with him to get control of the inheritance. My daddy has plenty of money, but he wants more. With my money to use, he can take advantage of opportunities to expand his business. Don't misjudge him, now. He is not a cruel man. He loves my mother, I believe. I feel that when he was young, he had ideals, but they went by the wayside when he was thrust into the world of the wealthy and unscrupulous men that he encountered in business. He has never mistreated me. He kept the fact of my inheritance a secret from me. When I became interested in you, my mother told me about it. Then, I realized why Daddy acted the way he did when I had shown an interest in anyone not in the circle from whom he wanted a husband for me. I am almost twenty-one. He chose a husband for me and made all the arrangements for us to be engaged. He has signed away his rights to my inheritance, in exchange for a lifelong pension, because he is the youngest son of an old aristocratic family, who is penniless. I ran away. I will not marry him. They can have the money. I refuse to marry a man on those terms. I can't believe my daddy has become so blinded by the love of money that he would stoop to this level." Penelope's eyes brimmed over with tears again.

"Ian, I trust you. I know you are honest and good. I know you once had feelings for me. If you will help me, I will be able to give you anything you want. I will be a wealthy woman in a few months." she waited for his response.

"I don't want nor need your money, Penelope. I would help you as a friend. Friends don't need to be paid." Ian's eyes, full of compassion at first, had grown cold at her last words. "You may not realize it, but your values are much the same as your daddy's seem to be. Just what kind of help did you have in mind that I could give, anyway?" his words hid the pain he felt when he realized she had not come to him because she loved him.

Another sneaky woman, just like Millie, Matthew thought. She's trying to take advantage of Ian's good heart. He saw right through Penelope. She wanted that money just as much as her old daddy did. She just couldn't get her hands on it without help from outside the family. He watched Ian through narrowed eyes, hoping he didn't fall for her sad story.

"Let me stay here with you. If they come looking for me, tell them you haven't seen me. It'll only be for a few months. I have no money to go anywhere else. I know Daddy will think of coming here. He knows about your horses. He's heard about your success. He knows I cared for you." her eyes begged for understanding. .

Ian heard the past tense of her feelings for him. He wanted to turn her out into the dark. He wanted to tell her he didn't care what she did or what happened to her. But he couldn't lie. He did care. He would marry her now, tonight, if she gave any indication that she loved him. "Penelope, what you're asking is impossible. Matthew and I are staying here. I could not allow you, a single woman to live here with us. Your reputation would be ruined. Then, you're asking me to lie if your daddy comes looking for you. I can't do that either." He stood and walked to the door, going out onto the porch.

Suddenly, Belle, who had been silent through the whole episode, looked straight at Penelope and spoke softly. "Penelope, why don't you tell Ian the truth about your feelings for him? You admire him for his honesty, and then you've asked him to lie for you. He cannot be the man you know him to be if he were to compromise himself to please you. Would you agree for us to pray together about this situation? I feel that you have slipped away from your commitment to the Lord and you have become entangled in a web of Satan's devising. Greed and love of money are not of God. Why don't you go after him, now? Be honest, totally honest. That is the only thing that will work with my brother."

Penelope reached across the table as Belle spoke, clasping her hands tightly, she began to weep. This time, she was not weeping in self-pity, but in sorrowful repentance. Amelia came and stood behind Penelope, gently laid her arm across her shoulders and began to pray for her, tears running down her face also. Phillip bowed his head, but Matthew stared at them in astonishment. He had never seen such sincere caring before. He had been reared by people who professed to have the love of God in their hearts. He could not remember seeing Uncle James and Aunt Martha and the girls praying in such a way. All he remembered was harsh words and whippings. In his mind, most, if not all people who claimed to be Christians did not live the way the Bible said a person had to live to be a Christian. He felt uncomfortable, not really knowing what he should do. Finally, he bowed his head. He heard Amelia tearfully entreat God for Penelope. He heard Belle's gentle voice like water running softly over smooth stones, calming and soothing. He heard Penelope sob brokenheartedly, asking God to forgive her for losing her way, for straying from the right path, for allowing herself to become caught up in the love of money more than a love for Him and his ways.

Matthew remembered the cave down in the woods behind Uncle James's house. He saw the box hidden under the leaves and straw. Inside the box, he saw the smooth white stone with the writing carved into its surface. Funny, he should think of that now. He had not thought of it in awhile. Someday, he would go back and get the box. He felt a need to hold the stone in his hand. "If only I knew what the coin and the stone mean for me," He thought. The praying had stopped. Penelope looked different, Matthew thought. Her eyes had lost that dull, lifeless cast. Her face seemed to shine; her eyes danced. She hugged Belle, then Amelia.

"Thank you, thank you so much. I love you, Belle, Amelia. Now, I have to have a talk with your brother." she walked out onto the porch to join Ian.

Ian had heard the praying. He had been praying for direction. Asking God to show him what in the world he was to do about Penelope. When he heard the girls start praying, his heart was suddenly filled with peace. He knew he only had to wait, for God would take care of the situation himself. He heard her step behind him. He turned and she came into his arms and he knew. He kissed her face and felt the tears still wet on her cheeks.

"I love you, Ian MaceIlwain. I love you now and forever." her voice was soft and husky with her crying.

"I love you, Penelope. I love you now and forever." he held her close and they prayed together, their tears mingling, even as their lives were joined for always.

Inside the house, the sweetness created by the prayers of the women hung in the room. Gentleness pervaded the air and touched each of them with peace and joy. Amelia smiled at Matthew as he raised his head. Her face was radiant; her eyes sparkled with a light he had never seen in her before. She looked different, as though she had washed her face. He smiled back, for something made him want to smile. Then, embarrassed by his show of emotion, he stood and went to check the coffee, shaking the pot to see if there was any more. Belle stood too, for it was getting late and she felt they needed to start back home.

Phillip still sat with his head bowed and she looked at him, wondering. Beckoning to Amelia, they went on outside, after telling Matthew good night. Matthew poured himself another cup of coffee and sat back down at the table. He felt awkward, out of place, somehow. Phillip raised his head finally. Seeing only Matthew, he got up to go. Almost to the door, he turned and faced him again.

"Matthew, have you ever been baptized with the Holy Ghost?" he asked, surprising Matthew at such a question.

"I've been baptized in the river. A few years ago, before I came here. Is that what you mean?" Matthew grinned. "The preacher almost drowned me, too. I guess my sins were washed away pretty well."

"No, I mean have you ever spoken in tongues, received the Spirit of God into your heart, as the Bible says? You know, like the disciples, on the Day of Pentecost." Phillip persisted in his questions.

"No, Phillip. Matthew shrugged his shoulders. I've never done that. I know people who have, though and most of them who say they have the Spirit of God don't act much better than those who don't." Matthew answered.

Phillip said no more, just, "Good night, Matt, see you later." before he joined the girls outside.

That night, Matthew had a lot to think about. He lay awake long after Ian returned and went to his room. Remembering the sweet touch of Amelia's lips brought a smile to his face. He tried to sort through all his conflicting emotions women seemed to cause in him. The praying had touched something deep inside his spirit, he admitted reluctantly. Then, he was reminded of Annie's words, warning him of the danger of holding on to his anger toward Uncle James and Aunt Martha. Have I ever prayed? The question startled him. Have I repented? He had heard Penelope weeping and asking God to forgive her, and then the difference afterwards. He remembered being overcome with rage and nearly beating the life out of the man at Mr. Reeve's ranch. Was that a sin that he should ask God to forgive him? He decided finally that he would talk with Ian. He can trust him, he knows.

Chapter 19

Ian and Penelope were married three months later. She spent the intervening weeks with her mother and daddy. She had stayed with Belle and Amelia that night after they had prayed and she and Ian had decided to bring William and Constance into their plans. William had insisted that he and Ian go to Penelope's father together, asking his permission for them to marry. He knew they could not be in God's will if they were in rebellion against her parents. Mr. Harris received them cordially enough, but when he discovered the reason for their visit, his manner became cold. in. Ian asked for his permission to marry Penelope. He vehemently refused, becoming very angry, though he kept his anger under control. William then intervened, suggesting that Mr. Harris give him a few minutes to explain the situation they found themselves in at the moment.

"Mr. Harris, you are a businessman of great success. You have been very generous in contributing to our community. Penelope is your only child, your most important treasure. Her happiness, I know, is of paramount importance to you, just as my own children are to me. Every father wants to ensure the security and happiness of their own children. That is why God, our Heavenly Father, gave us earthly Fathers. You and I have two fine young people who care for each other deeply. They have prayed and asked for God's guidance as to their future together. They want your blessing, for they want to give you the honor you deserve as Penelope's father. If you withhold your blessing, you will be denying your child the most important thing you can give her in this life. Your blessing and approval are far more important than all the money in the world. Ian has worked hard. He has a fine place, a home he has built himself, a prospering business. He cares nothing for Penelope's money. He would rather not have it, in fact. She has permitted me to tell you that you may keep her inheritance. They know that if they live for God, he will supply their material needs, for that is a promise in His Word. They do want you to be a part of their lives. It is your choice, Mr. Harris. What do you say? Will you give the bride away to a man who will love and cherish her more than his own life?" William's words were wise and eloquent and Mr. Harris could not possibly say anything, except "Yes."

Amelia's eyes were full of stars, as she watched Penelope come down the aisle on the arm of her father. She was seeing herself in such a gown as Penelope's, meeting Matthew at the altar, becoming his wife. Her heart yearned for the love she saw in Ian's eyes as he and Penelope left on their honeymoon to Europe. Mr. Harris had given them the trip as a wedding gift. William and Matthew promised Ian that the horses would not suffer at all in his absence. They would be gone for three months, seeing all the sights they had only read about. It was a once-in-a-lifetime experience. They promised to send postcards to keep everyone informed of their travels. Amid tears and laughter, they boarded the train. Those left behind found themselves having a hard time adjusting to the routine of everyday life again. All the excitement and heart-touching experiences of the last few months seemed to have drained everyone. Amelia found herself in a predicament. Her frequent visits to Ian's house came to a halt with his departure on his honeymoon. William had told her straight out that she was not to be going there unless accompanied by a companion. He reminded her that she was a single young woman who needed to guard her good name and reputation carefully. Matthew would be alone, taking care of Ian's place. He would certainly have no respect for her were she to be so bold as to visit there alone. Amelia began to spend a lot of time in prayer and reading her Bible again, something she had tended to neglect in the excitement of the last few months. Her enforced separation from Matthew caused her to renew her commitment to God. She got her Mother to invite him to eat with them as much as she could, because she felt sorry for him, spending so much time alone.

Caleb loved the horses and had begun spending a lot of time with Matthew since school was out. Matthew was teaching him all about caring for them. So, every day, Amelia joined Caleb, feeling glad to have an excuse to visit Matthew while he worked. Amelia cooked and cleaned, pretending this was her house and she and Matthew were married. After cleaning up the supper dishes, she and Caleb would hurry home before dark.

The summer drew to a close too soon and before you could blink, it seemed, Thanksgiving was coming. Ian and Penelope had written they would be back by New Year's, so once again excitement built.

A couple of weeks before Christmas, Amelia and Caleb hurried down the path, bundled up against the cold wind. She knew she was being foolish, getting out in this weather, but she couldn't stand the thought of Matthew being alone. She was going to invite him up to the house. Several of the young people she had gone to school with were coming over. They were building a big fire outside.

Phillip and Belle would be there. Nathan and his new bride, Lilibeth, would also be there. Levi would be there, too, for she could not leave him out. She just wished he would not look at her with that hurt expression. Amelia knew that as long as there was any chance of Matthew loving her, she could not be interested in anyone else.

Matthew was in the stables. He seemed glad to see them. Was it her imagination, or did he look at her differently? He was usually rather reserved with her, not given to long conversations. She had tried to draw him out of it, but so far had not made much progress. She told him about the gathering that evening, invited him to come for supper and stay later, then she and Caleb hurried back home to the warmth of the fire.

Matthew had been doing a lot of thinking since Ian had left. Being alone, with no one to talk with was a lonely kind of life, he realized. He had never been in a house totally alone in all his life. Not for an extended amount of time, like this, anyway. On the days that Amelia and Caleb didn't come, the quietness, the solitude, began to get on his nerves. One night he noticed Ian's Bible beside his chair. He sat down and opened it at the marked place Ian had been reading.

"Come to me, all you who labor and are heavy laden and I will give you rest," he read aloud slowly. What does this mean?" he asked into the silence. The need to know suddenly gripped him and he felt the presence of the man on the creek bank all those years ago when he had felt so lost and unloved. The shining eyes of the man had been full of love that seemed to go inside him. He wanted to keep that feeling, but the hurting inside caused him to be filled with angry thoughts. *"I am the light. Walk with me and you will walk in the light and the darkness will* have to go." He froze, afraid to move. Who is it? The same voice he had heard call his name. What does it mean? He sat very still, holding the Bible, as something sweet and peaceful flowed into the hurting place deep inside his heart. Finally, laying the Bible aside, he walked out onto the porch and looked into the night sky. Millions of stars covered the darkness and the moon illuminated every tree. The light caused the dark night to become like day.

He went to bed but not to sleep, for the feelings that had been awakened in him had thrown his thoughts into confusion. While it was still dark outside, he threw back the covers, built up the fire, made coffee, and cooked his breakfast. Sipping on another cup of coffee, he waited for daylight so he could start working. What should he do about his plans to go to Texas and what do his feelings for Amelia mean. He couldn't just keep working for Ian. He wanted his own place. He wanted to make money, have respect, wear fine clothes, like Mr. Harris, and maybe have a big, fine house like his, too. He didn't feel he would ever become wealthy working for Ian, even though he liked it here. Ian is a good person. They had not had a cross word. They get along fine, Matthew thought, while he was working all that day. He decided he would find out more about the wagon train and just what a man would have to have to go along.

That evening, Matthew walked up to the farmhouse to attend the gathering. After supper, which Matthew thoroughly enjoyed, the young people gathered outside, building up a big bonfire, laughing and joking together. Matthew noticed one young man in particular who was always with Amelia. He was tall and sandy-haired. Once, he saw her lay a hand on his arm as they laughed together over something. Matthew experienced a new feeling that night. He felt jealous. He didn't want her laying her hand on that man's arm. She had said she loved him. She must have lied. His eyes darkened with anger and disappointment. He thought Amelia was honest and good. Now, he saw she was just like the others. He felt helpless as he saw her enjoying herself with someone else. Clenching his fist to keep from going over and punching the man, Matthew slipped away into the darkness and down the path to Ian's house to spend another solitary night. He couldn't sleep, however, once he was in bed. He kept seeing Amelia's face as she laughed at the man with her.

Then, he saw her face when she told him she loved him. How could it be both ways? Well before dawn, having hardly slept at all, Matthew was building a fire, brewing his coffee. With his feet propped up before the fire, warming, he drank his coffee and thought some more. He couldn't leave before Ian got back. Well, as soon as he returned, Matthew thought, I'm leaving for Texas. Amelia can have that fellow, whoever he might be. She doesn't need me hanging around. I don't need any woman, not even her. Having settled the matter, Matthew cooked his breakfast, then took the lantern and headed to the barn to check on everything.

Amelia didn't come that day, or the day after. The weather was very cold and she and Caleb stayed home. They had put up the Christmas tree and were getting excited about Ian and Penelope returning. Belle was waiting to hear from a position she had applied for at a school in South Carolina. It would be an excellent position if she was accepted. Phillip had been pressing her for an answer to his ongoing proposal of marriage. He had agreed to go anywhere she wanted to go to further her career. For some reason, Belle could not bring herself to say yes to Phillip. She felt that if she really loved him, she would have no problem at all in giving him an affirmative answer. So, she continued to put him off.

Amelia would be eighteen in January. She had begun to wonder if she had made a mistake by staying home from school, giving up her dream of becoming a teacher. Then, she would remember Matthew's face when he kissed her that night. He did care for her. She knew he did. It was just a matter of time before he figured out how to approach her and make his feelings known. She had seen him leave from the bonfire that night. She didn't know why, except, maybe he felt uncomfortable with so many people he didn't know. She had meant to spend most of her time with him, but Levi had kept her talking so long, that Matthew had already left by the time she got rid of him.

After a whole week of bitter cold, the weather changed and became almost spring-like. The sun shone brightly, though the wind had a bite still. Amelia decided she and Caleb would venture out and visit Matthew. He must be pretty lonely by now. Soon, they arrived at the house, just as Matthew was knocking off for lunch. He gave her a black look, scorn in his eyes. He spoke to Caleb, went on into the house and started building up the fire that had burned low. She and Caleb followed him, though he still ignored her. Finally, Amelia had enough of his silence.

"Matthew, what are you mad about? Have I offended you in some way?" she asked him.

I don't guess you've offended me. Do you think you have?" his voice was detached, as though it didn't matter one way or the other to him.

"No, I don't feel that I've done anything to offend you. I noticed you left the other night rather suddenly. I'm sorry I didn't get to introduce you to everybody, but Levi Nichols kept talking to me about that time he scared me down at the creek. I was trying to get away from him, so I could be with you, but you left." Amelia finished apologetically, and then sat down at the table.

"That was Levi Nichols you were talking with?" Matthew didn't want to appear interested, but he had to know.

"Yes, that's what I said. He used to tease me unmercifully all through school. Then, you know, Ian told you about what we did to break him of his practical jokes. Then, he wanted to be my friend. Now, he wants to be more than that." Amelia raised her eyebrows, showing her dislike of Levi's attention.

Matthew felt his heart lift at her words. "You don't like him, then?" he had to ask.

"Matthew, what did I tell you that night on the path? Do you think I lied? No, I didn't lie to you. I'm not lying to you now, either. I do not intend to wait on you forever to make up your mind about me, though. I'm not beautiful like my sisters, but I'm sure that somewhere there is a man who will love me for who I am."

Amelia's eyes flashed angrily at Matthew. She looked so cute, with her hands on her hips, he felt his lips twitch as he tried not to laugh. He wanted to put his arms around her and kiss her, he realized. Caleb looked from one to the other, not knowing what in the world they were talking about.

"Amy, why are you mad at Matthew?" he asked his sister curiously.

"Because he's blind, that's why," she replied, getting up from the table and standing before the fire.

"Matthew, you're not blind. Blind people can't see. You can see, can't you? Caleb was concerned, looking anxiously at Matthew.

Grinning in spite of himself, Matthew assured Caleb that he wasn't blind, that Amelia was only joking. "Caleb, let's you and I go out and check on the colts, make sure they have plenty of hay to keep them warm," he told the young boy. With a glance at Amelia's stiff back, he ushered Caleb out the door.

In just a few minutes, he returned without Caleb. Amelia was sitting at the table, her head on her arms, sobbing. Matthew stared in confusion. He didn't know what was wrong with her. He stood in front of the fire, his back to her, trying to think what he should do. Then, he heard her blow her nose and sniff a few times. Turning around, he waited a moment. When she didn't say anything, he spoke. "Amelia, why did you say that I'm blind? Just what is that supposed to mean?"

"Matthew, will you ever love me?" the words caught him by surprise and he fell silent. How can he answer her? She talked of love so easily, as though she knew exactly how it felt. She got up and put on her coat and gloves, tied her hat under her chin and walked out the door without another word. He wanted to go after her, tell her something to change the sad, forlorn look on her face, but what could he tell her? Should he share his experience of the night before with her? No, he couldn't share that with anyone.

Amelia spent a miserable day, standing at the window, watching the path, hoping Matthew would come. After Christmas, she would make her plans to go away, she decided. She was giving up on a future with him. He didn't love her. She wondered if he even knew the meaning of the word.

Chapter 20

William told Matthew that he, Caleb and Amelia could look after the horses if he wanted to go to Buck and Willie's for Christmas. He felt he might want to be with his own family during that time. Matthew seemed surprised at the suggestion, but after some thought, decided he would go. So, on Christmas Eve morning, he saddled up and rode out, enjoying the chilly air. The sky was cloudless and the sun shone on the remains of a light snow that had fallen a couple of days before. Matthew's horse was a fine black he had picked from Ian's stable. Big and muscular, he covered the ground in powerful, but smooth strides, eating up the miles. Matthew enjoyed the feeling of the power under his control as he sat astride the big horse. The pain of Firefly's loss was only a dull ache in his heart, now.

Remembering the peace he had felt when reading Ian's Bible and hearing the Voice, he realized the feeling of belonging and being loved that he longed for did not come when he thought of the injustices he had suffered when he lived with Uncle James and Aunt Martha. It was as though the rage that always simmered just below the surface overcame the good feelings. He wants what he feels when he is with Amelia and her family, he decides. What he sees in her eyes when she looks at him puzzles him because she has not known him very long. Any feeling that he was being given orders or told what to do brought such a violent reaction on his part, but he did not want a hard heart like Uncle James. Many a young man who had come against him had learned quickly that his fists were powerful and not to be taken lightly. But, he didn't enjoy   fighting any more, he admitted. He just doesn't know how to control the anger. A chill gripped him as he remembered where his anger has taken him many times.

Startled out of his thoughts, he pulled back on the reins as a big buck deer dashed across the path in front of him. It has been a long time since he has been hunting. He wondered if Aunt Martha missed all the meat he used to provide for them. He remembered that Uncle James had died. He hadn't gone to the funeral. He had closed the door on that part of his life. Buck had told him Aunt Martha had been sick but had recovered. He had not gotten any news lately from Annie. She wrote to him once in a while, giving him the news about everyone. He never wrote back. As he rode through the countryside, Matthew's thoughts eventually got around to Amelia. Funny, how he felt her absence, yet didn't know how to deal with her in person. He was no closer to a solution to resolving his feelings about her than before, when he cantered up to the hitching post in front of Buck and Willie's, mounted the big wide steps and went in, calling Willie's name. She always made him feel welcome and today was no exception.

"Why, Matthew, what a pleasant surprise. I was just telling Buck I wished I had sent word to you to come be with us for Christmas. I'm making candy, so I know how you are about divinity. Come on back to the kitchen and you can be our official taster. Bertha and I will surely look like Santa Claus before all this cooking is done." Willie laughed her cheerful laugh and Matthew was enveloped by the warmth of her acceptance, as always.

Later, when everyone gathered for dinner, Matthew noticed a young woman about his age, that he had never seen before. She is very pretty and smiled at him when he looked her way. After dinner, she followed him out onto the porch overlooking the garden.

"Hello, Matthew. I know you don't remember me. I'm Bethany Carlisle. You and I are cousins twice removed, if you can figure that out. My great-grandfather and your great-grandmother were brother and sister; I think that's the way it is. Anyway, we're kissing cousins." she laughed delightedly at her own self and Matthew had to smile in return. She took his arm and drew him over to the swing, where she seated herself, pulling him down beside her.

"Aunt Willie has told me all about you. May I call you Matt? You may call me Beth. We live in Alabama. Mama decided we needed to pay a visit to all our kin people, so here we are. No telling how long we'll be here, making the rounds. I can't wait for Christmas. Wait until you see my dress tomorrow night. Mama said I look like a princess in it. Would you like to sit with me at the Christmas party?" she paused for breath.

Matthew was overwhelmed by this girl. She talked a mile a minute, her hand resting on his arm. She wore something that smelled like a field of daisies under a summer sun and her soft brown hair curled in little wisps around her ears and over her smooth brow. She paid no attention to his lack of input in the conversation but took his silence to mean agreement.

"That's wonderful, Matt. Now, I'm going to change into my riding clothes and we'll go riding. It's such a beautiful day. We must take advantage of it while we can."

Then, she was gone in a swirl of skirts, leaving Matthew feeling a little dazed, as though he had come through a whirlwind. He stayed in the swing and in a few minutes, Beth returned. He had to admit, she looked good in her riding clothes. Matthew had never seen a riding habit. She wore a long skirt that fit over her hips, then flared out at the bottom, with a bright blue jacket of the same color. Something white and frothy spilled from the neck of the jacket. Shiny black riding boots of soft leather showed beneath the hem of her skirt and a little hat with a feather sat on top of her curls. Her eyes were bright with excitement as she once again took Matthew's arm, urging him toward the stables. She chattered all the way across the yard and Matt didn't have to say a word, just nod and smile. Finally, once they were mounted, she had to stop talking, for a while, anyway. Once out of the vicinity of the house, on the trail, she suddenly grew silent. Matthew looked at her, wondering if she had finally run out of something to say. They rode in silence, the crunch of the horse's hooves on the patches of snow the only sound.

Suddenly, with a mischievous grin, Beth looked over at him. "I know what you're thinking right now, Matthew. That I'm a terribly talkative person, I imagine," she said.

He didn't know how to respond. He didn't want to hurt her feelings by agreeing. He grinned back.

"Well, you said it, Beth," he admitted, reluctantly.

"I'm not really that way at all. You're such a handsome man. I didn't want to give you a chance to get away." her candid way of speaking her thoughts shocked him. He had never had a girl talk to him this way. Then, she shocked him even more. "I plan to marry you. Oh, I know you don't even know me right now, but that only takes time. Once you get to know me, you'll want to marry me.

My daddy has lots of land and lots of money. When you marry me, you'll be set for life. You'll be wealthy and have prestige. You'll wear the finest clothes, ride the finest horses, travel, and see the world. And, you'll have me. We'll have beautiful children, you and I. With your looks and my brains, they'll be unstoppable when they grow up." she pulled up and dismounted.

He stared down at her in amazement. This girl is crazy. Why, they only just met today, a few hours ago. How can he get away from her as soon as possible? He got off his horse and followed her up a small rise where the snow had completely melted. Tying her horse to a small tree, she turned as he came up, walked up to him, faced him.

"You think I'm crazy, Matt. I know how it must sound. Someone you never met before today proposing marriage. I won't have my daddy choose a husband for me. I'm choosing my own and I've chosen you." she came close, put her arms around his neck and before he realized what she intended, pulled his head down to her, kissing him. Matthew found himself kissing her back. He couldn't help himself. Just when he started to enjoy it, she pulled away, went to her horse, waited for him to help her mount. He placed his hands around her small waist and sat her atop her horse with hardly any effort at all. She looked down at him appraisingly.

"You're quite a man, Matthew. You'll suit me, I think" She turned her mount and walked the mare she rode back to the trail.

Matthew mounted up and followed her, his emotions in turmoil. He could be wealthy without working like he had always had to do. He could have anything he wanted, handed to him. All he had to do was accept Bethany as his wife. His heart began to pound at the thought of the feelings her kiss had aroused in him. Love must make you feel like that. He had not experienced such a kiss before. He remembered the touch of Amelia's lips that night. This feeling was different. Bethany's boldness brought out a response in him that he didn't fully understand. He didn't like the way she seemed to think he would go along with whatever she proposed, though. He felt out of control with her. He was silent, deep in thought all the way back to the house. When they reached the stables, Bethany dismounted and walked away, leaving him to tend to the horses.

He didn't see her the rest of the day until supper was served. Then, she was seated too far from him to even gain eye contact. He listened to the talk going on around him. He heard someone mention the forming of a wagon train and his attention immediately focused on the speaker. A distinguished-looking middle-aged man with a neatly trimmed beard and shrewd eyes sat directly across from Matthew. He was talking to the gentleman next to him and his voice carried easily to Matthew.

"Should be about a hundred or so wagons ready by the time we pull out. It takes a lot of preparation for that kind of venture. There's got to be plenty of water, food, good horses, and determined people" he concluded his statement, and then turned his attention to his food.

Matthew was disappointed that the man didn't talk some more. He was desperate to get information. Maybe Uncle Buck would know something. He would talk to him later.

After supper, Matthew followed the rest of the men into the library where they all congregated to talk. Making himself inconspicuous, he listened to the talk, seeing what he could learn. He heard mention of some scientist by the name of Pasteur who had made some kind of discovery about bacteria. Matthew had a vague recollection of what bacteria were. They evidently caused people to get sick. The man giving this information was very excited by the discovery, saying it was a breakthrough in medicine.

Matthew wandered across the room and stood near Uncle Buck and a couple more gentlemen deep in discussion. The subject seemed to be women's rights, whatever that might mean. It seemed to his way of thinking that women had all the rights they needed. They seemed to boss everybody they could. It seemed that the State of New York was about to pass a law giving women the right to keep any money they earned. Well, that seemed fair, Matthew thought. Anybody ought to be able to keep their money if they worked for it. It shouldn't matter if it were a man or a woman.

Disappointed that no one was talking about the wagon train, he finally slipped out of the room and went outside. The night was cold, now that the sun had gone down and he shivered, not having on a coat. Turning to look out into the garden, he didn't see a figure slip through the door behind him. When he felt arms go around his waist, he instinctively raised his fist, whirling around, ready to inflict a crushing blow on his attacker. He quickly realized who it was when he heard Beth gasp in fright.

"Don't ever sneak up on me like that. I won't be responsible for what happens." Matthew held her by her arms, shaking her fiercely, as he spoke. "Another thing, I want you to understand, Bethany. When you deal with me, you're not the boss. I am. You remember that. You don't tell me what I'm going to do. Didn't your mother ever teach you that nice girls don't go around kissing strange men?" he released her suddenly and walked away, leaving her to think about what he had said.

Before he went to sleep that night, Matthew came to a decision. Amelia would never have acted the way Bethany had acted toward him today. How would it be to be married to a woman like Beth? She reminded him too much of Millie and Katherine, the bossy women in his life, telling a man what to do and when to do it. She didn't even ask him if he wanted to marry her, just told him he would. In spite of the feelings kissing her had caused, he would leave tomorrow right after dinner, he determined.

He avoided Beth the next day, going with Uncle Buck down to the stables and staying most of the morning. He found out the wagon train would probably be a year at least in preparation. At dinner, he kept his eyes away from the other end of the table, where he knew Beth was sitting. As soon as the meal was over, Matthew hurried to his room, gathered up his things. Thinking he was getting away free, he went to find Willie to say his goodbyes and to thank her for a wonderful dinner. Rounding the corner of the dining room, he came face to face with Bethany.

"Matthew! I need to talk to you." she grabbed his arm, her eyes going to the bag he carried. "Are you leaving?" her tone was disappointed.

"Yes, Beth, I'm going home." as he said the words, Matthew realized that was how he had come to see the Macellewain farm. It was the place where he had received acceptance and great kindness. It is the place where people respected him and seemed to appreciate his hard work. Yes, he replied., "I'm going home."

"Oh, I see." she sounded resigned. Then, she smiled brightly. "Is she very pretty?" she suddenly asked.

Matthew thought for a moment. Then, with a lopsided grin he replied. "She is to me. Goodbye, Beth and good luck."

Chapter 21

In spite of Matthew's absence, Amelia enjoyed Christmas with her family. She had talked with William and to his delight, told him she would be going back to school in the spring. She felt that Matthew could not return the love she felt for him and she certainly didn't want him without love. She felt suddenly carefree, for the first time since meeting Matthew. Her feelings for him had weighed her down, forcing her to choose between him and fulfilling her lifelong dreams for herself and her future. Now that she had made a decision, she was anxious to get started on the rest of her life. Her family felt relief at seeing her natural good nature restored. She laughed freely and often during the holidays, enjoying herself, like a child again. Christmas Eve, Levi had appeared, in a fancy buggy, inviting her to go for a ride. She had accepted. Bundled up against the cold, they laughed and talked the whole time. Then, they had hot chocolate before the fire. She walked him to the door, where he reached for her hand, then pointed to the mistletoe, laughing. Then, suddenly serious, he placed his hands on each side of her face, looked into her eyes.

"Amelia, I love you. Will you marry me?" Then, he kissed her softly on her forehead.

She didn't know what to say. She stood, captured by his gentleness. His kind face was so familiar throughout her childhood. Amazingly, she knew without doubt that Levi would be a good husband and a loving father to his children. She was tempted to say yes. She really wanted to keep that light glowing in his eyes. She could not. Not because she didn't love him, but because she did. She just didn't love him the way she loved Matthew. Hating herself, she felt hot tears sting her eyes and she squeezed her eyes shut. Levi felt her tears on his hands and wiped them with his fingers. Then he smiled and kissed her again, this time on her cheek, with her tears salty to his mouth.

"Good night, Amelia. Merry Christmas," he left then, closing the door quietly behind himself. She stood there, under the mistletoe, crying, the tears coursing down her face unheeded.

The next afternoon, Christmas dinner over, Amelia was lying on her bed. Later on, she thought, she might go for a walk, get out of the house for a while. She must have dozed off, for suddenly, Victoria was shaking her awake.

"Amelia, Matthew is here. He wants to see you," she whispered, as though it was a secret.

Disoriented, Amelia did not grasp what she was saying. Matthew had never come to see her. What could have happened? She hoped nothing was wrong with Buck or Willie. Hurriedly, she washed her face, straightened her hair. Then, deciding, she snatched a fresh gown from the wardrobe, one that Aunt Faith had bought for her. It was a deep purple, with tiny pearl buttons down the front, fitted at the waist and falling in soft folds over her hips. Feeling prepared for whatever news Matt brought, she went to greet him.

He had been standing at the fire, his back to the door. She walked softly and he didn't hear her. She stopped in the doorway, gazing at his broad shoulders, his hair so black, it glistened. The sight of him caused her heart to beat faster and a longing to overcome her doubts of being with him. He must have felt her presence, for she didn't speak.

He turned and they looked at each other for a long moment. She waited for him to speak. Finally, he did.

"Hello, Amelia. I just got back" he held his hat in his hands and his knuckles were white as he unconsciously gripped it tighter and tighter. Her eyes reflected the brilliant color of the dress she wore and her skin was so fair, the freckles almost all gone, but still showing across her cheekbones. She is pretty, he realized, to me.

"Did you have a good time? Are Mr. Buck and Mrs. Willie alright?" there was a stillness about her, as though she had stopped breathing and was suspended in the moment.

"Oh, well, I suppose so. Uncle Buck and Aunt Willie are fine. They sent their love to you" his dark gaze bored into her, a question in their depths. She would not help him, she vowed. She felt the uncertainty in him. She wondered what could have happened to cause him to act this way.

"Amelia, how do you feel when you love somebody?" His question was childlike, sincere.

"That person means more to you than your own happiness. You want to be with the one you love. You're miserable when you're away from that person. You want to see them laugh and be happy. You want to laugh and be happy with them." she felt herself starting to cry again. She didn't care. She didn't care about anything right now. She felt as though Matthew stood on the brink of a great revelation and she was afraid to move, lest the spell be broken.

He saw her tears. He heard the words she spoke, her voice soft. Then, he crossed the distance between them. She closed her eyes, for she could not bear it if he did not tell her what she longed to hear. She felt him standing there, so close, yet not knowing what he should do next. Tentatively, he touched her arm.

"Amelia, don't cry. I always seem to make you cry." She opened her eyes, then, and there was a shining hope mirrored in their blue depths. He realized he had seen that look once before, directed at him. He wanted to put his arms around her, for he needed to absorb some of that shining. He held back, not sure he should. His eyes were dark with an emotion she had never seen as her heart filled with joy.

"That's the way I feel inside, Amelia. That's the way I feel about you," he whispered. He drew closer, his face so close, she could see the green flecks in his dark eyes. She closed her eyes, anticipating his kiss. He stared at her closed eyes and he so wanted to kiss her. Instead, he drew her gently into his arms and with his head on top of hers, just held her closer than he had ever held another person since he was a child. She lifted her head, tears wet on her cheeks and filling her eyes with shining light. He could not help himself. He touched his lips to her forehead, and then grinned, his eyes looking into hers in amazement. "Amelia, I've never felt this way about any girl."

Her heart was beating so fast, she wondered if she would faint. What has happened to him? He's telling me he loves me, she realized. She looked at him in surprise, unable to believe she was being held in his arms where she had so longed to be.

"What are you saying, Matthew?" she asked.

"While I was away, I thought about you. I missed you, being around you. I want to be with you all the time."

He knew he had never felt this way about any other human being in his life. What it was about her that pulled at him, he could not figure out. They seemed always to disagree, but something in him, a force he did not understand at all, drew him back to her each time.

"Are you saying you want to marry me?" Amelia persisted, wanting to hear him say it.

"If that's what you want, then that's what I want, too." he sounded humble, unlike himself, she thought.

"We'll have to talk, Matthew. We'll have to make plans. Are you sure, I mean, that you want to marry me?" she seemed unable to believe what she had heard.

He grinned, then, his eyes lighting. "Well, unless you want to live in sin, I think that's what I mean. We can't get married right away, but later on. I have to go talk with your daddy. He may not let you marry me. I don't think he has a very high opinion of me."

She put her arms around his waist, laying her head on his chest. What will her daddy say, she wondered, when Matthew tells him he wants to marry me? What if he forbids us to marry? Sudden fear made her shiver and she tightened her arms around Matthew, feeling his arms tighten in response. Now that she knows he loves her, she cannot give him up, no matter if it means going against her dad's wishes. "Oh, Jesus, she whispered silently, please make a way for us to be together." As he held her tightly to him, her love flowed into his spirit, touched the hurting place that had never healed. She is the answer to the emptiness inside him, he suddenly knows within his heart. He can never let her go, for she will dispel the darkness in him with the brightness of her love. Here was someone who could belong to him, who wanted to be with him. Just like Firefly and Tippy, Amelia loves him.

"Matthew, we have to talk with Papa. We have to have his blessing before we can go any further with our plans." Amelia held his hand as they sat together before the fire. In spite of the dread she was feeling at the thought of talking to William, she could hardly contain her happiness at being held in his arms. She listened in astonishment as he told her about his experience with Bethany over Christmas. "When she grabbed me and kissed me, I didn't know what to do." Matthew grinned as Amelia's eyes flashed angrily at such behavior. Without thought, she threw her arms around his neck. "Matthew, I love you." She kissed his cheek, and then quickly stood, pulling him by his hand. "Let's go talk to Papa so we can make our plans to be married.

"Amelia, wait a minute." He placed his hands on her shoulders, forcing her to look at him. "We cannot get married any time soon. I have no place of my own, much less a home for you right now. At her expression, he kissed her softly on her cheek and pulled her into his arms again. We need to get to know each other better, don't you think? We will tell your family about our feelings for each other. I have great respect for your papa and I will talk with him. Let's go together."

Hand in hand, they knocked on the door of William's study. When they walked in, holding hands, William felt his heart sink, for he knew what was coming.

He forced a smile, shaking hands with Matthew, asking about Buck and Willie. Then, he motioned for them to be seated. They did and he waited.

Matthew swallowed a few times, then, nudged by Amelia, stood up again, and faced William.

"Mr.Macellwain, I would like to ask your permission to come calling on Amelia. I know that right now, I'm not in a place to be marrying. That's why I want to court her. In spite of himself, William felt sympathy for the young man, for he remembered his own discomfort at a certain time in his life. He smiled at them, but then became serious as he looked earnestly at Matthew.

"Matthew, I agree with you about waiting. You and Amelia have not known each other long enough to plan marriage." William hesitated. "There is so much more to marriage than just feeling attracted to each other. It is a lifetime commitment created by God. There is much the two of you need to ask each other, so that you can know if you are in agreement about what matters in a marriage. The most important is that your plans must be pleasing to the Lord and that both of you are filled with His Spirit, for without the Spirit of God, you cannot walk together in unity and agreement. I will ask you to spend the next year in prayer as you get to know each other and share your plans for the future. I don't know your dreams and ambitions, but I know Amelia has always wanted to be a teacher, so it is necessary for you both to find out if your goals for your life can be reached once you marry." William saw disappointment cloud Amelia's eyes, but Matthew seemed relieved, for he grinned at William.

"Thank you Mr. Macellwain. I'm not ready to take care of Amelia any time soon. I don't even have a home of my own right now. We will have a lot to talk about, like you said." He stood, pulling Amelia up with him. William put his arm on Matthew's shoulder, kissed Amelia's cheek.

"I will be praying for the two of you to hear the voice of the Lord and be willing to obey. Now, I give you my blessing, Matthew, to call on Amelia and I thank you for showing me and her mother the respect of asking for our permission. You are welcome to be a part of our family, for I know you are a hard working young man and I believe you will respect Amelia. I trust you will be filled with the Holy Spirit of God, as she has been so you can love her even as Jesus loves the church He bought with his blood on Calvary. Let's go share the news with Constance." He said, walking with them to the door.

Later, when he finally left, after having eaten supper with them and sharing the news with the family, Amelia walked him out, just as she had done with Levi, only the night before. It seemed like an eternity ago, she thought. She remembered Levi's gentle touch and kind eyes, his acceptance of her unspoken refusal of his proposal. What if she had said "Yes," she thought. What a terrible hurt she would have inflicted on Levi. Her heart was glad, as once again Matthew put his arms around her. He looked down at her, waiting. With a little quirky grin, her eyes dancing with mischief, she shook her head at him.

"Matthew, we must be very discreet, you know. No kissing until after our engagement is official."

He immediately dropped his arms and looked at her in dismay. "Oh, I didn't think about that." he sounded disappointed.

She laughed out loud then and he realized she was teasing him. He reached out, suddenly bold and pulled her to him. This time, when he let her go, he was the one grinning, as he pointed over their heads to the mistletoe hanging there. With another kiss on her cheek, he was gone, his dark eyes leaving her heart pounding with a promise sealed.

After that night, Amelia could think of nothing but the future she and Matthew planned together. Gone was her determination to further her education. She forgot about her desire to become an author, a teacher. The focus of her life became a tall, dark-haired young man with dangerous lights in his dark eyes. She lived for his appearance each evening when he finished his day's work. She viewed her appearance with critical eyes and went to great lengths each day to look her best when he came. He had captured her heart without even trying. She did not understand why she felt such a strong yearning to get inside his mind, understand him. She wanted to nurture the sweetness she knew was there, hidden behind the wall of self-preservation he had erected from childhood.

She began spending more time in the kitchen with her mother and Belle, sharpening her skills as a cook. She delighted in surprising him with some dish or sweet she had prepared.

Matthew suddenly realized that he had committed himself to marry Amelia. He had not really intended for things to move so quickly. He had not had marriage on his mind until Amelia brought it up. Then, he saw no way to back up without hurting her, which he really didn't want to do. It was true that he felt himself missing her, wanting her company, and he enjoyed the feeling of holding her in his arms. He wondered at her Pa's words about praying for God's will for them. How can they know such a thing? He and Amelia are not in agreement with much of anything, he admitted. She seems ready to be married, but is he really ready to take on the responsibility of a wife and family at this time in his life. After all, he is barely twenty years old.

Ian and Penelope returned in the middle of January, in the midst of a cold winter. They were wrapped in furs and bearing gifts like visitors from some foreign country. Their happiness and love for each other reached out to all the family and it was suddenly Christmas again, as presents were given and received amid cries of surprise and pleasure. As soon as the flurry of homecoming had settled down a little, Ian began to talk with Matthew about the work and all that had developed while he was away. He praised Matthew highly for the smooth running of his business in his absence.

"Matt, I can't begin to tell you what a great job you've done around this place. I found something I think you're going to like. This is just a little token of our friendship and I want to welcome you as a future brother-in-law." Ian grinned as he handed Matthew a long box.

Matthew's face was a study of conflicting emotions as he took the gift Ian held out to him. He never expected anything and he suddenly realized he had bought no gifts, not even for Amelia. Cursing himself for an idiot, he vowed to make up for it just as soon as he could get to town.

As the paper was ripped away and the lid of the box lifted, Matthew's eyes widened in disbelief. Ian had given him a brand-new rifle! It was an unbelievable piece of workmanship. He was speechless with pleasure.

"Man, I can't possibly accept such a gift. Why, this must have cost a fortune." he protested, even as he ran his hands over the shining barrel and carved stock of the gun. Ian laughed at his pleasure. "Just call it an investment in your and Amelia's future. Of course, I didn't know about you two until I got home, but you'll never be without fresh meat, that's for sure."

He was delighted at his friend's pleasure in his gift. "I want to talk to you about an idea I had while I've been away. In fact, my wife has quite a business head and she's actually the one who came up with the suggestion. How would you feel about doing a little traveling? I've realized that I could sell a lot more horses if I had time to visit around, meet with businessmen who are interested in a better breed of horseflesh than the wild broncos we used to catch. I would pay all your expenses, set up the meetings and you could go, transact the deals and then we could make arrangements to get the horses there." Ian's face was alive with the anticipation of his new business venture.

Matthew was unable to take it all in. The thought of traveling, meeting strangers was not too appealing to him. The thought of making money, however, was certainly appealing. Could he pull it off? "I don't know, Ian. That sounds like a great deal, alright. Do you think I could do it?" He sounded doubtful.

"Well, I'm in no hurry for your answer. Think about it. We really can't do much until spring gets here. Traveling will be much easier, then. Now, let's see just how many foals we're expecting in the spring." They walked companionably through the big stables, assessing the stock for the spring sale. As they neared the stable door, Matthew cleared his throat, swallowed a couple times and then, spoke hesitantly. "Ian, I've been wanting to talk with you about something."

"Sure, Matt, he replied. Let's go on to my house. Penelope is with Mom and the girls.

A few minutes later, they sat down on the porch in the rocking chairs. "Matt, I want you to know that you can talk to me about anything and trust me with your confidence. I consider you a real friend and now your relationship with Amelia means you are a part of our family." Ian's smile and his words calmed Matthew's fears of sounding ignorant.

"That means a lot to me, Ian. I have a lot of questions about what I read in the Bible. I need to know how to read it so it makes sense to me. I know I feel something in your family that I have never felt before. I feel accepted and appreciated and that is a new feeling for me. I want the kind of love I see demonstrated by your daddy for your mother and all of you for each other. Amelia talks about loving me, but I am not sure if what I feel for her is the same kind of love. I don't want to hurt her, but I am not ready to marry her until I know. I want to be with her, but we sure don't agree about much so far." Matthew grinned sheepishly and Ian laughed heartily at his words. "Where in the Bible, Matthew continued, can I find how to love Amelia in the right way?" Matthew felt as though a burden had lifted off his heart and mind as he shared his feelings with Ian. He ran his hand through his hair and got up from the chair. He stood and looked out across the beautiful acres of planted fields and wooded forest. When he turned to face him, Ian saw a longing on his face that he understood. "I want a place like this some day, Ian. A place of my own. I'm afraid Amelia will not be willing to leave her family and her life here to go with me to Texas. I don't want to leave her, but I don't think I can be satisfied until I have my own land and be in control of my life without being in the control of others. I know enough about the Bible from hearing preaching all my life to know a man is to forsake all other women and even his parents when he marries. What about a woman, though. Is she told to go wherever her husband goes, even if she does not want to?" Ian could see Matthew is troubled and seeking answers and he wanted to give him the answers according to God's Word. "I trust you to help me understand." Matthew sat down again and looked expectantly at Ian. Ian took a deep breath, realized Matthew is sincerely needing Godly counsel and praying for God's wisdom as he spoke. "What you are asking, Matt, is not a quick thing. You are right about a woman going with her husband after they marry, but there is so much more to the marriage covenant than just that requirement. A man and a woman must be filled with God's Spirit before they can love each other the way God intended in the beginning. As a husband, you are to love Amelia so much that you are willing to give your life for her, like Jesus did on the cross for his bride, the church he bought with his blood." Ian paused, as Matthew's face filled with confusion. "Do you understand what that is all about, Matt? Have you read in Matthew about Jesus and how he suffered and died on the cross so all men could be set free from sin?" Ian realized Matthew's knowledge of God's Word is limited. "I tell you what, my friend. Let's you and I get together and start at the beginning, when God created man and woman and put them in a beautiful garden and what happened afterwards so you can fully understand how to be a Godly man married to a Godly woman." Ian grinned as he stood up. Let's have some coffee and a piece of Penelope's pound cake. "I will be glad to meet with you alone and we will begin at the beginning, just like you do when reading a book. Let's agree on a meeting once a week to read and talk about what we are reading so you can learn how to get understanding of God's Word, because that is the only way there is given to us to know how to live pleasing to the Lord." Ian grinned. "I can't tell you, Matt, what it means to me for you to be my friend and trust me with your questions. Now, when do you want to have your first Bible lesson?"

"How about as soon as you have the time for us to get together?" Matthew replied, his eyes full of excitement. He felt like he had just made a step in the right direction to understanding himself.

Chapter 22

Winter gave way to spring and though they had been spending time together talking about their future, Amelia has not brought up the subject of her desires to go to college and become a teacher. She has set aside her dreams and allowed herself to focus on nothing except being married to Matthew. Even though it had only been a few months since their talk with William, Amelia began to push Matthew to approach her Daddy again. She wanted to have an official engagement party, so she and Matthew could begin to receive household gifts for their future home. So far, Matthew had made no effort to begin a house or even discussed any plans for where they would live. This bothered Amelia. If he were serious about them, why hadn't he already discussed the subject with her?

Early April found them sitting in church together. Their appearance had caused some heads to turn, for they made an attractive couple. Matthew's dark handsome figure beside Amelia's red hair and fair skin was a picture of contrast when they came down the aisle and took their seat next to Constance and William in the pew. Amelia could feel the eyes of all the single girls and she felt a little smug at having such a handsome suitor as Matthew. Her friend Holly's eyes were wide with excitement and Amelia knew she was about to burst wanting an explanation of Matthew's presence with her. She kept her eyes straight to the front, paying strict attention to the sermon and noticed Matthew seemed very uncomfortable himself. He too felt the stares and wished he had stayed home. He found, however, that he was expected to attend church with Amelia. He felt, somehow, that his refusal would have seriously affected his prospects of making her his wife. He found himself interested in spite of his reluctance in attending, for it was Easter and the sermon was concerning the crucifixion and resurrection of Jesus Christ.

"When you feel yourself tempted by sinful pleasures, get a picture in your mind of the cross. Hear the hammer of the nails as they were driven into his hands and feet. Think about a man willing to die in your place. For, dear friends, that is what he did, you know. He died in our place. But, Praise God, He also arose. That is our hope, too. If we die in the Lord, we shall also rise, just like He did. That's the difference between men and animals. Our soul is different from all other creatures. We will never die. We may die here on earth, but we will live forever, either in heaven or in hell. God forbid that any of you should neglect so great a salvation as was given to us by the apostles. We have the Word of God ever before us. We have no reason to not be ready to meet the Lord when he returns, or when death claims us on this earth. Today is a glorious day for all mankind. It is the day of resurrection. Because He lived and died and rose again, we have a blessed hope that we shall also rise from the grave." Pastor Haney looked out over the congregation as he brought his message to a close. If we gain the whole world and never know Jesus as our Savior, we will have spent our lives in vain."

Matthew's attention was caught by the earnest message. He remembered the day he and Robert had talked about his mother going to heaven. Robert told him they could see her again. But they would have to live like the Bible said to live. They had to repent of their sins, be baptized and receive the Holy Ghost, just like she did.

Matthew had been baptized, he thought, but as far as repenting went, he hadn't done much of that. He was still pondering when he realized the minister had closed his message and everyone was standing for the final prayer.

Later, having dinner with the family, Matthew watched Constance as she laughed and waited on her family. He wondered if his mother had acted like that. He wondered how she looked if she was tall or short, slim or plump. He always pictured her as a beautiful, slim, Indian princess, in a buckskin dress and a feather in her hair. He knew deep down that she had worn regular dresses and had become a Christian, giving up her Indian ways. It just seemed more natural, somehow, thinking of her in her Indian clothes.

Constance seemed to feel his gaze, for she turned and looked his way. She smiled, giving him a little nod, as though she understood his thoughts. Her eyes were brown, too, but her hair was not black, only a dark brown, with little hints of red here and there.

He smiled at her, accepting the piece of pie she offered, but not before she had seen the longing on his face.

After dinner, he and Amelia walked down the trail, stopping at the creek to watch the little minnows and enjoy the sound of the running water. She seated herself on a fallen tree. She smiled, remembering how Levi had changed when he gave her the locket.

"What are you smiling about, Amy?" Matthew wondered.

"Oh, just remembering how Ian and I used to walk down here during the summer. He suddenly came close to her, as though to take her in his arms. She looked up expectantly, but his eyes were on the neck of her dress, which was round, without a collar. He pulled the chain holding the little locket from inside her dress and held it in his big hand. "I never noticed that before. Have you worn it long?" he asked her, curiously.

"Ever since my fourteenth birthday party. I got it then." For some reason, she blushed, and his eyes narrowed strangely. Amelia suddenly felt guilty, but knew she had done nothing wrong.

"Who gave it to you?" the question was mildly put, but sudden tension was there, between them. He still held the little locket in his hand, waiting for her answer.

"Why Matthew, I was only a child then." she laughed, making light of the gift.

"I want to know who gave it to you. Did your parents give it to you?" his voice had become hard and suddenly Amelia was afraid to tell him who gave her the locket.

"No, Levi gave it to me. He had always been mean to me all through school. He gave it to me as a friend." Amelia reached up and tried to remove the locket from Matthew's hand. He closed his hand over the locket and Amelia felt the pull of the chain against the back of her neck. He was very close to her and she looked into his eyes, pleading with him to understand. He saw the fear in her eyes.

Suddenly, he released the locket and strode away from her, up the trail, without a word. She sat on the fallen tree, trembling, her heart beating so hard, she felt it in her head. Reaching her hand up, she grasped the little locket in her cold hand and felt its warmth make a little spot of comfort in her palm.

Matthew didn't go to the house but turned off blindly and found himself further up the creek, where the trees were thick. His anger had cooled somewhat and he sat down on the ground beside a tree to sort out his thoughts. He had almost jerked the locket from Amelia's neck, wanting to throw it as far as he could. The rage had come on him and he had to get away before he did something he would regret. Deep down, he knew Amelia had done no wrong, but he was consumed by anger toward Levi. Anger that Levi had given her a gift that she still valued enough to wear; even though she said she loved him. How could she love him and still wear the locket? The locket represented another man. Why would she wear it now, when they were planning to be married?

Maybe she really didn't love him. Maybe she was just like all the other women in his life. Out to use him, and then discard him. Maybe he should give her something to show that he loved her. Maybe then she would not care about the locket. Getting to his feet, he walked rapidly back to the trail and made his way to Ian's house. When he got there, he suddenly remembered to knock on the door. Since Ian and Penelope had come home, he had to do things differently than before Ian was married.

"Matthew! Come on in." Ian opened the door, grinned his welcoming grin.

Penelope turned from the sink, drying her hands. "Hello, Matt. Wasn't that a wonderful service this morning?" she stood beside Ian, her arm encircling his waist.

"Why, yes, I guess it was, Penny." Matthew seemed distracted. The couple looked at each other. What's going on, they wondered.

"I need your help, Penelope. I need to buy a gift for Amelia and I don't know the first thing about buying anything for a woman." he sounded desperate, Penny thought.

"Oh, Matt, that's wonderful. I'll be glad to help you. What did you have in mind?" She exclaimed with excitement at the prospect.

Matthew looked blank and Ian and Penny laughed together, bringing a wry look from him.

"Do you want to buy her jewelry, some scent, maybe gloves, or just what were you thinking about for her? That's what Penny means." Ian explained.

"Well, where would I get something really nice? Maybe a ring, I thought. She wants us to be engaged. Maybe that's what I need to do. Buy her a ring." Matthew's face lightened at the idea.

Ian and Penny again exchanged looks. Then, Penny clapped her hands excitedly. "I know," she exclaimed, rushing from the room. The men looked at each other, Ian shrugged his shoulders. Then she was back, something in her hand. She held it out to Matthew. "Give her this, Matthew," she said triumphantly.

Matthew opened the little box and there on a bed of royal blue velvet was a dainty gold ring. In the center was a beautiful pearl and on each side were tiny little diamonds, giving off blue sparkles of light every time it moved. It was a thing of exquisite beauty. He had never seen anything like it before. He knew it was expensive, but he didn't care. He had to have it, he thought recklessly. It would suit her. Looking up at Penny, he asked her, "How much?"

"Matthew, that ring was given to me by my grandfather. He gave me many rings and a lot of jewelry while I was growing up. He could afford to, because he was a jeweler. That's why I can offer it to you because he gave me so many. I am offering it to you as a friend. I hope you will accept it on those terms, as it cost me nothing." her voice was sincere, hoping he would not let his male pride cause him to refuse the ring.

Matthew could not believe anyone would give him something so expensive after Ian had already given him a brand-new rifle. He studied the situation, wondering what he should do. Finally, he came to a decision.

"I'll accept it on one condition" he finally smiled; the dullness gone from his eyes. "Let me make you a cradle for your first baby."

"How did you know?" They both cried in unison. Then their laughter filled the room and Matthew had to join in, looking at them in surprise. "Sit down, Matthew, I have coffee and cake." Penelope went to the cabinet, bringing three cups to the table. He and Ian pulled out chairs and sat down as she poured coffee and sliced the cake.

"This is delicious, Penelope." he grinned after his first bite of the cake. "I appreciate all you and Ian are doing for me, he said, meeting Ian's eyes across the table. I'm anxious to give Amelia the ring. I know she will love it." He drank the coffee quickly, finished the cake and stood. Ian laughed. "Go on, Matt," he urged. I know how you feel."

Matthew hurried to the corral, saddled his horse and rode quickly toward the MaceIlewain farm. He didn't know what he would say to Amelia. He had frightened her, he knew. It would be alright, he told himself. When he gave her the ring, it would be alright between them again.

Matthew rode up to the house, jumped quickly off his horse, took the steps in one leap, knocking on the door loudly. Constance came to the door, seeming surprised to see him.

"Are you looking for Amelia, Matthew? I haven't seen her since earlier today." she volunteered.

"Uh, you mean she's not here?" he looked confused and disappointed, Constance noticed.

"No, I thought the two of you were together. I haven't noticed her in the house all afternoon. I'll go check her room, though. Come on in and have a seat." She went toward the back of the house where the bedrooms were located. Matthew walked up and down the length of the front room, nervous and anxious about seeing Amelia after the way he had acted earlier. In a moment, Constance returned.

"I was right, Matt. She's not in her room. When did you see her last?"

"A couple of hours ago. I thought she would be here. I've been back at Ian's house. I had something to take care of." he seemed at a loss as to what to do next. Finally, he turned back to the door.

"I'll be going, now, Mrs. Macellwain. I'll come back later." he walked slowly out, mounted his horse and rode away in the direction of Ian's house. Constance watched him go; wondering what was going on with him and Amelia. She went to Belle's room, knocked on the door, then, when Belle answered her knock, went in.

"Belle, what do you think about Amelia and Matthew?" Constance sat beside the window in the small rocker that had been Belle's since she was very young.

"Mama, do you want my honest opinion? I think he's all wrong for her. They just have nothing in common. What they talk about is a mystery to me. Amelia has always loved to read. You know how she has always read any and everything she could get her hands on? Matthew cares nothing about reading. He cares about making money and being able to tell other people what to do. He's been mistreated all of his life, from what I can gather, and it has really affected his dealings with other people. She is closing her eyes to his true character. All she will allow herself to see is how he makes her feel and that's a poor reason to marry somebody." Belle finished, her eyes concerned, looking at her mother.

"I couldn't agree with you more, Belle. Your father and I are very fearful of this relationship. I don't mind telling you that we feel Matthew is a person who can be totally out of control in an instant, with very little provocation." Constance rose, smoothed her skirts, and then turned to go.

"Belle, what is your suggestion as to how to convince Amelia to see the danger of pursuing a relationship with Matthew?" she stopped when she reached the door.

"Mama, we'll just have to pray that she will see him as he really is before they get married and she will back out." Belle gave her mother little comfort with these words.

Amelia was high in the place she had always gone when facing problems or wanting to escape the routine of life. From her perch in the fork of the spreading branches of the oak tree, she was able to look up into the heavens. She could look down upon the earth and she could see far into the distance.

She saw the horse carrying Matthew approaching from the direction of her home. She saw him looking in every direction, stopping every few steps, scanning the countryside, searching. She knew he was looking for her, but some part of her wanted to make him wonder about her. He had wounded her and made her afraid of him. She hated what had happened between them. "His eyes were the eyes of an uncontrollable force, she thought. I was hardly breathing; I was so frightened." She had seen the demon look at her through the dark eyes of the man she had planned to marry. She was beginning to get a premonition of what was in store for her if they married.

She remained very still, watching him come closer and closer to the tree where she sat. She would not call out to him. She kept silent as he stopped his horse not more than ten feet away. He looked carefully in all directions, and then reached inside his shirt, pulling out something.

But she could not make out what it was. He held it between his hands, looked at it intently for several seconds, and then replaced it inside his shirt. Reining his horse around, he rode back toward Ian's house, his shoulders not quite as straight as they usually were when he rode.

Ian saw Matthew ride up to the barn and start to unsaddle his horse. Thinking to find out Amelia's reaction to the ring, he smilingly hurried out to talk with him.

"Matt! What did she say when you gave her the ring? I bet she cried. You know Amelia cries when she's happy and cries when she's upset" Ian's smile faded when he saw Matthew's face. "What's wrong, buddy? Do you want to talk about it?" his tone turned serious. "I'm here for you, you know. Just like we agreed, we need to have that Bible study so you can know God's direction for you and Amelia."

Matthew didn't answer, just watched his horse as he let him into the pasture. He then leaned his arms on the fence, looking off into the distance. How much should he tell Ian about him and Amelia, he wondered. After all, he's her brother. He wouldn't be agreeable to Matt's behavior; he knows that without even thinking about it.

"I didn't get to give it to her. She wasn't at home. I'll probably see her tomorrow. I may ride back over before dark. She must have gone walking or something." he never did turn and look at Ian as he offered this information, just kept his head averted.

Sensing Matthew was not being truthful with him, Ian didn't question him further. "Well, Penelope was anxious to know if she liked the ring. You know how women are. They get all excited over things like that." he laughed as he gave Matt a friendly slap on his back. "Will you be here for supper? You know you're welcome, Matthew, to eat with us."

"I don't know, Ian. Just go on and eat if I don't show up. Maybe Penelope would save me something for later if I don't eat at Amelia's house."

Matthew still hadn't looked at Ian. His body tensed at Ian's touch, then relaxed as he reminded himself that Ian is his friend. As he still kept his eyes turned into the distance, Ian gave him a thoughtful look, then left him and started back to the house.

"Okay, I'll see you later, Matt," he called back over his shoulder.

"I do know how women are," Matthew thought after Ian had gone. He felt sometimes like an idiot when he was around women, even Amelia. The same way he had felt all those years, growing up with Millie, Kate and Annie. Aunt Martha was continually hollering at him to do this or do that. She never could stand to see him idle, not for one minute. He remembered the way Katherine had talked to him the last time he had seen them. They had all been there, because of Uncle James being so sick. He had built a fire, just like always and they were sitting there, talking about what to do about the place and Uncle James's condition. He had sat down near the edge of their circle, silently listening to the discussion. Suddenly, as though realizing he was present, Katherine had given him a sharp look.

"Matthew, you have no business here with us. You have nothing to say about any of this, you know. You are not our brother, after all." her eyes were cold, her words cruel.

Matthew had said nothing, but his eyes met hers in a look of pure hatred. Her face whitened and then turned red, as he directed the full force of his feelings at her. Then, he had walked out. That was the last time he had been in the same room with them, except Annie. Thinking of it now, he felt his stomach heave with hurt and rage. The scene before him blurred. He could have hit Katherine that day. He could have beaten her with his fists. There she sat, being warmed by the fire he had built, with the wood he had cut, talking to him like a dog. Sometimes, he seemed to get his feelings toward those women who raised him all mixed up with his feelings for Amelia. He knew deep inside his conscience that there was a difference. It just seemed like his mind just got mixed up sometimes. Thoughts of hurting Amelia when she is innocent filled his heart with shame and remorse. *Why do I get so angry? What is wrong with me?* With no answer for his question, he felt a sense of hopelessness as to what to do to make things right with Amelia. Pastor Haney's words came back to him. "Jesus died for us before we were born. When we didn't love him, he still loved us. We must have Jesus inside our soul before we can love others like he loves us." *How can I get Jesus inside my soul? Who can I ask?* He remembered the conversation with Ian and how they had agreed to meet to study the Bible. So far, he had been busy and his questions are still unanswered. He has to get with Ian soon, before he messes up with Amelia more than he already has. He promised Amelia's Pa they would pray, but he doesn't even know how to pray, he has realized. Ian said he must love Amelia like Jesus loves all people, willing to give up what he wants for her sake.

Matthew turned suddenly from the fence and walked rapidly across the yard, reaching the trail that wound through the woods and onto the MaceIlewain land. As he reached the edge of the woods and started across the pasture, he stopped in amazement. A big oak with spreading branches grew about halfway between the pasture and the woods. He could see someone was sitting at the base of the tree. It was a woman, for he could see the bright color of her dress. His heart told him who it was and he quickened his pace, quickly reaching her.

Amelia saw him coming. She didn't want to see him, but there was no place to go, so she waited to see what he would say to her.

"Amelia! Where have you been? I've looked everywhere for you." he stood between her and the sun and she could not see his eyes.

"I've been here." She did not look at him.

"You couldn't have been here. I rode within a few feet of this spot. I didn't see you." he just couldn't help himself. He implied that she was lying.

She looked at him then, her eyes distant, without feeling. "Matthew, I was up in the tree. I saw you. I kept quiet. I had nothing to say to you. I have nothing to say to you now." She kept her voice low, but she wanted to scream at him to go away and leave her alone. He had become a stranger.

"Oh, well, why didn't you say so at first?" He acted as though he didn't hear her last words, continuing to stand there, the air between them charged. Suddenly, he dropped down beside her, his shoulder touching hers. She moved just enough to break the contact. Seeming not to notice, he reached inside his shirt, pulling out a small box, which he offered to her.

Amelia made no attempt to take the box from him. She kept her head averted, refusing to meet his eyes. She felt his arm go around her shoulders and she stiffened her body, resisting the effect his nearness had on her. His arm drew her toward him, until he held her next to him, his arm strong around her shoulders.

"Look in the box, Amelia. I want you to have this." he placed the box in her hands where they lay in her lap. She made no attempt to open the box. He reached and took her face in his free hand, turning her head toward him, until she was forced to face his eyes. She was lost, then, just as she knew she would be. Closing her eyes, she felt the tears forming and willed herself not to cry.

"Amelia, open the box and then if you want me to go away, I will."

At his words, her eyes flew open and they were bright with unshed tears. "I don't understand you, Matthew. I love you. I don't want you to go away." She swiped helplessly at her face, trying to stop the flow of tears.

"Stop crying, Amelia, and look in the box," he ordered.

At his tone, she picked up the box. Glancing up at him, she was surprised with an anxious look on his face. Wondering, she lifted the lid of the small box. She said nothing, just stared at the ring, and then raised her eyes to his once more. She was crying again, tears rolling down her face, dropping onto her hands still holding the box.

"Are you happy, Amelia? Ian said you cry when you're happy." his voice was softer than she had ever heard it, hopeful, even. He reached, removed the ring, lifted her hand and slid the ring onto her finger.

Amelia knew this should be the most exciting, joyful event of her life, but the feeling that swept over her was not joy, but a fearful acceptance. A feeling of being pushed along by unexplainable emotions, dangerous emotions that have gotten control of her mind. She knew she should not accept the ring, even though she had longed for him to give her a token of his love. After the episode with the locket, she had strong misgivings about him. Yet, she seemed unable to pull back. Even as she smiled through her tears, she was not happy, just swept along by her feelings for him.

Matthew suddenly felt great, as he saw Amelia's acceptance of the ring. He knew she would not be able to resist such a gift. Thanks to Penelope, everything was fine between them again. She could not resist as he pulled her to her feet and drew her quickly into his arms. She saw his eyes fill with emotion before he kissed her hard on her lips. Suddenly, her arms were around his waist and she was overcome with love for him, though her legs trembled. He had never acted in such a way with her and she felt overwhelmed at such treatment. Then he grinned triumphantly, holding her tight, his arms strong around her. She had no strength to free herself from his arms or from his will.

"Now, you and I are officially engaged, Amelia. Once we're married, everything will be alright, you'll see." his tone was confident, exultant. He released her then, took her hand and they started walking back toward the house.

Amelia was silent, thinking of her parents' reaction to the ring. She felt she should have talked with William before allowing Matthew to give her a ring. Now, she was fearful of Matthew being offended, angered, if her Daddy objected. Praying all the way to the house, she was nervous, her stomach in a knot. Realizing that she had made Matthew feel as though he needed to give her a ring, only made her feel more responsible for the situation. They have not done what her daddy had told them to do and now she realizes there is much about Matthew she is now finding out.

When they reached the house, it was close to supper time and the family was about to gather around the table. Amelia drew Matthew into the kitchen.

"Matthew and I have something to tell all of you" Amelia exclaimed, anxious to get it over with.

She held out her hand, the ring sparkling on her finger, showing it to them. Her eyes went to her Papa, begging him to be glad for her. He felt her fear, knew immediately how she felt. He rose to the occasion, shaking Matthew's hand, hugging Amelia. Her eyes were full of grateful love as she felt her daddy's arms holding her close. Then, they were all exclaiming over the beauty of the ring, as they sat down and bowed their heads for the blessing of the food.

Matthew felt good, as he heard William give thanks for the food and ask the Lord to bless him and Amelia. He felt a part of them now, accepted. The ring had somehow elevated him to a higher position in the family. He knew, deep down, that William had misgivings about him as a husband for Amelia. Well, he would have to show him that he deserved respect.

Matthew stayed awhile after supper was over. He and Amelia sat on the porch with the rest of the family, watching the sun go down in a blaze of glorious color. They talked about the success of Ian's horse venture, the planting of the crop, wondered about the weather conditions for the coming summer. Nothing was mentioned concerning the date that Amelia and Matthew were to be married. They had not discussed that as yet. Then, Matthew rose, saying he had an early day tomorrow and needed to go. Bidding them all good night, he struck off down the trail, his heart lighter than it had been in a long time.

After Matthew left, nothing was said for a while. They all watched his figure disappear into the dusk of the spring evening.

"Amelia, have you and Matthew discussed when you would like to be married?" Constance spoke into the silence. "You know it will take some preparation, so we do need to know."

"I don't know right now, Mama. I don't even know for sure that I will ever marry Matthew. Sometimes I feel that he is not really for me, after all. I'm realizing more and more how different we are. I couldn't refuse the ring. I couldn't stand to see him disappointed. So many people have disappointed him, all his life. I told him I love him. I can't tell him I don't" Amelia did not sound like a young woman who was happy about her engagement. She could still see the blackness in his eyes when he held the locket.

"Amelia, do you realize that what you are doing is crueler than if you had refused the ring? If you are in doubt about your feelings, please don't lead Matthew on, allowing him to care for you more each day, then let him down later" William's voice is firm, scolding, almost. "Have you and Matthew been in prayer concerning your future? Unless you know God's will, Amelia, you will make decisions based on your feelings and not on what is best for your happiness." Amelia's heart felt torn afresh, knowing she has disappointed her daddy. Even as she had said the words, she knew she would marry Matthew. She knew she would never have the strength of mind to turn away from him and let him go out of her life. She knew she would die, surely, if she always had to wonder where he was and who he was with.

"Yes, daddy, I know you're right. Maybe I'll talk with him some more. We don't really know each other. I think that's the biggest difficulty to overcome. I think I'll go in now. Good night, everybody. Sleep tight, don't let the bed bugs bite." she smiled at them then, hugged and kissed them all before she went into the house.

Constance and William exchanged helpless looks as the door closed behind their daughter. Clasping their hands together, they began to earnestly pray for God to intervene in Amelia and Matthew's plans and work his will for what he knows is best for them.

****

The following Sunday afternoon, Amelia and Matthew walked hand in hand to the garden that is now a beautiful, peaceful refuge that she loves. He sat down in the chair Amelia had put in the gazebo, as she walked through the garden. The roses, wisteria and jasmine filled the air with an intoxicating fragrance that seems to give peace to

Matthew's heart, as he watched Amelia go from flower to flower, like a butterfly, sticking her nose in the blooms. He smiled indulgently when she turned to him with her eyes shining with pleasure. She came to where he sat. As though in a dream, she placed her hands on his shoulders, leaned close, touched his cheek with her lips, looked into his eyes. "I love you, Matthew."

Something swelled up inside his heart at her sweetness and the innocence he saw in her eyes. She is giving him a gift, he suddenly realizes. She is trusting him with her loving heart. He reached and pulled her down beside him, wrapped his arms around her, and wanted so desperately to love her the way she loves him. Would she love him if she could see the darkness inside his soul? A terrible fear caused him to tighten his arms around her.

Amelia felt loved and wanted in the tightening of his arms and the touch of his lips as he tried to express his feelings for her.

He looked into her eyes and saw himself in their clear blue depths. "I love you too, Amy. I want us to be together no matter what happens." And then, with that lopsided grin that made her heart quicken, he revealed the plans he had been making for their future.

"Amelia, do you remember hearing about the forming of a wagon train over a year ago? Well, I met a man in town yesterday who is getting his supplies together. He and his wife are buying a covered wagon, stocking it with food and bedding and everything they can carry. They're going to Texas to claim a homestead."

She said nothing for a moment, for her breath caught in her throat and fear gripped her heart. She looked away toward her garden and spoke softly.

"I imagine that must be an awfully hard thing to do, you know. Just pack up and leave your family, friends, everybody you've always known and go off, be a stranger in a strange place. I would never want to leave here."

"Well, I could leave. I've been thinking that would be where a man could claim himself a fine homestead. Make a name for him in a new place where no one knows him. Have a new life." Matthew replied. "Amelia, I'm thinking really strong about joining up with that wagon train. If you don't feel like you can leave here, its best we don't marry, for I don't intend to work for Ian all my life. I want my own barn and stables. I want my own house."

"Matthew, you know Papa will give us some land. You can have your own place, right here. You don't have to move to Texas, or some faraway place, to have all of that." She felt desperate to make him realize what her family means to her. But, suddenly, she saw his eyes fill with impatience and though his arms were around her, she felt separated from him in disagreement.

"I've always wanted to see more of the country than what is around here. I'm going next week with Ian to meet some men interested in buying horses. He asked me awhile back if I would be interested in making some trips for him to meet buyers. We're going together this time so I can decide if it is something I want to do. When I get back, I will have made up my mind whether I will go to Texas or stay here and work for him. You need to make up your mind while I'm gone what you want to do. If I go to Texas, we have to be married this summer. That is, if you want to go with me."

Matthew's words struck Amelia as so matter of fact that she felt herself at a loss for words. He sounded as though he didn't care if she stayed or went with him.

"I won't try to force you to do anything you don't want to do, Amelia. If you really love me like you say you do, you should want to go. That's how I feel about it." He waited for her to reply, his expression revealing nothing of his feelings.

He sounded so cold, she thought. What if he left without her? How would she feel? He has just told her he loves her and now he wants her to give up her family. How can she be happy among strangers, miles away in a strange place? She wanted to tell him she would go with him wherever he wanted to go, but she felt as though he didn't care that she would be heartbroken. Resentment at his ultimatum, suddenly realizing she would be the one giving up everything for him to carry out his own plans for their future turned her voice cold. She stood up, walked away from him, turning her back as she spoke. "I'll let you know, Matthew. Perhaps if you find someone else between now and then, you will want your ring back." She heard her own words as though someone else were speaking them. Matthew shot her a strange look. "What is she upset about?" he wondered. Her words are so unlike her.

"Now Amelia, why would I want someone else when you and I are engaged to be married?" He sounded sincerely confused by her sarcasm and she regretted her words.

"Oh, Matthew, I wonder sometime if you really love me at all," she sighed and turned away to look into the distance, across the fields beyond her flower garden. Her expression bothered him and he stood up and went to her, putting his arms around her back and drawing her close to him.

"Amelia, would I have given you a ring and asked you to marry me if didn't love you?" He spoke softly into her ear and she could do nothing but rest her head against his chest and whisper. "I guess not." *"How can two walk together when they do not agree?"* *The scripture reminded her.*

Chapter 23

Hannah Wilson glanced once more at herself in the mirror, and then gathered her purse and gloves, before she exited her room. She hurried down the hall to her parent's room, knocked, then entered. "Good morning, Mother, Father. I'm sorry to keep you waiting, but I didn't sleep well on such a mattress as this hotel provides for its guests." her pretty face was wearing a complaining look this morning.

Mrs. Wilson, a slim, attractive woman in her late fifties, greeted her daughter affectionately.

"Now, Hannah, I slept very well. You shouldn't be so critical. This is a very nice hotel. Try to enjoy yourself. We'll be leaving after your father's meeting this afternoon."

"Yes, daughter, listen to your mother. She has a very good outlook. That's why we get along so well." Mr. Wilson, putting on his coat, smiled at his wife. Balding, but still distinguished looking, he had put on weight as he neared his sixtieth birthday. Being six feet tall kept him from appearing overweight. His well-cut suit and expensive shoes gave him the look of a prosperous banker, which in actuality, he was not. Mr. Wilson owned a large ranch in Texas and was meeting with Ian MaceIlewain today. He wanted to see the thoroughbreds Ian was raising in his place. Mr. Wilson was looking to buy stallions to add to his stable. He had brought his wife and daughter with him so they could shop and see the sights. Hannah, however, he had to admit, had been much too spoiled by him. She tended to look down her nose at everything and everybody outside their little kingdom of the ranch.

"Well, dear, it looks as though we can descend to the dining room for some breakfast if you're ready." he offered his arm to his wife, then his daughter, as they left the room.

The waiter seated the family at a table where they could see the rest of the diners as they entered. Hannah immediately noticed the two men who came in soon after they were seated. One of them seemed to know his way around, for he indicated to the waiter a table with a view into the back garden of the dining room. The younger man seemed uncertain of himself, following the other one's lead. They were both handsome men, but one of them, the one with the olive complexion and the dark eyes, appeared to be some foreigner, or perhaps he was just an Indian, Hannah, decided. She observed them boldly, for she had been raised among cowhands and had none of the timid demeanor of most young girls her age. She spoke her mind and didn't care who didn't like it.

"Father, do you know those men who just came in?" she indicated at the table where the two men were giving their order to the waiter.

Hiram Wilson turned his head, looking surreptitiously toward the back of the room.

"Why, I do believe that is Ian MaceIlwain. I don't know who the other young man is. Perhaps he is one of his men, or a possible buyer, like me." He replied.

"I want you to introduce me to them. Is Ian married?" Her green eyes were calculating as she again looked at the men.

"Now, Hannah, dear, how would your Father know such a thing?" Mrs. Wilson is sometimes overwhelmed by this young woman who is her daughter. Her direct way of going after what she wants and making no secret of it is totally different from what Mrs. Wilson considers acceptable behavior for young ladies. She knows her husband has spoiled and pampered Hannah all of her life. All she had to do when she was small was climb into his lap, put her little arms around his neck and whisper to him her desire and it was hers. Now, she very seldom asked, she just took. She is a beautiful, but calculating woman at twenty-three and many of the young men on the ranch and acquaintances of their friends aspired to court her. Her forthright manner, however, was too much for most of them to deal with. Mrs. Wilson feared that her daughter would become a veritable shrew if some man didn't conquer her soon.

She discarded most of the would-be suitors after just a few minutes of conversation, considering them below her mentally. She had been sent away to an expensive boarding school for two years, in an effort to acquire social graces. She had learned absolutely nothing about fluttering her eyes and dropping her handkerchief as a means of attracting a man. She scorned the other girls as too sissified and delicate for her taste. Now, she was determined to become the manager of her Father's holdings and the large empire he had built from scratch. She was happiest when astride her big gelding, and could rope and brand a calf as good as any man on the ranch. She wore britches, too, which appalled her gently reared mother.

Now, as she ate her breakfast, she watched the two men much as a cat would view a canary just before it attacked. Once, her glance coincided with the time Ian happened to look in that direction. Their eyes met. He looked quickly back at Matt, for he knew that look. He did not need such a woman in his life. He wondered why she was focusing her attention on them. He was soon to find out, for the Wilsons had finished their meal and were approaching the table where he and Matthew sat. Matthew didn't see them, for his back was toward their table.

"Mr. MaceIlwain? I thought I recognized you. I'm Hiram Wilson. We've corresponded, concerning your horses. I'm to meet with you later, but just wanted to speak to you and your friend." Mr. Wilson cordially held out his hand as Ian rose to greet him.

Taking his cue from Ian, Matthew also stood and shook hands with him, then looked at Hannah, as her Father introduced her and Mrs. Wilson to them. Hannah offered her hand to each of the men in turn. She turned the full force of her strange green eyes on them. Noticing that Ian wore a wedding band, she smiled demurely, murmured a soft greeting to him. Then Matthew bowed over her hand, as he had seen Ian do.

"Mr. Carlisle, I hope you and I become better acquainted. You may escort me to dinner tonight." her eyes took in his handsome features and she smiled, revealing perfect white teeth. Her luxuriant hair was casually dressed in a simple fashion, pulled straight back from her face. Her green eyes were arresting in their color, for her skin was unexpectedly tanned from being in the sun. Her face was almost perfect in symmetry, with a slim nose. Her lips were full and touched with a hint of color. She wore a green dress of expensive fabric, which made her eyes even more brilliant.

Mrs. Wilson watched this extraordinary behavior from her daughter and wondered why she was putting out all this charm on this dark young man. She was pretending to be a sweet young thing, which her mother knew she could never be. She suddenly felt sorry for Mr. Carlisle, for he seemed at a loss to deal with her daughter.

Matthew suddenly felt awkward under the force of the green eyes of this young woman. He dropped her hand and waited for Ian to finish talking with Mr. Wilson.

"I'll see you later, Mr. Macellwain. Sorry to interrupt your meal. Let's go, Hannah, Mrs. Wilson and let these gentlemen finish their breakfast." he ushered his womenfolk out of the dining room.

"Matt, it looks as though you have an admirer. What are you going to do about her?" Ian asked, grinning at Matt.

"Can you believe she asked me to take her to eat? I mean, just like that. I never knew there were women like that in the world. That's the way Bethany acted." Matthew then told Ian about meeting the young woman at Buck's house during the Christmas visit he had made. "She didn't even ask me if I wanted to marry her. She just told me I was going to, then grabbed me and kissed me." he sounded incredulous.

Ian laughed outright, then, at Matthew's innocence where women were concerned. "Matt, there are all kinds of women in the world. Some of them are like predators, you know, like a wild cat stalking a deer. They see a man they want, and then go after him. Others, more timid, have to wait for the man to come to them. Hannah and Bethany are definitely the stalking kind. You shouldn't have a problem with Hannah, though. Just tell her you're engaged to be married. She will still try to ensnare you with her charms, because some women, and I think she's one of these, don't care if a man is committed. That just makes the chase more exciting; to take what belongs to another woman. A man has to be strong in his resolve to remain faithful to overcome these temptations." Ian's face had taken on a more serious expression as he cautioned Matthew. "One of the signs of Godly love of a man for his wife is resisting the temptations of other women."

They finished their breakfast, finally, had a second cup of coffee, and then left the hotel to see the town before they met with the other men. Ian wanted to buy something for Penelope and his mother, so kept his eyes open for the right shop as they wandered through the town. Matthew watched him purchase a pin on the watch that looked like a brooch for Constance, then a beautiful jeweled comb for Penelope. While the shopkeeper was wrapping his purchases, he pointed out a comb, hinting that it would look nice in Amelia's auburn hair. Matthew looked surprised at the suggestion he should buy a present for Amelia. Looking at the price, he saw it was almost a month's wage for him, as it had real jewels set into it, not just glass. Not wanting to appear cheap to Ian, he purchased the comb and had it wrapped to give to Amelia.

They ate lunch in a small restaurant, and then returned to the hotel to rest.

That evening, when Ian and Matt descended the stairs, Ian wore a tailor-made suit, purchased when on his honeymoon. He had lent Matthew one also. It was well-cut and fit his slim, broad-shouldered body to perfection. It turned him from a rough-appearing cowhand into a prosperous appearing businessman. Feminine eyes were drawn in their direction as they walked through the dining room to the private room reserved for their meeting. Some of the gentlemen were already seated at the table, conversing, getting acquainted. They rose and greeted Ian and Matthew cordially, shaking hands all around the group. The table was laid out and white-coated waiters served their plates. Matthew felt nervous, but he thought he could get used to this kind of treatment. He knew he was only receiving this attention because of Ian, but someday, he thought, he would be honored for himself. He had completely ignored Hannah's bold invitation to escort her to dinner. She scared him, just as Bethany's overtures had scared him. Yet, something about their attention excited him. Ian's warning came to his mind again about Godly love resisting temptation.

When Mr. Wilson arrived, Matthew was amazed to see that Hannah accompanied him. She was even more stunningly dressed tonight, in a white, beaded gown, her dark hair swept up, then allowed to fall loosely over her bare shoulders. The gown emphasized her tanned skin and brilliant eyes. Matthew noticed how all the men could not seem to take their eyes off her. He felt a touch of male ego that she had singled him out to escort her. He suddenly realized that a beautiful woman like her could probably have any man she wanted. Why she should want him was a mystery to Matthew.

"Well, Mr. Carlisle, you know you're never supposed to disappoint a lady." she stood beside him, her eyes assessing him and his reaction to her. The scent she wore enveloped them, as though they were alone. He was not skilled in the give-and-take of social conversation. The hidden meanings and flirtations that were carried out by men and women were an unknown thing to Matthew. So, he looked embarrassed, feeling that he had committed a social blunder, taking her words seriously.

"I'm sorry, Miss Wilson, but I'm engaged to be married. I don't feel it would be quite right for me to be escorting you to dinner. I should have told you that earlier, when you first told me that you wanted me to." he sounded like the country boy that he was and Hannah realized that all of her charm was totally lost on him. She laughed then, at herself.

"That's very honest of you, Matthew. Most men would not pay any attention to such a fact when approached by a woman such as myself. I admire you for your faithfulness. You can't blame me for knowing a good thing when I see it, though." Hannah smiled and Matthew saw she really meant what she said.

The air seemed cleared, somehow and they sat together and talked. He told her about his dream to go to Texas, acquire his own land, and start a new life. He listened to her describe how her daddy had built an empire out there, where land was abundant. It was fuel for his desire. He would get Amelia excited with his plans, he determined, as soon as he got back home. She would be happy after they were married, he told himself, though doubt whispered differently.

His chance came immediately upon their return, for Amelia had missed him terribly. She took his hand and led him out to the gazebo as soon as she could get him away from the family. Once alone, she put her arms around him.

"I love you, Matthew. If you want to go to Texas, I'll go with you. I could never be happy if I didn't go, I know that." She sighed in resignation.

Surprised at her words, he hugged her tightly. "You won't be sorry, Amelia. I promise you that. I'll be a rich man, someday. You won't be sorry." he vowed.

The thought of Amelia leaving for parts unknown, so far away, was a blow to her family. Realizing that once a woman marries, she is obligated to follow her husband, they kept silent, not trying to change Matthew's mind. They would be married in the fall, for the wagon train would leave in the spring .

Amelia dreaded the moment she would leave her family, but the change in Matthew gave her hope that she would be happy once they were married. She allowed herself to be caught up in the excitement, finally, that drove Matthew. He smiled and hugged her often as he shared his progress in making the arrangements for joining the wagon train. He felt that he was finally being seen as a man capable of making his own decisions. With the confidence to carry them through and with no one to control his life, he was boyish in his enthusiasm for the adventure they faced.

Constance, Belle, and Amelia, with the help of Caleb and Victoria, were quickly preparing for the wedding that Amelia wanted. She wanted to be married in her gazebo, for she would be leaving it and this was a heart-rending thing. She could not imagine going to a place where there were no flowers, having to start over. But, she thought, "I'm young and strong. I can do it."

The busy days sped by on wings and the day of the wedding approached far too rapidly for those preparing for it.

Amelia had noticed Victoria clinging to her more and more, as the day for her wedding drew near. Still sleeping with her older sister, Victoria was faced with the fact that Amelia was leaving. Not only was she leaving their room, but leaving their house and also the state. Now ten years old, Victoria is beset by fear of being left behind, alone, by her sisters. One night, only three days before the wedding, Amelia is awakened from a deep sleep by a shrill cry.

"Amy! A---a----mee-e-e-e! The sound ended in heart-wrenching sobs, as Victoria sat up in the bed, shaking and trembling.

Amelia gathered her little sister's trembling form close into her arms, rocking her back and forth, like a baby, soothing her with comforting words.

"I don't want you to marry, Amy. Please don't marry Matt and go away. I'll never see you again. Please stay here with us, in this house. I love you, Amy." her arms gripped Amelia desperately, as she begged pitifully.

Amelia felt her heart torn by the desperate appeal. "It's alright, baby sister. I'm not going right away. I'm going to stay here until next year. You'll be older, then. Someday, you know, you'll be getting married yourself."

At these words, Victoria suddenly looked at Amelia, tears wet on her face. "Will I have a long white dress with a veil over my head and satin slippers, with heels like yours Amy?" Amelia forbid herself to laugh, as she felt her lips twitch with the effort. "Yes, little princess. You will have all of that and when that day comes, I will be there to help you dress up in all your finery. Now, you want to try and sleep, since you have school tomorrow?"

"Will you sing my song, Amy? The one you made up, just for me, when I was a little baby?" Victoria lay back on her pillow, her eyes expectant. Amelia began to sing softly.

> *Jesus loves you, Amy's baby,*
>
> *Jesus loves you, yes he does.*
>
> *He will never, ever leave you.*
>
> *He will always hear your cry.*
>
> *Jesus loves you, Amy's baby,*
>
> *It matters not where you go.*
>
> *Around the world, His love will find you,*
>
> *He will always bring you home.*
>
> *You belong to Jesus, Baby,*
>
> *He will never let you go,*
>
> *Give him all the love within you,*
>
> *Just because He loves you so.*

Amelia's voice sank to a soothing hum as Victoria's big eyes closed in sleep. Placing a gentle kiss on her smooth brow, Amelia lay down, closing her own eyes. Sleep did not return, though she tried to sink into oblivion again.

"I wish I were as confident inside as I appear to be outwardly," she thought, staring into the darkness. "Am I making a mistake?" the question was spoken aloud into the stillness. The answer came from deep within her soul.

How can she change her mine now, after accepting Matthew's ring and pushing him into this marriage? Fearful images of the future attacked her mind, reminding her of Matthew's reaction to seeing Levi's locket around her neck.

She knows she is caught up in an attraction and a personality stronger even than her desire to please God. "Oh, dear God, please change Matthew's heart and give him a heart like yours." She whispered desperately.

Chapter 24

Thankfully, the day chosen for the wedding turned sunny after a cloudy morning. Amelia's image of a fairy tale was about to come true.

She stood before the mirror as her mother adjusted her long veil over the beautiful jeweled comb nestled in the auburn curls clustered atop, he heads. The comb, which caught the light at every movement of her head, Matthew had given her, surprising her with it just a few days ago. He had bought it months before, he had told her, but wanted her to wear it when they married. Her long white dress hugged her waist, and then fell to the floor in shimmering folds. Her high-heeled slippers gave her slim figure added height as she turned slowly, viewing herself from all sides. The reflection in the mirror gave her confidence, suddenly, for the woman whom she saw in the mirror was the woman she longed to be. Confident, poised, her blue eyes sparkling with anticipation, she was to be the center of attention. Today was the day of her wedding.

The house was filled with flowers and their fragrance added to her intoxicated feeling. She felt herself moving inside a dream, going through motions and feelings that she had already experienced many times in her imagination. She was the main character in her own fairy tale. Soon, she would marry the handsome prince and live happily ever after. At the thought of the man to whom she was about to commit her future, her heart thumped in her chest and a queasy feeling was felt in the pit of her stomach. Is she making a mistake? Should she listen to her Papa and wait? No, she can't wait. He won't wait for her.

It's now or never. With one last critical look at herself, she realized her face had gone pale and her hands felt clammy with nervousness. Determined to go through with her decision, Amelia turned and left the sanctuary of her room, to greet the friends and neighbors who would soon gather to help her celebrate her marriage to Matthew.

They had come from miles away, even Matthew's daddy, Wiley Carlisle. There had not been an event like this since Ian and Penelope had married. Since she had wanted so desperately to be married in the gazebo, there would be no music, but Belle would sing the wedding song, for she had a beautiful, clear soprano, which needed no accompaniment.

Mrs. Willie had gotten involved in the preparations, stripping her garden of every rose and blooming flower. Amelia's garden was truly a fairy tale setting and when she walked from the house on her Papa's arm and caught sight of her prince, all her misgivings fled in a great rush of love. He looked every bit the part of the princely bridegroom. His long white coat over dark navy pants accentuated his dark coloring and black hair. His eyes admired her as she drew near. Accepting her hand from her Papa, he held it tightly in his warm clasp, for it was cold.

She could not know that his heart was beating just as rapidly as her own, that his stomach was in a knot. When he stood, watching her approach on William's arm, he was struck with the reality that he was actually getting married. He had never really expected to be married, nor thought about it at all. His dislike for women prevented him from even having romantic dreams or showing an interest in girls, as is natural for any maturing young man. Had Amelia not pushed the issue, he may not have married for years in the future. Now, he stood before the minister, her cold hand in his, repeating his vows to love, cherish and provide for her. He didn't really have any idea of what was expected of him as a husband. Beyond his plans to go to Texas, he had no idea what kind of future awaited them.

Then, they were no longer Matthew Carlisle and Amelia MaceIlwain, but Mr. And Mrs. Matthew Carlisle, for better or for worse, for richer or for poorer, in sickness and in health, as long as they both should live.

Lifting her veil with careful hands, Matthew kissed his wife. Then, the family and friends were all laughing, slapping him on the back, offering their congratulations. The cake was cut and the young couple ate the first piece. The rest of the day was a blur in Amelia's mind, later, when she had time to look back on it all. She wished many times that she could have been an observer, for it seemed that the whole event was over in a moment. Her place of importance, of being the center of attention, of feeling beautiful, didn't last very long at all. Until the beautiful dress was hung carefully away and the veil was stored in tissue, was as long as the feeling lasted.

She and Matthew had not planned to go on a honeymoon, for he felt they needed to save every nickel for the trip to Texas and all the supplies they would have to buy. Her disappointment was acute. Penelope, realizing how she felt, had offered to let them stay in their house that night and the next day. She and Ian would be glad to stay with Constance and William, they said, in order for the newlyweds to have a little time alone. Then, when Mrs. Willie discovered that Amelia was not going on even a short honeymoon, she presented her with a sealed envelope, just after the ceremony. Amelia had not even looked in the envelope, for she had been too excited, greeting the guests, accepting well wishes. That night, in the spare room at Ian's, she pulled out the envelope and she and Matthew looked at what was inside it, then at each other in astonishment. Mrs. Willie's generosity was overwhelming, to say the least. The gift was $500.00. With Matthew's salary from Ian, if they were very thrifty, they would have enough to outfit themselves for their coming adventure.

Later, lying beside her new husband, Amelia relived every moment of the day.

"Matt? Are you asleep yet?" her voice was a whisper, just in case he was. She had a need to hear confirmation of his love once more.

"No, I'm remembering how you looked in your wedding dress." he rose up on his elbow and looked down at her, barely able to see her face, for the room was dark. "What are you thinking about?"

"I was remembering how I love you and how handsome you looked, waiting for me. You looked just like a prince and I felt like a princess." she smiled to herself.

"Is that how a prince looks?" he grinned at her foolishness. But he was pleased, for he had felt rather silly in the outfit Ian had persuaded him to wear. Now, he was glad he had listened to him, for Amelia thought he looked like a prince.

"Matthew, do you love me?" the question had to be asked again, even though she knew his answer.

"You know that I do." Always, when she asked the question, he answered in the same way. His answer had never satisfied her and it didn't now. In spite of the fact that they were now married and on their wedding night, his answer was not what her heart longed to hear. Taking her in his arms again, he kissed her and she forgot all her doubts and fears. This was the expression of his love.

Chapter 25

Life after her marriage soon settled down to a routine that lasted until Amelia and Matthew left to join the wagon train in May of the following year.

Though they had planned to stay with her parents until they left, Ian and Penelope offered them their spare bedroom for the time remaining. Matthew was really glad, for he felt much more comfortable with Ian and Penelope than with Amelia's parents.

Each morning, Amelia and Penelope cooked breakfast for their husbands, with laughter and lively conversation. Then, Ian and Matt would go to work, returning at noon for a light meal. After a few more hours of work, they would return to the house to clean up and eat supper. Then, the two couples would sit on the porch, talking, enjoying the beauty of the nights, now growing chilly. Sometimes, they would go riding together, but Matt and Amelia frequently rode off alone, carrying a picnic basket. They would spend the day walking through the woods, now bright with orange, red, and yellow. Matthew brought down many squirrels that fall, thanks to Ian and his gift of the gun. They made some precious memories then and on through the winter months, as the time for their leaving drew closer.

Amelia tried to store every scene of her home and family in little compartments in her heart. Here, she would put the picture of her mother, busy preparing a meal, her hands continually being wiped on her apron, skillfully making bread, baking a cake or cooking chicken and dumplings. Right here, she would carefully place Victoria's face as she was now, for she had no idea how she would change as the years went by. Then, Caleb would have his own special place in her heart. Sweet, shy, but growing up so fast. How she would miss him. He spent most of his spare time now with Ian and Matt, learning the horse business so that he could be a rancher, he said. Belle was finally able to pursue her career as a teacher. She was accepted for the spring term at the very school she had attended just across the creek. Finding themselves without a teacher, the school board members suddenly realized they already had an excellent teacher in residence. Amelia felt that Belle and Phillip would marry, now. He had certainly been patient, waiting for her to decide.

Her Papa deserved the place of honor in her heart, for he was surely the best Papa any girl could ever have. In spite of his doubts concerning Matthew now that they were married, he was always most kind to his new son-in-law. He treated him with the same respect he showed Ian, and Amelia was so grateful to him for making Matthew feel like a part of their family.

Ian and Penelope will have a baby in January, so Amelia and Matt would see it before their departure.

Christmas was a bittersweet occasion. The Christmas Eve service at the church seemed even more sacred. This was the first Christmas for Amelia and Matthew as a married couple. They sat together, their hands clasped, as they listened attentively to the ever new, but old story of how the Savior came to earth, robed in flesh, to die for lost mankind. At the end of his message, the minister said something that would forever return to haunt Matthew, in the days and years ahead.

"Dear friends, the story of the infant in the manger is always such a sweet, beautiful story, that sometimes, that is all that it is, just a story. We forget that these were real, flesh and blood people. They had hopes and dreams. They lived, ate, worked, and yes, played and enjoyed life, even as we who live today. We cannot, though, forget that this sweet, helpless baby no longer exists, except in our minds. Jesus Christ was born a babe in a manger, but he is now the King of Kings and Lord of Lords. He is God, who only came to this earth for a short time, then returned to his throne. He will return to this earth, not as the innocent babe, but as the righteous judge of the sinner and the bridegroom of the saint. All those who overcome the world and the sinful pleasures will be given a white stone and in the stone will be a name written, which no man can know except the one receiving it. If you want to receive the white stone from Christ the Lord when he returns, you must receive Him into your heart and life today. Receive him as Jesus, the Savior, not Jesus, the babe in the manger. Open your heart to him and He will open up heaven to you."

The church was silent, hushed, as the message ended. The closing prayer was over, yet they were still waiting. No one moved, not even the children. Amelia had never heard such a message. She was stirred to the depths of her soul. Tears fell from her closed eyes, for she felt like a sinner, in this reverent atmosphere. Many others must have felt the same, for some made their way to the altar and knelt to pray. Some remained in the pews, their heads bowed. Much later, quietly, they exited the church. The night sky was so full of stars that it seemed as though the very heavens were rejoicing. Matthew wrapped her in his arms as they looked up in awesome wonder.

Riding home in the buggy Matthew was silent, though their hands were clasped together. His thoughts were far away across the miles. He remembered a small metal box hidden beneath leaves and the glow of a white stone, waiting for him to come and claim it. *"Is he worthy to receive it?" He wondered.*

"What can the white stone given to him by his mother mean for him? How can he find the answers for all the supernatural experiences he has had through the years? He has never shared any of the strange events with Amelia and though he meant to talk with Ian, it never seemed the right time."

****

Amelia began to get excited as the actual time for their departure drew closer. Matthew was a bundle of energy, making sure everything was just right. He grinned at Amelia constantly and she realized what this meant to him, for them to go off together. She discovered that Nathan and his wife, Lillibeth, also joined the wagon train. Amelia was delighted, for she had talked with her at church and other gatherings and liked her good-natured disposition.

Belle and Penelope planned a big party to give them a good send-off. Belle presented her with a beautiful quilt they had been working on in secret. Amelia cried, just like always. Lately, it seemed she was always crying, either because she was happy or because she was leaving.

The long-dreaded day moved toward Amelia, and they were in the midst of the going away party. She saw Levi and met his new wife, a shy, pretty young woman named Charity. They seemed very much in love and

Amelia was glad Levi had found someone. He kissed her on the cheek and wished her and Matthew good luck in their new home. Matthew didn't like Levi kissing her, but he kept himself under control this time. He even shook hands with Levi when they left.

Bright and early the next morning, amid tremulous smiles and held back tears, Amelia hugged her family again and again, until Matthew grew impatient and took her by the arm, urging her to the wagon. She tied her bonnet under her chin, and then he lifted her onto the wagon seat. As they pulled out of the yard, she waved until she could no longer see anyone for the tears running down her face. Then, she resolutely turned her eyes forward, dried her tears and smiled at Matthew, who had begun to look a little aggravated at her. They were to meet the other wagons by noon, and then they would start for the Three Notch Trail, which would lead them through Alabama, Mississippi, Louisiana, and Texas.

Matthew felt more excited than he could ever remember. After all his plans, they were finally on their way. His dream of making a name for himself was on the way to becoming a reality. All he needed was a chance. Now he had a wife, some good horses, a milk cow, and enough to start building his own future. He had two strong arms and quite a bit of knowledge that would come in handy in their new life. He looked at Amelia. He knew she had felt bad about leaving her home and family. He couldn't really understand the depth of her feelings, though, for he had no family he hated leaving. He had gone by his Pa's place the last time he visited Uncle James before he died. Becky had run off with that man, Wiley didn't want her to marry. He could do nothing about it, though, for she was plenty old enough to marry by then. He had told his Pa then, that he might leave Georgia and go to Texas. His Pa had wished him good luck. He had meant to take Amelia to visit him before they left, but it had slipped his mind. He had come to their wedding, though, which surprised Matthew. William seemed to like Wiley, realizing immediately that he was a good man, who had a lot of regrets where Matthew was concerned.

Well, he was leaving all that behind him, now. No more being told what to do. No more working for the other man. He will be working for himself from now on. He would show them that Matthew Carlisle is a man. He felt Amelia slip her arm through his and glanced over at her.

"I'm glad you finally got through crying, Amelia. Crying doesn't change anything, you know. Only makes you feel worse." he told her, trying to get her to cheer up.

"I suppose you're right, Matthew. I just can't seem to help it. That's the only home I've ever known, you know. Everyone I grew up with is there. Since I was very small, I've known most of the people there. It's hard, leaving everything that's familiar." she tried to explain.

"Maybe you should have not married me, just stayed with your family the rest of your life. Or, if you had married Levi, you would always live here." His voice was sarcastic and she looked at him in astonishment. He immediately regretted his harsh words, for he didn't want to hurt her.

"Why Matthew, why would you say such a thing? I love you. I married you. I want to be with you. I just have to adjust, that's all."

"Well, you couldn't prove it by me, the way you've constantly complained about leaving. I practically had to drag you away, when you knew we had to meet the others on time." He is upset with her for making them late, she realizes.

His words pierced her heart. She was silent. She looked straight ahead, her expression hurt, disappointed that he would talk to her in such a way. Is this the way he felt toward her? He surely didn't love her. She had made a terrible mistake, coming off with him. Her thoughts went back to all the times she could have backed out of her commitment to Matthew. Now, it was too late. She was married for better or for worse. She didn't know why he had suddenly begun acting in such a way, but she decided she would have nothing to say to him until he apologized.

So, Amelia rode all the way to the meeting place, silent and withdrawn. Once they arrived, at least a hundred wagons were being lined up. Children yelling, dogs barking, cows lowing- a noisy gathering. Matthew had been told to try to get his wagon toward the front, so as not to eat so much dust. He was upset with Amelia for lingering so long. Now, they would have to take whatever place they could find. He knew she was hurt by how he talked to her. She needed to learn that when he had some place to be at a certain time, he meant to be there on time. He had learned that early in life. After getting several beatings for being late with his chores, he soon adopted the habit of being punctual. He could not stand being late for anything and he got upset with anyone who caused him to be late. Of course, he had failed to explain to Amelia the importance of their getting there early.

"Amelia, can you hold the horses while I check to see where we're supposed to be in the line?" He held out the reins to her.

"Yes, Matthew." She took the reins, refusing to look at him, her face closed.

He jumped down and went to find the wagon boss. She sat there, firmly holding the reins, in the midst of all the noise and commotion and wished herself back safe at home with people who loved her. When Matthew finally returned, almost thirty minutes later, she had made up her mind. She spoke up as soon as he climbed up beside her, taking the reins and clucking to the horses.

"Matthew, I've decided that I want to go back home. I feel that you don't love me and if you're going to treat me the way you've begun to, I don't want to be with you. I want to go, now. If I have to walk all the way, I can do that." Her voice was resolute.

"What in the world has come over you?" He exclaimed. "You can't go back. I'm lining us up so we can leave with the others. They had reached the end of the line and Matthew pulled their wagon behind the last one. Soon, more wagons were lining up behind them, until one hundred wagons were ready to pull out for Texas.

"I'm not going with you, Matthew." She stood up, as though to get down off the wagon.

Matthew reached out and took her by her arm, holding her. She twisted her arm, trying to get free, but he held her fast. "Sit down, Amelia. You're not going anywhere. I don't know what has come over you, but you need to sit down and stop making a fool of yourself in front of the whole wagon train." he sounded very calm, but his hand held her like a vise.

She sat down, her face crumpling as her tears began to flow. Matthew looked at her disgustedly. "For heaven's sake, Amelia, why are you crying now?"

"You don't love me. That's why. You're mean and cruel. I don't want to be with you." She sobbed.

Suddenly, he laughed and she stared at him. He reached down, tied the reins to the wagon, and then turned to her. "Amy, don't cry." He pulled her close and kissed her. She pushed against his chest and he saw the hurt mirrored in her eyes. "Amy, don't be mad." He held her tightly, lifted her chin and kissed her again until she began to kiss him back. Finally, she put her arms around him and laid her head on his chest. "Amelia, now do you still think I don't love you? Do you still want to leave and go home?" his voice was persuasive, soft.

"No, Matthew, I don't want to go home. You know I love you too much to leave you. You hurt my feelings when you talk so mean." she persisted.

"Well, I want you to do what's right, Amelia. You made us late this morning and that's why we're so far back in the line. When you continually complain about leaving home, how do you think that makes me feel? I'm your husband. I'm supposed to be more important now, than your family." He still held her to him as he explained himself.

"Why didn't you tell me that before and I would have been ready earlier. I can't read your mind, Matt. My mother and father never fussed and I don't like to be criticized when I don't even know what I've done." Amelia tried again to make him understand how she felt.

"I'm telling you now. Always remember one thing. I was raised up and taught to be on time. If I wasn't, I got a beating. I guess that's why I get upset at being late for anything now." He kissed her again, gently, "I'm sorry I sounded mean. See if you can find us something to eat because I don't know how long it'll be before we pull out. It may not be until morning." he released her then and she climbed over into the wagon where their supplies were stored.

The day wore on and Amelia could not imagine all these wagons and animals strung out over the trail all the way to Texas. She had not seen Nathan and Lillibeth. She had been hoping they would be near each other but had not been prepared for the enormous number of wagons and people she now watched. She decided it looked as though they would not be leaving that day. Matthew had gone off to consult with the other men, so she climbed into the wagon and lay down to nap, having gotten up early that morning. He returned to inform her they had decided to start out, even though it was now afternoon. With the length of the train, the lead wagons would be miles ahead of the last ones. If any others wanted to add themselves to the back, there would be room, once they started. It was still an hour later before their wagon actually moved forward. Then, it was a snail's pace. Amelia could not see how they would ever reach Texas if this were the speed they would attain.

Matthew's face was animated, and he was excited to start out finally. His previous irritation at Amelia was forgotten in his anticipation of actually leaving the familiar and launching out into the unknown. Three hours later, they had covered very little ground. Their pace was slow due to the number of wagons ahead of them. It was still light enough to see clearly, and they hoped the leaders would go on a little further before calling a halt. Finally, after another two hours, the order came down from wagon to wagon to halt to prepare the evening meal. As fires were built, people began to visit back and forth, cheerful talk floated through the air and children's voices rose excitedly.

After they ate, Amelia and Matthew decided to walk down the trail and maybe find Nathan and Lillibeth. Their earlier conflict seemed resolved in his mind, but the memory of his hard words was added to the memory of the locket in Amelia's mind. A barely discernible reserve had taken over her heart, and her natural open and honest outspoken personality was affected by Matthew's criticism. It was as though she didn't know where she stood with him. Now, as they walked side by side, he took her hand, but quickly dropped it as they approached anyone. She looked up at him in surprise, remembering the emotion in his kisses moments ago. 'Matthew, are you embarrassed to be seen holding my hand?"

He looked down at her then with a strange expression.

"Well, I don't think I would call it that, Amy. I'm just not used to showing affection in public. I guess I have never had the affection that you have had with your family." He stopped and faced her. Putting his hands on her shoulders, he looked into her eyes and his widened at what he saw in the clear depths. The tender gaze of the man on the creek touched his heart again. "How can I hold on to the feeling from so long ago," he thought. He ran his finger down her cheek and watched her expression become expectant, her eyes close. He drew her close, pressing his lips to her forehead. Amelia felt such a powerful surge of love flood her whole being for this man who has been wounded and scarred that she wrapped her arms tightly around his waist, wanting desperately to share it with him. If only she could impart God's love to him, she thought. She raised her head and with all her strength and all the love of her heart, touched his lips with hers so gently and tenderly that Matthew felt it to the depths of his soul. Joy flooded his heart and he clutched her to him, absorbing the healing power of love flowing from her. Something from another world held them in a holy silence. Matthew looked at Amelia in amazement, speechless. He did not want to lose this moment. He cupped her face in his hands. Her eyes were shining pools of blue with depths that seemed endless. He touched her hair with his lips and then kissed her forehead, her shining eyes and finally her lips with all the longing of a lifetime for the love that seemed to elude him. "Amy, don't ever leave me," he whispered. "I have bad feelings that I don't want to have. I have a hard time trusting others with my heart."

"I love you Matthew," she smiled. "I will not leave you. You are my prince, you know. We have to love one another no matter what it takes, because we promised the Lord on our wedding day 'forsaking all others' and I, too have to overcome bad feelings."

He took her hand then, with a grin, and they went on in search of Nathan.

After walking for what seemed like a mile to Amelia they finally saw Nathan in conversation with an older man. They stood beside a wagon holding a woman, with a small child on her lap. When they saw him, Amelia smiled and hurried up to him. Seeing her, Nathan grinned delightedly. He hugged her, and then turned quickly to shake Matthew's hand.

"Man, it sure is good to see the two of you. Lillibeth had been pestering me to go find you, Amelia. She's been kind of lonesome already for her family. Maybe you can cheer her up." Nathan sounded hopeful. Then, turning to the man beside him, he introduced him.

"Mr. Jacobs, meet my friends, Amelia and Matthew Carlisle. Matthew and Amelia, this is Mr. Jacobs and his wife and that's Joshua, their baby. They have three more, scattered around the camp somewhere." Nathan gestured toward the woman on the wagon seat as he introduced them.

Amelia walked over to speak with Mrs. Jacobs, whom she quickly found to be worn to a frazzle. She said she was trying to care for her children in the close confines of a wagon. She was already regretting her agreement with her husband to go to Texas. She told Amelia wearily that she hoped she could endure the next months on the trail, her face resigned at the prospect.

Suddenly, Amelia wanted to cheer up the sad-faced woman. "Mrs. Jacobs, if you need help with the children, I love children. I have a little sister and brother that I took care of when they were small. I'm pretty good with children. When we have some time later, I would gladly teach them their lessons. I've had some training as a teacher and I brought some books with me." As she talked, Amelia felt her spirits lift. The thought of teaching the children had just occurred to her. That would be a way for her to use her talents. She smiled sweetly at Mrs. Jacobs, encouraging her with her kind words. By the time she and Matthew returned to their wagon, she was full of plans, talking excitedly, waving her hands in the air, as she told him what she wanted to do.

"Matthew, I feel so strongly that God has led me to think of this idea. Think of all the children on this train. Oh, I'm so excited. She clapped her hands delightedly, her face alive, her eyes sparkling again, as she took his arm, hugging it to her side.

"Well, you better be careful or those kids will worry you to death, once you get them started coming to our wagon." he cautioned her, not realizing he was throwing cold water on her excitement.

"Oh, I'll just have certain times for them to come. It won't interfere with us, Matthew." she immediately doubted her plan. How strange how his least word of opposition seemed to confuse her thoughts. When her mind was made up about a situation, so sure that God was leading her, he could cause her to doubt the goodness of her intentions.

That night, Matthew slept almost immediately. Amelia lay awake, her thoughts a jumble of hope, doubt, fear. Matthew didn't seem to approve her wanting to teach the children wholly. Surely, he could not object to her doing something that would give her a sense of accomplishment, of self-esteem. The miraculous happenings of the day came back to her and she remembered the look on Matthew's face and his revealing of his thoughts to her. "Fear not, little flock, for the Father knows what you have need of." As she remembered the scripture, peace overcame the doubt and fear trying to discourage her so quickly after the

Lord had overwhelmed them both with such a powerful manifestation of His love. Matthew had been so loving and tender. Finally, she began to pray, silently, lest she wake him. Tears seeped from her closed eyes and she could feel them running down her face. Her spirit screamed out in the darkness, pleading for help from God, whom she knew was her only source of strength. As she prayed, the anger melted away and was replaced by a prayer of submission. Dear God, if it is your will that I teach the children, please help my husband to agree." Then, she slept.

****

Amelia awoke to the sounds of the camp and realized Matthew had left the wagon. She quickly dressed, nervously trying to hurry. She had no idea what time they would be starting out and she didn't want to be late. As she was fumbling with her buttons, he startled her by sticking his head through the opening in the wagon.

"Well, sleepy head, I see you finally woke up." he grinned. Seeing that she was dressed, he climbed into the wagon with her. Looking at her with a little smile, he pulled her close and kissed her. Holding her, he looked down into her face.

"You're so little, Amy. You know I could probably crush you with my bare hands." Her heart jumped at such words, but, then he gave a little chuckle and kissed her again. "Amy, I'm only teasing. You don't have to be afraid of me." His kisses were making her legs weak, and she clung to him for support. She felt powerless in his arms, and even though he had said he was teasing, she knew what he was saying was true. If he ever turned against her, she would have no chance against the strength he possessed.

Part of his attraction for her had been his strong, muscled arms, his manly appearance. Now, she was made to wonder if that very thing would become a threat to her. Finally, with a last, lingering kiss, he released her, though still holding her by her shoulders. Her eyes were clouded with emotion and he grinned, for he knows her feelings for him would not let her stay upset long.

"I built a fire while you were asleep and made us some coffee. Come on out if you're ready and I'll cook our breakfast. It won't be long before we have to pull out." He drew her close again, surprising her. "Amelia, if you want to teach the little kids, you must do it. I've been kind of missing May's boys. They used to really think a lot of me. They looked up to me, you know. They were the only ones who looked up to me and showed me affection." Matthew smiled, remembering the joy he had seen on the faces of Sammy and the other boys when they met. She saw the longing in his face as he talked. "All that's behind me now. Someday we'll have our own children. I know we've never talked about having children, but I sure would like to have a son to hunt and fish with. They'll never be treated the way I was treated when I was a kid." The anger was back in his voice and his arms tightened around her. His eyes were dark and unreadable and his face was set in hard lines. She felt a shiver go through her and he must have felt it, for he looked down at her, as though he had forgotten she was there.

"You're not cold, are you?" he asked.

"No, Matthew, I'm not cold. I'm ready for that coffee, though." she replied.

His expression changed and he grinned boyishly before releasing her. As they left the wagon, he jumped down, then turned and lifted her down, his hands strong, holding her around her waist. They had eaten and were ready to leave when the call came down from the front to fall into line. Excitement rippled through the long line of wagons, for this was the first full day of travel and they hoped to cover some ground before night fell.

The days passed slowly for the next thirty days, as the wagons ponderously made their way southwestward, ever rolling toward Texas. The beauty of the country through which they travelled filled Amelia's senses with hope and anticipation, for it was as beautiful as the home she had left behind. Each day, she gathered the Jacobs children together. She prepared lessons and told them stories, capturing their attention, love and affection with her animated gestures and changes of voice when she told the stories. Her gift as a teacher soon caused many of the other parents to bring their children to join the little group and Amelia's heart filled with joy as she fulfilled the desires of her heart at last. Thoughts of anyone who would mistreat an innocent child as Matthew had been treated brought anger and pain to her heart. "Dear Lord, please heal my husband's heart as only you can," she prayed.

They entered the borders of Louisiana the second week of July. The first day, they camped by a spring that bubbled up out of the ground, crystal cold, and then made its way between sandy banks, becoming a large pool. As soon as the weary travelers had replenished their water supply, the children were turned loose and they went wild. Amelia and Matthew, along with all the other parents gathered in the cool shade beneath towering pines and oaks, with sighs of relief. The sound of the children, laughing and shouting in childish abandon lifted the spirits of everyone on the train.

Matthew walked on down past the swimming hole, following the creek as it wound through the beautiful land surrounding it. Much like the woods where he was raised, it called to him, like a lovely woman, offering herself to him. He heard squirrels chattering high above him in the towering pines. He caught a fleeting glimpse of a deer quickly moving away from him through the trees. His heart was captured. He knew he would stay here, in this place. Reaching a low-hanging branch, he broke off one of the huge magnolia blossoms for Amelia. With a little pleased smile, he quickly started back toward the wagons.

The land lay fertile and pregnant with possibility. Soft murmurings and rustlings can be heard as its inhabitants move about. Loud twittering and raucous calls identify songbird and crow alike. Deep shade harbors swaying three foot ferns. Languid honeysuckle scented breezes sigh among the shade filled hollows. Stately oaks and stalwart pines lifted themselves high into the blue of the sky. Cold waters flowed from underground springs, singing to themselves on their journey between banks edged with lush vegetation.

Tiny wild violets nestle in the pine straw piled beneath the trees. A doe drank from the cold creek, her white tail swishing slowly, while a mother possum, babies hanging like ornaments along her tail and back, waddled towards the creek. Long and sinuous, the water snake makes its way through the damp undergrowth edging the bank. Water bugs skitter rapidly across the surface of the crystal clear water. Small minnows and tiny bream darted busily here and there. Sunlight dappled the water with colorful beams under the cedar, cypress and oak interlocking branches. Bees drank thirstily, buried in the heart of the honeysuckle and wild violet blooms. Their industrious sound adds a peaceful note to the song of the land.

Hot and humid summers breed pests such as mosquitoes. Winters are sometimes very cold, but more often tend to be mild. Blackberries, wild grapevines and huckleberries abounded in the forest depths. Huge creamy white magnolia blooms exuded a heady fragrance into the sultry summer air. Indians moved silently on soft carpets of fallen pine straw and leaf mold. Their campfires burned brightly in the dusk.

Soon, the sound of axes and saws will be heard for the first time in this virgin land. Men and women of another tongue will invade the peace and tranquility, bringing their hopes, dreams, frustrations, despair and faith. The land will open its innocent heart and receive them all, giving up the treasures of centuries without reserve.

20 Years later

Louisiana

Golden fingers of dawn inched across the plowed field. Nimble seekers of worms hopped and fluttered in the furrows, satisfying themselves on juicy offerings of the rich soil. The man walked slowly behind the plow, straight and strong, broad-shouldered in overalls and cotton shirt.

The yellow dog trotted ahead of the mule, ears pricked and tail held high. As the distance lengthened between them, she stopped and looking back, waited patiently until the mule drew close. Then, as if to offer her encouragement, a sharp, short yip is given before the yellow dog takes the lead once more. As the trio progressed up and down the field, rich loamy furrows appeared in the flat, fallow ground.

Nearing a huge oak with spreading branches, the man paused, removed his hat and ran sun-browned fingers through his thick, dark hair. Matthew Carlisle is still a handsome man at forty. His six-foot, three-inch height is all hard muscle from years of hard work.

He's come a long way from the half-breed orphan raised by James and Martha Carlisle. He looked at the fruit of his labors, laid out before him. His fields, his cattle, his horses, stables and barns. Back there, sitting on a little knoll, is the beautiful home with tall chimneys and a white fence just as he had promised Amelia all those years ago. Yellow roses climb the trellis beside the shady porch and the strong scent of honeysuckle fills the air.

Matthew remembers how this land looked the first day he laid eyes on it. He smiles now, for the memory is sweet. He and Amelia worked hard that first year, just to survive. Then, realizing she was carrying their child, he grew anxious and wouldn't allow her to help him. Their sweet little baby girl, Sara was born and her love for her daddy was balm to his soul. He and Nathan had helped each other through those first years. Nathan and Lillie had left the wagon train with Matthew and Amelia, along with several other families. The land was theirs for the taking and Matthew quickly laid claim to a hundred and sixty acres, which included an underground spring that ran continuously, dividing itself many times as it progressed through the countryside. It formed a creek, further down, but it began on his land as a bubbling stream pumping up from an underground source.

This spring morning, as he has done for the last twenty years, Matt plowed his own field. He could well afford a tractor that would do the work for him but, strange as it seems, even to him, he continues to do it himself. This will be the last year, he thinks, for he now has other pursuits more exciting, though not as rewarding. At the direction his thoughts are taking, he feels the same nudge from his conscience that has been bothering him more and more often lately.

As he stands beneath the oak, resting himself, a sudden moving of the air through the tree sets the leaves in motion. He lifted his face and felt a sweetness as the unexpected breeze touched him, caressed his face with delicate fingers, and then was gone. Without warning, he remembers the same feeling the day he and Amelia had been enveloped in a supernatural presence. What had happened to that feeling and the love they had shared?

"Come on, girl," he beckoned to the yellow dog sprawled in the shade, then gathered up the reins, shocking the dozing mule awake with a loud shout.

"Get up, you lazy Jenny. I'm getting mighty hungry. Let's get this job finished."

Amelia had awakened early, as she usually did. As she poured a cup of coffee, she looked through the window to her flower garden, wet with dew. Matthew had kept the promise he had made her before they left Georgia. If only he had kept his marriage vows, she thought, almost bitterly. But how could a man who had never understood the meaning of love know how to cherish. Her thoughts went back to the years following their arrival in Louisiana. Their first child, Sara had been followed by another daughter, Hope and then their first son, whom she thought would change Matthew's heart for showing the love of a father to his children. After the birth of another daughter, Felicity, named after her mother's sister, she thought her child bearing days were past. But, then, her sweet little son, Jonathan arrived after five years. Matthew played with the children and took the boys fishing and hunting and outwardly appeared to be a good father. No one knew the real man like she and the children, though. His anger controlled them all and the children feared being around him. Their only escape from the tension of their home was to go to church and be loved and strengthened in the body of Christ, their spiritual family. She had taught her children to pray and had seen them all be filled with the Spirit of God, after being baptized in the Name of Jesus. The joy of knowing her children love the Lord as much as she does has given her courage to never give up on seeing Matthew become a man after the heart of God.

This morning, as is her custom, when Matthew is out in the field, she had gone to her knees to pray. Memories of the past divine encounters they had experienced continually reminded her of the faithfulness of the Lord and kept her believing that he is working in answer to her prayers. The memory of the words Matthew had spoken, entreating her not to leave him, tormented her. "Lord, how can he be so loving at times and then be so angry and violent towards me and our children? Is it your will for me to stay when I am so unhappy? I know I did not seek your will all those years ago when I did not listen to my daddy's words of caution." With tears running down her cheeks, Amelia once again turned to her Heavenly Father for only in these times in prayer can she find the strength and hope to face each day. Though she wears no uniform and carries no apparent weapon, she engages in a life-and-death battle. The weapons she possesses are not natural, but spiritual. They are mighty weapons and Amelia has learned well how to use them against the enemy of her marriage and her family. Strongholds built up over time by Satan are being bombarded consistently by her faith and persistence. The fervor and intensity of her focused attack send shock waves of alarm through evil ranks. The power of her desire causes an essence of such strong incense to rise up to the Father's throne, that His mind is filled with the image of her and her travail. His response sends waves of love that bathe her soul in joyful strength. His powerful presence fills the room where she kneels, moves through the house and across the field, caressing the face of Matthew as he rests beneath the tree.

Miles away, Sara Carlisle Perkins rocks her fretful baby in a small log house. Her eyes are red from lack of sleep and weariness covers her like a heavy weight. The chair is still as she dozes, her head resting against the wooden slats. The tiny face of her three-month-old baby is screwed up into tight creases of discomfort, as he squirms uncomfortably, obviously in pain.

A waft of fresh air lifts the soft down on his round little head and moves through the small house with a delicate sigh. Suddenly, his little face is transformed as the frown lines relax and he drifts into sleep. Sara feels the sweetness of a loving presence as her mind is filled with a comforting thought.

"Mama is praying. Mama is praying right now, this very minute." she smiled. Rising stiffly, she went slowly to the handmade cradle beside the flickering fire. She brushed a kiss on the soft head and deposited Matthew Carlisle Perkins gently into it. Stretching her arms above her head, she flexed her tired back.

"What a night!" she thought. Tiptoeing across the rag rugs, she peeped into the bedroom. All she can see is a wild head of straw-colored hair. Smiling, she closed the door and went to the window. The sun is well up and the animals need attention. John needs to wake up, but he hasn't slept any more than she, dealing with a colicky baby. Well, the little rascal seems to be recovered. Maybe he'll sleep awhile and she and John can rest. Going to the stove, Sara poked at the hot coals and added kindling. As the flames caught, she set the big coffee pot on the iron eye. Gathering cups and sugar, she then skimmed some cream from last night's milk. Then, pouring the strong brew into thick white mugs, she entered the bedroom.

John opened one eye and viewed her questioningly. "He's sleeping," she whispered. Groaning, he opened the other eye as the aroma of the coffee penetrated the fog of sleep. Easing down beside him, Sara leans her head close to his. Grinning, he framed her face with huge hands and kissed her gently on the lips. Then he took the steaming cup from her and propped himself against the pillows, taking a tentative sip.

"Ah--h---h---h!" he whispered. "How tired I am!"

"I know, darling. That bed looks greatly inviting, but Bessie is lowing so pitifully," Sara sighed. "Maybe Mattie will sleep and we can nap after dinner. How do hot cakes and grits sound right now?"

"How about a real good morning kiss, Mrs. Perkins?" he teased, mischief in his hazel eyes.

Setting her cup carefully on the table beside the bed, Sara put her arms around her husband and felt the warm strength of his love flow into her tired body. His lips are soft and tender upon hers. His arms are a strong and safe haven. "I love you so much, John. I feel so blessed that God brought us together." Sara sighed contentedly.

Perhaps tomorrow they should ride over and visit her mama and daddy, she thought. It had been several weeks since they had been over there. She wondered again, with a feeling of pain for her mother why her daddy was so volatile, almost like a lighted fuse. Her mama is an unbelievable woman, but Sara cannot see how she has endured years of humiliation and verbal abuse. She is forever putting herself between her children and her husband, being a buffer, trying to smooth things over, and explaining away his unreasonable outbursts. Sara sighed as she looked back into her life before she married John. Thank God, she had found a way of escape from the tension and unhappiness of her home!

Chapter 26

The biscuits are light and deliciously fragrant as Amelia lifted them from the oven. The bacon sizzled, and the freshly ground coffee sent out its tantalizing aroma, which melted in the misty air. She smiled with satisfaction as a sharp "yip, yip, yip" pierced the morning's calm. Just in time! She heard Matt's footsteps on the porch as he washed up, and then he came into the warm kitchen with a pleased smile.

"It sure smells good in here." Matthew put his arms around her, drew her close, kissed her longingly. His lips are soft and seeking her response. She feels his need and responds as always, sending love and tenderness into the empty place in his heart. He looked into her eyes for long moments, for he saw the shining of the man by the creek. With a groan, he whispered, "Amy, I need you."

He released her then, as though embarrassed, but something sweet and comforting filled the room. She turned away to put the food on the table. She could not speak lest the moment be lost. She quickly filled their plates and sat down across from him, bowing her head. Unexpectedly, she realized he had bowed his head as she asked the blessing. He raised his head quickly and began to eat, but then looked at her, a question in his expression.

Her heart leapt with new hope at what she saw in his eyes, but his words were not what she wanted to hear.

"These are good biscuits, Amy. You seem to get better all the time. I finished the south field. It's ready to be planted. I'll get Charlie and old Jake to do that next week. I need to make a trip to New Orleans to meet with a buyer for my beef calves. I'll be gone for at least a couple of days. Depends on how everything goes." he spooned black berry jelly onto his buttered biscuit. Have you been crying?" he suddenly noticed her eyes were slightly red.

"Well, I've been praying, Matt," she replied.

"Seems to me praying should make you happy, not make you cry. What do you have to cry about, Amy? You have a nice home, just about anything you want. Plus, a hard-working husband that a lot of women would like to have. Not bad looking, either, I've been told." he added with a teasing grin.

Amelia glanced up at him at the reference to his looks. Matthew had been shy and reserved with her when they first met, seemingly unaware of his good looks. She had noticed that, in the last few years, he had frequently made remarks such as the one he had just made. Almost as though he is reaching for a word of confirmation from her that he is a handsome man. She realized, with a surge of guilt that for so long, his behavior toward her and the children had practically eradicated from her mind the positive things about him. She continually focused on all the wrong, she had to admit. Now, she saw an unspoken need reflected in his dark eyes. Impulsively, she went to him, wrapping her arms around his neck, she kissed him sweetly, holding his dark head against her cheek. Surprised, he responded to the affection, holding her tightly, feeling the longing rise in his heart to have what she has in her spirit. So they stayed for long moments, silent, a precious space of time that gave her hope for the future. Reluctantly, she released him, but he drew her down onto his lap. Held in his arms had been what she longed for all those years ago. His angry outbursts had stolen her longing. But as he brushed his lips across her face with soft lingering kisses, her heart responded as always. "Oh, she whispered, you are my prince, Matthew. You are my love. She saw love in his eyes then and there was no darkness. She felt his heart beating as fast as hers and never wanted this moment to end.

With a sigh, Matthew allowed her to stand, for they heard the children coming down the stairs. She went to the stove to prepare their breakfast so they could be off to school. Felicity and Jonathan joined them in the kitchen and took their places as Amelia placed a kiss on each of them and then placed their plates of bacon and eggs and biscuits on the table.

Felicity, with her dark hair, so like Matthew's and dark eyes, is a beautiful young girl. "Good morning, Daddy." She smiled sweetly at them. "Good morning, Momma." She nodded at Jonathan and they both bowed their heads. "Thank you, Jesus for this food. Bless it for the use of our bodies. Amen."

Jonathan quickly began to eat his breakfast. At eleven, he is the baby of the family and has been mothered by all the girls. After taking a few bites, he looked at Matthew and asked, "Daddy, when can we go hunting?" Mr. Nathan and Carlyss are going tomorrow." Matthew felt guilt as how he has been neglecting his son lately. "I have to go on a trip in the morning, but we can go next week."

Jonathan grinned excitedly, and then finished his breakfast. Going to Matthew, he hugged him. "I'll see you, Daddy. Be careful." He hugged Amelia, endured her kiss and then was gone out the door.

Felicity finished her breakfast, took her plate to the sink and then turned back to face them. "Will it be okay if I go home with Isabel today after school?" she asked, looking from one to the other of them."Her daddy will bring me home."

Amelia looked at Matthew, waiting for his answer to their daughter. He looked back at her. "Amelia, do you know these people?" he asked.

"Yes, she replied." Isabel's parents are members of our church. You've probably met her dad. He owns the farm on the other side of Nathan."

"What is the purpose of this visit?" Matthew asked. "You aren't meeting a boy over there, are you?" His tone is teasing but Felicity's face showed fear, for her visit is not altogether what she would have her parents think.

"No, Daddy, we're not meeting boys. We're working on a school project together." Matthew conceded. "You are too young to be thinking of courting, so remember that." Felicity turned quickly as though expecting her daddy to change his mind. Amelia watched her leave with an uneasy feeling that all is not what Felicity is telling.

"Would you like another cup of coffee before you head out?" Amelia picked up the coffee pot from the stove and refilled her cup. When he nodded, she filled his too. "When did you plan to leave?" She asked, sitting down at the table again. "I would like to go with you, but I guess you need me to stay here." she said, wistfully.

He looked at her in surprise. Still feeling the afterglow of their intimate moments, he wanted to say he would take her with him. He sipped the coffee, racking his mind for an answer that would not hurt her feelings. He is pierced with shame at the treatment of his wife. He remembered when he had taken her with him and how close they had been, enjoying the sights of New Orleans. Before he had gotten himself in a situation he could not figure how to get out of. She loved the delicate china cups that came with her set of dishes he had bought for her on that trip. They stayed at a fabulous hotel and ate delicious Creole food with strong coffee. She had worn a beautiful green silk dress in the newest style and had looked beautiful. She told him she felt like a princess again and he was her prince. Lost in memories, he didn't realize Amelia had asked him a question. He shook his head to clear his mind and then looked at her with a strange expression on his face. "What did you say?" he asked.

"I just wanted to know when you are leaving on your trip." She looked inquiringly at him over the rim of her cup, wondering where he had gone in his thoughts.

"Oh, I'll leave in the morning and should be able to finish up by Tuesday, depending on how long it takes to get my business done. He finished his coffee, retrieved his hat from the rack by the door and left her sitting there, having never replied to her hopeful comment about going with him. She wondered why he never asked her to go with him on his trips any more. She had been so caught up in raising the children and keeping their home she had not shown any interest in going with him. She remembered the expensive suits and hats and boots Matthew had begun to purchase that she never saw him wear anywhere they went together. He had always been very frugal when they were first married, but as their ranch became profitable, he had changed drastically. He never went to church with her except on Easter or Christmas. Niggling unwelcome thoughts caused uneasy feelings to disturb her peace as she went about her routine. She made beds and gathered dirty clothes to be washed, and then put on a pot of soup to simmer for the evening meal. She had gotten into the habit of constantly praying in her head, sometimes out loud, if alone, during the day. She felt the burden of her family heavy on her mind and knew it was up to her to ensure her children were saved. Amelia had seen Matthew's attitude toward the church and religion in general become scornful and critical. She knew he had been baptized as a young boy, but he had never shown any faith in God. She had ignored her daddy's warning all those years ago. She had come to understand that God had been trying to speak to her because he knew what her future would be if she married Matthew.

At times, thoughtful and loving to her, but then, at the slightest provocation, he became verbally abusive, using language that appalled Amelia. He had come close to striking her many times. She had been pushed to the limits of her self-control. She constantly had thoughts of leaving Matthew. She had even threatened him with leaving. He never took her seriously. "Dear Lord, she whispered, please make me to know what your will is for me and my children. Help me love him with your love and bring him to repent and give his life to you." She went to her place of prayer, opened her Bible and began to read. After reading for a while, she picked up her pen and began to write.

"And now the pain is a living organism. It grows with every passing day. Word by word, act by act, it is nourished. Its tentacles inch outward like a terrible infection has taken hold of the body. Natural emotions become tainted with fear of criticism. Acts of genuine love are viewed with suspicion. The spirit retreats further into the deepest recesses of the mind, closing each door in self-preservation. Hope is bombarded constantly by hopelessness until she falls, weak, and stripped of her power to revive. Life becomes a charade, a pretense, a façade. The mouth speaks, the eyes see, but the pain continues gaining power. What is life? How have I arrived at this place, this void, this non-living condition? What deceiving thought, wrong choice or moment of blindness propelled me to this "Now?" Amelia read the words she had penned. They told the depth of her utter disillusionment with her marriage and her husband. She wondered where the years of her life had gone so quickly. In the beginning, she had such high hopes. Memories of tender, loving actions collided with angry, hurtful scenes in her mind. The loving moments earlier tormented her with hope until the next angry encounter.

Hearing the door open, she quickly hid her writing, smoothed her hair and left the bedroom.

"Amelia, where are you?" he called, walking through the house, looking for her.

"I'm here, Matthew." she smiled a greeting as she put her arms around him, looking up into his face. The closeness they had shared earlier returned and her face glowed with gladness. He too, felt a difference in himself, as though his heart is happy and everything is all right. How can he hold on to this loving feeling he asked himself. *Forgive others as I am willing to forgive you.* The words drifted through his mind and he felt that presence again. He returned her embrace, holding her close. "How about a cup of coffee?" He grinned in that way that always caused her heart to respond and she had to reach up to pull his head down and kiss him again. "Mrs. Carlisle, you better be careful, kissing a married man like that." He teased as his eyes lit up. You better get our coffee because I need to ride over to Nathan's in a little while. I'll pick up the mail on the way.

He released her and sat down at the table as she poured coffee for both of them. Setting the coffee and fresh cinnamon rolls on the table, she sat down across from him. "I thought we might visit Sara today if you get through in time." She said, sipping her coffee.

"I won't be long, I hope. I should be back by 3, if that's time enough." He replied, biting into his cinnamon roll. He took a drink of his coffee and started to say something, but seemed to change his mind, causing her to look at him with a question in her eyes. He looked out the window, avoiding her eyes as he took another bite of his cinnamon roll.

"Did you want to talk to me about something?" Amelia's soft words invited his confidence, but for some reason, he held back telling her about what had happened in the field that morning.

"Nothing important" he replied, finishing his coffee and the last of his cinnamon role. He carried his cup and saucer to the sink. "I'll see you after while." He went out the door and left her wondering what has happened that he almost told her about.

Amelia had hardly seen him off, it seemed, before he was back, holding an envelope in his hand. He didn't say anything, just handed it to her. Scanning it quickly, she saw it was from Annie. Wiley Carlisle, Matthew's daddy, was very ill. Annie said she knew that Matthew would want to know. She hoped he would come before Wiley died, although she wasn't sure he would last that long. She said he had asked her to write to Matthew.

"Are you going?" she looked at him curiously, wondering at his reaction to the news.

"No, I haven't lost anything back there. He'll probably die before I can get there, anyway." His voice is matter-of-fact, unfeeling for the man who fathered him.

"Matthew, he is your daddy. Don't you have any feelings for him? He may want to ask you to forgive him. How can you let him die without giving him a chance to make things right with you? That's a horrible thing to do, Matthew."

Suddenly, Matthew hears the nagging voices of all the women who have pushed and shoved him all his life. All those women who cut him to shreds, criticized him and made him feel worthless with their sharp tongues and spiteful ways. He feels the pressure building up in his chest as though he will explode. With an effort, he speaks calmly.

"No one asks you to understand. He's my daddy, but he never acted like a daddy. He gave me away and let them talk him out of taking me to live with him and my brothers and sister. I felt like an orphan all my life, Amelia. That's why I can be so cold. I've been treated cold, that's why."

"Matthew, I know that, but we can't return evil for evil. We have to turn things around, try to be better than people who have mistreated us." Amelia's voice is convincing. "You cannot hold on to the past, Matthew. You have to let go of the hurt before it destroys your chance for happiness with me and our children."

"I don't care what he wants, Amelia. Do you understand? I owe him nothing!" His voice rises. You weren't treated like I was. You were spoiled and petted. That's easy for you to tell me. You don't know how I feel."

"Matthew, you don't realize I do know how you feel, because you have cursed and belittled me and our children just like you say you were treated. Please, Matthew, if you love me and our children, you have to let go of the hatred and anger. You have to forgive them all. Can't you see that we all need to try to do better?" She pleads softly, hoping to calm him.

"I don't want to hear another word about it, Amelia. If you love me, you wouldn't take up for those who have hurt me." His eyes filled with angry tears and his hands that only that morning had touched her in gentleness are now clenched into fists. His face is dark with suppressed anger. She looked at him with pity, turned, and left the room.

Matthew, left alone, crushed the letter in his big hand and threw it across the room. Striding to the door, he went out of the house, slamming the door behind him. The wonderful feelings of the morning were now gone and his heart was full of anger again. He had seen the pity in her eyes and he hated what he is doing to their marriage. A terrible premonition flooded his mind and he knew a fear he has never known since leaving Uncle James.

The next morning, Amelia awoke to sounds in the kitchen. Looking at the clock, she saw it was four o'clock. Matthew was not in bed. The door opened and he came in, carrying two cups of coffee. He handed one to her. "Amelia, I'm ready to leave." He sat on the bed, sipping his coffee. "I wanted you to know the men know what to do while I'm gone. You don't have to concern yourself about anything.

"Nathan's not going with you?" she asked." She knew Nathan had cattle to sell, too.

"No, he said he's not ready to sell right now. I think he needs to get his buyers lined up ahead of time, but that's his business. Do you think you can manage while I'm gone? I probably won't make it until Thursday night."

"I'll manage. I always have." He was ignoring his outburst so she would too, she decided. Jonathan and she would do something together, since Matthew was leaving. She felt her spirit lift somewhat at the thought of her sweet son.

She saw his bag was packed and he was dressed already. She watched him make a final inventory to ensure he had everything he needed. He approached the bed again. He sat down beside her, leaned over, drew her into his embrace and kissed her. As always after his anger subsided, he acted as though he had done nothing wrong and never apologized. He just held her for a long time. She wondered at this. As he drew back, she tried to read his eyes, but they were dark and unreadable. He kissed her again before rising, taking his bag and going toward the door. Then he turned and looked at her from the doorway. A feeling of dread washed through her from his expression.

"Amelia, whatever happens, I love you." Then he was gone, leaving her to wonder what his thoughts were. She tried to recall the beautiful morning and how the presence and love of God filled their kitchen and brought them together in a closeness they had not had for many years. Now, the same spirit of anger and hatred had gained control of her husband again.

Chapter 27

Matthew leaned back in the overstuffed chair. His eyes narrowed speculatively as the woman entered the hotel. She paused briefly, eyes quickly scanning the room. For a fraction of time, her gaze was arrested by the man in the dark suit. His eyes assessed her, but quickly moved past her as a roughly dressed individual entered behind her. He, too, seemed to be looking for someone. When he saw Matthew, he turned and went towards the stairs on the opposite side of the lobby. Mounting the stairs with long strides, he disappeared onto the second floor.

"Good afternoon, Miss. May I assist you?" The man behind the desk spoke kindly to the young woman at the register.

"Thank you, yes. I need a room, please. My husband will join me shortly." She signed the register, accepted the offered key, then turned and ascended the stairs also, her long skirts trailing behind her.

The hotel is grand and elegantly appointed. Red carpets, massive chandeliers, and gilt everywhere exude an atmosphere of luxury. Located in the heart of New Orleans, it is a favorite meeting place for businessmen. A large dining room draws the well-to-do for expensive, lavishly prepared meals served by white-coated waiters. Down a hall, a smaller, more intimate dining room is reserved for those who desire privacy or anonymity.

Matthew has been sitting in the lobby for quite some time. Pulling out a large pocket watch, he checks the time. Frowning slightly, he replaces the watch into his vest pocket, rises, and strolls into the dining room. He chooses a table partially hidden behind a large artificial plant and seats himself so that he may watch the entrance. Ordering coffee, he sips it slowly, presenting a calm, patient picture of the prosperous businessman. His suit is tailor-made and finely cut. His white shirt and gold watch chain all speak of good taste and wealth. He stretches the cup of coffee as long as he can. Just as he had decided to get up and leave, he saw her at the entrance. With a rustle of skirts and an enveloping fragrance of expensive perfume, she makes her way to his table. She waits for him to rise and seat her. He only lifts an eyebrow and smiles lazily at her. Jerking out the chair, she seats herself, furious at his lack of deference towards her.

"You have the manners of a country plow boy." she hissed.

"If you don't like it, you know what you can do." he smiled at her again, beckoning to the waiter. "You're thirty minutes late, you know. You almost had the opportunity of eating alone."

"You seem to think you're the only man interested in dining with me. You are so full of yourself, Matthew. I could have any man I wanted tonight." She tossed her head, her diamond earrings glittering. She is a beautiful woman, which is her main attraction to him.

"Who are you trying to convince, me or yourself? You know you can't leave me. You're in love with me." He laughed mockingly, a challenge in his dark eyes.

"I can't?" Do you really think I can't leave you? Do you want me to show you how I can, Matthew Carlisle?" By now, her eyes are flashing with pure fire.

"Oh, simmer down. Our food is coming. Let's eat before you leave me." He anxiously surveyed his meal. He loved this New Orleans cooking style and thought he needed to teach Amelia how to cook it. He relishes every bite.

After the meal, they left the dining room, crossed the lobby and left the hotel, and climbed into a waiting carriage. In the dining room, Levi Nichols and his wife looked at each other in dismay.

Hours later, Matthew mounted the stairs to his room. He had just closed the door when a tap was heard. He quickly opened the door, admitting the man who had earlier entered the hotel.

"What did you find out, Sam?" He watched the man remove his hat and run his fingers through his thinning hair. Then he began to talk. It was almost morning before he exited Matthew's room and went down the hall. After he left, Matthew sat, staring out the window. Finally, he undressed and fell into bed, where he slept until noon.

Thursday night, Amelia watched the road leading to the house until dark. She had thought Matthew would return before dark, but finally, she went to bed. The children were sound asleep, and they had to get up early for school.

She had received a letter from Hope that day. In it, she wrote that she had met a nice young man and wanted to bring him home with her for Christmas break so she could meet her mother and daddy. She read the letter again before she went to sleep.

The next morning, Matthew had still not returned. Another letter arrived from Annie. Wiley had died the same night that she had written the other letter. She just wanted him to know. Amelia cried, then. She cried for Matthew, who had never really had a mother or a father to love him. She cried for herself and her children who could not seem to bring healing to him, despite all their love for him. She cried for the people who had molded him into the person that he became.

Inside the letter from Annie was a folded piece of paper, old and creased, almost in tatters. Amelia stared at the faded writing, not believing her eyes.

On Friday evening, Matthew came riding in. He unsaddled his horse and hurried into the house. Amelia was at the stove, her face flushed from the heat, her hair damp. She heard the door, turned, and there he was, kissing her and hugging her tightly as though he would not let her go.

"Matthew, she gasped, what is wrong?"

"I love you, Amelia." he still had his arms wrapped around her. She had never seen the expression on his face that it now wore. Whatever has come over him, she thought.

"I love you too, Matt. I expected you back yesterday. Did you have a good trip?" She fixed him a plate from the food on the stove and set the table with silverware and glasses for supper.

He sat down at the table and looked around the room, expecting to see the kids.

"Jonathan went to spend the night with Nathan's little boy, Carlyss. They came over this afternoon and the boys begged so hard, that Nathan said let him go. He'll bring him over tomorrow. He said maybe you would get back and he wanted to talk to you about something." Amelia sat down and bowed her head, giving thanks.

"Where's Felicity?" he nodded toward the empty plate Amelia had placed on the table. "She'll be here soon. She's doing her homework."

"Did you get a good price for the cattle, Matt?" she was making conversation, she knew, trying to fill up the silence with talk.

"Yeah, I'm pleased with the deal I made. I'm glad Nathan's coming over tomorrow. That'll save me a trip over there."

As soon as the meal was over, Amelia cleared the dishes and entered the bedroom. When she returned, she held something in her hand, which she handed to Matthew. He noticed her strange expression: excited but sad.

After reading Annie's letter, he looked at the paper Amelia had handed him. He narrowed his eyes, trying to make out the faded writing. Then, he realized who had written the letter.

To my baby son,

You will never know me, your mother. That is why I am writing this letter to you. I have told your daddy to ensure you get it and the box. He promised to. I trust God to take care of you for me, for I know I will soon be with Him. I know that you will not be able to understand why you have no mother, like other boys. I pray that Martha will be a mother to you in my place.

I am leaving you three things. They are each very important. You must realize the importance of each before you will ever be able to find peace within yourself. The first thing I leave you is a noble past. I leave you the feather of the eagle. The eagle is the most noble of all flying creatures. The eagle flies so high, his nest is so high, no vulture's eye can see it. You must be like the eagle, my Matthew. Make your nest on high and build your house so the vulture cannot find it.

I leave you a coin. Money is man's way of getting what he thinks he needs. Love of money can destroy. Money has no power in God's eyes. Money controls men, not God. No one can buy God's favor with money.

Last and most importantly, I leave you the white stone. Read Rev. 2:17 to learn its meaning. The stone has a name, which you must find for yourself.

My son, I have prayed for the angels to always be around you wherever you go. I believe they will always be there for you. I believe you will find your name, and someday, you and I will meet again and get to know each other. I love you, my precious Matthew. I have given you the name of one of the disciples of Jesus. That is what I pray for you to become: a disciple of Jesus.

Your mother,

Morning Star

The room was so still she could hear the bees on the roses outside the open window. He sat as though in a trance, his eyes staring, unseeing. Finally, he looked at her, questioning.

"What does she mean? I must find the name for myself. What name is she talking about?" He's puzzled, holding the letter out to her. Now he knows why his mother left him a white stone. The coin represents money. The feather is the legacy of his Indian ancestors. He feels amazement at the revealing of the heart and love of his mother.

"Why don't you look in the Bible for the scripture she mentioned? Maybe it will tell you." Amelia's heart was beating fast; she felt like they were on the verge of a miracle in their lives. The thing she had prayed, something to turn Matthew to God, lay in his hand. If only he would take it to heart. She must let him find his own way, though. As much as she wants to rush in and help, she knows that one wrong word from her can instantly change his mood.

"You're the Bible reader. You find it for me." his eyes again go to the faded words, reading them. He saw the beautiful Indian princess from the cave. She wrote these words. She thought about me, he realized in awe, as she was dying.

Amelia now held her worn Bible in her hand, having retrieved it from the table beside her chair. "Is that moisture she sees in his eyes? "Oh, dear God, she prayed. Have your way, please, Lord, and lead my husband to you. She felt his eyes on her as she turned the pages, then she put her finger on the verse in Revelation, the last book in the Bible. She then handed her bible to him.

Matthew read the words she had indicated. Then he read them again. His eyes were puzzled when he raised his head. She was overwhelmed with love for him. He looked like a lost child suddenly, and she wanted to put her arms around him and weep. For the first time in their relationship, Amelia saw her husband vulnerable. Then, to her dismay, he suddenly got up, handed the Bible to her and walked out. She stared after him, unbelieving. What now, she thought. God had surely reached out to him in a very real way through his dead mother. What a woman she must have been. What kind of a man would Matthew have been had she lived to influence him with her Godliness and love? Amelia clasped the bible to her as though to press its power into her soul, to strengthen her for whatever lay ahead. Please, Matthew, please answer the call of God to you, she silently cried.

Matthew walked across the yard, through Amelia's flower garden, and then kept walking. Before realizing his direction, he stood beside the creek and heard its voice as it flowed softly downstream. His mind was being bombarded with memories, painful and disturbing after all these years. He could not allow Amelia to know that he felt stupid, at a loss to understand the words he had read. It had been long since he had thought of the cave and the white stone. The years had been good to him. He had prospered, becoming the man he had wanted to be. He had money, land, respect, and, yes, power over the lives of others. Something was missing, though. He refused to admit it to himself. He could not let her see the emptiness that existed inside of him. He had tried to fill it with Amelia's love, but that was not enough, either. He recalled the words he heard about forgiving. Does that mean he has to forgive Uncle James and Aunt Martha? Will that make his anger go away? Is that the way to have what he feels with Amelia in his arms? Is it possible to feel love he sees in her eyes all the time? The man and the angels on the creek bank came to him because his mother had prayed for him before she died all those years ago. Deep inside his heart came the yearning to see his mother some day. Robbie said he had to repent of his sins and be filled with God's spirit to be able to see her again. If only he could trust Amelia enough to share his fears and real feelings with. It would mean giving her power over him. No, he cannot let her know he is not the self assured man he appears to be.

Darkness was falling as Matthew stood beside the creek. He heard the sound of the crickets as they began their evening song. He realizes he has gotten into a dangerous situation, but he'll get out of it, just like always. Amelia would never leave him. She might threaten and cry, but she has always forgiven him, he reasons. *"What if she does leave you? You can have any woman you want."* The voice startles him but he knows it is not the voice he has heard before. A fearful awareness of something evil moves him to turn back toward the house. God would not speak such words to him. The presence of the angels and the love that he had experienced so many years ago was because of his mother's prayers. The day in the field, he suddenly realized, was that same presence. Amelia had been praying, she had told him when he had mocked her for crying. He had to get out of the situation he has created before it is too late, he realizes. Something tells him his life and his soul is at stake.

Chapter 28

It has been three months now since the letter came from his mother, telling him about the white stone. Nothing has gone right, it seems. A series of events have occurred, each adding to the growing tension between them.

A few days after her sixteenth birthday, Felicity ran away from home with the young man from their church. Matthew blamed Amelia, accusing her of knowing about the boy and of hiding the relationship from him. He had forbidden his daughter to have anything to do with the young man, but in response to her daddy's edict, she had simply run away. Amelia had been racked with pain and undeserved guilt over the whole episode. It had driven her to the depths of despair. Matthew had ranted and raved at her, his eyes full of hatred and scorn, refusing to listen to reason. She retreated further and further into a place within herself, trying to escape from the terrible hurt his cruel words inflicted upon her sensitive spirit.

Amelia had felt so hopeful over the letter, but Matthew had seemingly put it out of his mind, and had not spoken of it again since that first day. She had watched him anxiously for several days, expecting some response, but he had left again. This time, Nathan went with him. When he returned, he brought her a gift, a pair of soft leather gloves. He acted as though they had never had a disagreement, as though he had not left her in miserable tears, as though their marriage was not on the verge of dissolving before his eyes. She had been careful to speak of nothing that would cause controversy between them, accepting the gloves with a little spark of hope that maybe she had been blowing things out of proportion. Her hope was soon to be attacked in a much unexpected way, however.

Matthew and Jonathan had gone fishing early one morning, leaving before daylight. Amelia had been cleaning and cooking, as usual, when she heard someone at the door. Smoothing her hair, she checked herself in the mirror before opening the door to the visitor. She was startled to see a woman standing on the porch. A beautiful woman, perhaps slightly older than Amelia, she was tastefully and expensively dressed. Her hair was elaborately curled and a hat sat atop her dark hair, a gorgeous hat, Amelia noticed, with soft feathers trailing from its crown. Her eyes were an unusual color of green.

Her eyes took in Amelia's appearance in an instant and a little smile touched her full lips, which were painted. Amelia immediately felt pain in her simple house dress, blushing under the woman's scrutiny.

"Mrs. Carlisle?" her voice was soft, friendly.

"Yes, I'm Mrs. Carlisle. May I help you?" Amelia did not invite her in, but then felt even more ill-mannered at the woman's next words.

"May I come in? I'm a little weary from my trip."

Amelia stood back and allowed the woman to come into the house. She looked around the comfortable room, which was the parlor. Amelia had spent much time and given much thought to decorating and furnishing the house. She had felt pleased with the result and had received many compliments from her friends over her decorating skills. Now, suddenly, she saw it through the eyes of this worldly woman and it did not appear quite as satisfactory as before.

She motioned to a chair, asking her to be seated. The woman walked to the chair by the window and sat down. Amelia sat down on the edge of the sofa, her eyes curious as she waited.

"You don't know me, Mrs. Carlisle, but I feel that I know you. Your husband has spoken of you often. At Amelia's look of surprise, she smiled. Oh, I'm well acquainted with your husband. In fact, I feel that I know him as well as you." Her eyes pitied her and Amelia felt herself at a disadvantage. Who is this woman, sitting in her house, talking about Matthew this way?

"I've come to make you aware of the situation we are in, you and I. You see, Matthew is in love with me. He feels such an obligation toward you, however, that he has no heart to tell you of his feelings. I know that you would not want him to remain married to you under these circumstances." she smiled a satisfied little smile as she saw Amelia's reaction to her words. "You must let him know that he's free to go. I'm sure he will allow you to remain in this house. You have your children, your church, and your faith. He is not suitable for you. You like the quiet life. Matthew enjoys a more exciting lifestyle than you can give him." she stood, then, sure that she had won her point. How could Matthew ever have been attracted to his wife; she wondered. Well, she wouldn't be his wife much longer.

Amelia was in a state of shock. She could not believe the scene being played out in her home, her place of safety, of refuge. Now, her last bastion of hope had been destroyed by this gloating painted hussy of a woman. Well, if this is what Matthew wanted, she would let him go. She didn't want him, anyway, suddenly realizing the relationship between him and this woman. She still sat on the sofa, as the door closed behind the woman and she heard the buggy leave.

He and Jonathan had returned from the fishing trip after dark. She had prepared supper, as she had always done. They were full of the pleasure derived from the day. Matthew loved to hunt and fish. Amelia had gone with him when they first settled here. All of that ceased when the children were born. He gradually stopped asking her to go. She could not say anything about the woman in front of Jonathan, so she smiled and listened as Jonathan excitedly described the fish he had caught.

"I caught a bass, Momma. He stretched his hands apart at least a foot. "This big! Boy, did it ever put up a fight!" Matthew laughed and his eyes lit up with pride, suddenly so thankful he had taken his son fishing.

"It sounds like ya'll had a really wonderful time today" she said, with a smile. We will have fish tomorrow, I can see, with two such fishermen in the house."

"You bet, we will, Jonathan exclaimed. Daddy, tell Momma what you caught."

Matthew winked at Amelia. "Oh, mine cannot compare with yours, son. You're some kind of fisherman. You'll have to help me clean them so we can fry them tomorrow."

Amelia's heart hurt with the knowledge of the woman Matthew had been with. She could not say anything, though, in front of Jonathan. It was all she could do to even sit at the table with her husband. She wanted to confront him with his lies and deceit.

She got up from the table and cut them a piece of cake she had made that morning before the woman had knocked on the door. Jonathan took his cake and retreated to his room to study. She brewed fresh coffee and they went out onto the porch, as was their custom in the evening. For a moment, Amelia looked at the events of the day as unreal. The woman had to be lying. How could Matthew live with her, be a husband to her, yet carry on another life with that woman? To her naïve mind, it was just not possible. It must not be true. There must be an explanation. Tomorrow, she would pray and ask God to help her decide what to do with this information she now carried inside her, like a terrible wound, aching and filling her with pain.

The night was dark, for the moon was on the wane. The stars were brilliant, though. They sat in silence, Amelia going over and over the words the woman had spoken, feeling betrayed and angry, yet determined not to let Matthew know.

He too was silent, for his mind was full of his own thoughts. The day spent with Jonathan had given him time to be once again faced with his life and what a mess things had become. He had remembered the letter from his mother, for he had memorized it by now. Amelia did not know that he carried it inside his shirt. The day of the angel's appearance had also returned, vividly, the scene played out again, reviving the same emotion in him. He could feel Firefly's soft lips nuzzling him, the awe that overwhelmed him when he felt the touch of the man with the shining face. The need to return to the cave has become urgent. He must go to his cave, find the box and retrieve the white stone, along with the eagle feather. The coin had been returned to him by Annie, after being lost for so long. While he fished that day, he had heard, it seemed, the sound of his name, even as he had heard it that day when he rode home from church as a little boy.

He is confused, filled with conflict. One part of his mind wants to discard the strange events and pass them off as imagination. Another part wants to pursue the elusive source of the unexplainable happenings. His pride won't allow him to express his feelings to Amelia. She would think him weak. She would try to force him to go to church, seek God. She would tell him what he needed to do. He couldn't stand her telling him anything. Quoting the bible to him, telling him he needed to pray. He knows he needs to pray, if only he knew what to say to God.

They spoke of unimportant, safe things that night. Whether it might rain the next day. How nice the evening had been. The prospects of the flourishing crop, now nearing maturity. He complimented her on the cake, his favorite kind, and the strong coffee, which he demanded.

Later, Amelia lay awake all through the long night, rehearsing what she would say to Matthew the next day. When she thought of a life without him, she began to feel sick inside. She had never known what it was to be alone, never in her whole life. Her pillow was wet with tears when she finally drifted off to sleep toward morning.

She awoke to full daylight and the sun shining brightly outside. She felt awful. Her head ached and her eyes felt full of sand. The bed was empty beside her. She had not known when Matthew got up.

As she bathed her face over and over with cold water, trying to improve her looks and feelings, she remembered everything that had happened the day before. Fresh anger washed over her at the nerve of that woman who had invaded her life and home. Amelia dressed and left the bedroom, wondering where her husband could be. The house had an empty feel. Jonathan must have gone off fishing or roaming the woods, maybe riding his horse. He was a silent victim of the tension that filled the house almost continually now. He spent a lot of time over at Nathan's, with Carlyss. Amelia caught a sympathetic look on his face occasionally, as though he wanted to tell her something. She had been so consumed by her own heavy burden; she was unable to reach out to him. She wanted to avoid confronting Matthew when Jonathan was present in the house.

By now, she had walked through the house, even opened the front door, checking the porch, then going to the back, she looked out across the fields and pastures. No Matthew. Oh, well, he'd be back eventually, she supposed. Meanwhile, she would have coffee. Maybe her head would stop hurting after a little breakfast. She brewed the coffee, poured herself a cup, and then wandered into the front room, her favorite room.

Absentmindedly, she straightened a cushion, wiped a speck of dust from a tabletop and picked up a treasured figurine, finding comfort in the peace of this room. Going finally to the window, her gaze fell at once upon the yellow rose bush, spilling its opulent beauty over the trellis. The sun magnified the intense color and she could even smell the perfumed air through the open window. "Oh, God, what am I to do? Anguish rose up and the cry was torn from her soul as her eyes filled with tears. The roses swam together in a blur, as her hand gripped the curtain. There was no comfort to be found. She sank to her knees beside the window and felt the pain spread through her soul. A terrible grief born of hopelessness to be what she felt her husband required while trying to fulfill her vow to God brought from her lips groaning and finally, gasps of convulsive sobs. She heard her own voice giving vent to the roiling emotions deep inside her heart. Anger at her lot in life, despair towards the future, revulsion directed at herself for all the years she had given herself to her husband, to be discarded like a piece of trash.

Behind her closed eyes passed memories from childhood. She saw herself running barefoot, carefree, skirts held high, winning the races. What happened to that Amelia? Where did she go? That happy, laughing, loving person, filled with dreams and grand expectations? She was gone, gone forever. In her place is a pitiful excuse of a person, absorbed by the demands of a man who never loved her, only used up her life, leading her on until now she is old and it is too late. Amelia's fists clenched tightly and a fresh wave of regret scalded her senses. Pounding the floor in helplessness, she knew such self-loathing that she wished her heart would just stop and she would not have to face her future. "It's my fault, Lord, it's all my fault. I let it happen. All these years, I kept hoping for something that was out of reach. I give up, God. I give up on him."

As the words were torn from her suffering heart, Amelia lay on the floor, spent and exhausted, with no tears left, eyes swollen and hurting. Above her head, a soft sigh moved through the room and something sweet and gentle fell upon her prostrate form. A touch so light as to be imagined passed over her and from head to toe she felt love wash through her spirit. A subtle change was taking place deep within. Healing oil flowed over her wounded soul and hope raised her head and refused to die.

She made up her mind that as soon as Matthew returned, she would tell him of the visitor, while Jonathan was gone. She had bathed her face again, but could not repair the ravages of the sleepless night and terrible spell of weeping. Her face was swollen and puffy and she knew she looked horrible.

Matthew stared at Amelia in shock as she told him of Hannah Wilson's visit. His face darkened with anger. Then, to Amelia's astonishment, he had denied everything. Even laughed when she told him he was free to go to that woman.

"Amelia, I don't want that woman. She's lying to you. She's been after me for years. I met her through one of the buyers of my cattle. She's a married woman. Her husband has been abroad, involved in some kind of government position. She believes herself in love with me. Believe me, if I wanted her, I could have had her, that's for sure. She's mad because I won't fall in line with what she wants." he had such a convincing argument. She wanted to believe him. She didn't really want to have to go through with her plans for leaving, for she didn't know where she would go or what she would do, once she left him.

"Matthew, if you're lying to me, I will eventually find out. The truth will come out." She got up from the bed, then and went out, leaving him alone.

Matthew stood at the window, staring unseeingly at the view of Amelia's garden, full of color. He breathed a sigh of relief. Well, he had gotten out of that. Thank goodness Amelia is so innocent. She always believed whatever he told her. His hands clenched into fists and his eyes darkened with a fearful intensity. Now, he thought, to deal with that crazy woman. He could not believe she had the nerve to come here and tell Amelia such things. She had the nerve, alright. Well, he would take care of her. She wouldn't be paying any more visits to his wife. He felt himself being pushed into a position of defending himself and he knew he had to remain in control. He had to rid himself of those who were trying to control him.

Their relationship after this situation was strangely unreal to Amelia. She continued to have doubts that Matthew had told her the truth. She even at times wished that the woman had never come. Now, the nagging thoughts plagued her, filling her with sudden anger toward Matthew, causing her to dread his touch, to avoid his attempts at intimacy.

Finally, desperate for relief from the situation, she decided to go for a visit to her mother.

It had been over a year since she had been home and suddenly, she needed to be with people that she could feel confident loved her for herself, just as she is. When she told Matthew of her plans, he didn't argue. Summer was almost over and he would be in the middle of harvest, so would have plenty to keep him occupied. He missed her when she was gone, but he would not let her know he really didn't want her to go. Jonathan would go with her, she decided. It would do him good to get away, too.

Felicity had married David Montgomery, the young man she had run away with and was living with his parents at the present. Amelia had hoped Matthew would offer to help them build a house, but so far, she had not been able to get him to agree. She hoped that their differences could be worked out someday. Then, there was the matter of Hope and her young male friend. Well, it was some time until Christmas. Maybe when she returned from her visit to her family, she would feel more like making decisions for the rest of her life.

The last time she had seen her son, Mark, he had a pretty young lady with him. Her name, Joy, was something that seemed to promise a brighter future for him. He had a good job, working at the sawmill and would be able to provide for a wife. Through God's intervention, her splintered family would be brought into unity someday, if she continued to pray and trust God.

Amelia and Jonathan rode the train back to Georgia. As the miles were eaten up behind her, she felt a lightening of her spirit. She was young, not old. She made up her mind she would forget the past and enjoy herself.

She received a joyous welcome from everyone. Ian and Penelope had grown children. Belle and Phillip had married rather late in life, being close to thirty when he finally made her his wife. They had only two children, twins, a boy and a girl, who were now only twelve years old. Victoria, more beautiful than ever, was married to a doctor, for she had gone to nursing school for a couple of years until they were married. They lived in Atlanta in a fine home. Their two sons, Ralph and Colin, were both handsome young men. Caleb too had married and joined Ian in the horse ranch. His wife, Cynthia, shared his love of horses and aspired to be a veterinarian. They had no children as yet.

Constance and William, older now, but serene and as much in love as ever, watched the lives of their children with pleasure. Their grandchildren were a source of great delight to them and the fact that most of them were living within a day's journey only added to their joy. William enfolded Amelia and Jonathan in his arms, and then looked deeply into Amelia's eyes. "Baby, how are you doing?" She knew what he meant, but she pretended not to, for she didn't want to talk about Matthew. She didn't want her family to know how he treated her. She didn't want their pity. She remembered the rash promise she had made her daddy many years ago. She would stick to it, she decided.

Amelia spent a wonderful two weeks, walking the woods, still the same, yet different, too She went into town, now a thriving, bustling place with many shops and eating places. One day, walking into a dress shop, she spied a familiar face and rushed over to Charity, Levi's wife, embracing her.

"Charity, I'm so glad to see you!" Amelia greeted her friend with enthusiasm. The three of them then went to have lunch at a tea shop, recently opened, catering to ladies. After they had eaten and were enjoying catching up on each other's lives, Charity looked at Amelia speculatively, and then asked bluntly. "Amy, are you and Matthew still married?" her question was like a blow, so unexpected it was, coming from Levi's wife.

Amelia's eyes widened in surprise, and then she forced a little laugh. "Why, of course, we are. Why do you ask?" she watched as her friend tried to decide whether to tell or not to tell her the reason for such a question.

"You can tell me, Charity. It's alright." Amelia encouraged her.

Charity looked at Penelope, then, for she had frowned at her question, nudging her under the table with her foot. Suddenly, Amelia felt they knew something she didn't. Something concerning Matthew and her heart sank. "You have to tell me, you know. Whatever it is, I'll know eventually, anyway. I would rather hear it from a friend." she persisted.

"Well, it's probably nothing, Amy. Levi and I went to New Orleans a few months ago and saw Matthew in the hotel where we stayed. He didn't recognize me, but I knew him right off. He's not seen me in a long time, probably ten years or more. Then when they left, he didn't see Levi." she stopped, realizing what she had said. Amelia caught the slip, too.

"They? Who are "they" Charity?" her voice is light, hiding her fear.

"Amy, it was probably just someone he was having dinner with, a business acquaintance, maybe." she tried to back up, extricate herself from the position of being a bearer of bad news. Amelia would not let her off the hook, though. She had to know.

"It was a woman he was with, wasn't it?" she demanded an answer and Charity miserably nodded, sorry that she had divulged the incident, now.

Amelia explained it away, saying it was the wife of a cattle buyer that Matthew had already told her about. Then, she pretended that everything was alright. She laughed and joked with her friends, showing a side of herself that had been smothered out for years. They cooperated with her, bringing up incidents from their past and laughing at each other. Charity heard the story of Levi and his trial. She giggled like a schoolgirl as she pictured Levi being subjected to a dose of his own medicine. When they parted, all mention of the encounter with Matthew had been relegated to the back of their minds.

A week later, when the train pulled into the station, Amelia saw Matthew's dark head right away. He was watching every car, looking for her. Her heart quickened of its own accord at the sight of him. Then, they were wrapped in a bear hug of greeting and she and Jonathan were glad they had gone and glad they were back.

Amelia had been home a few days and was deep in her plans for Christmas. Thanksgiving would not be a big affair, but she would cook a big meal, as usual. Sara and John, with little Mattie, along with herself, Matthew, and Jonathan, she figured, would be all that would be eating Thanksgiving dinner. Felicity had still not come around to even show remorse for being so disrespectful to Amelia and Matthew. Amelia knew her baby daughter was expecting to have a child herself and her heart yearned to be a part of their lives. Mark and Joy were to be married in the spring, she knew, but so far he had not come to see his parents.

Since her visit home, she and Matthew had returned to a measure of peace. Amelia had not mentioned her conversation with Charity, just continued to be suspicious each time Matthew was away from home. He acted as though they had never had a disagreement, which was even harder for Amelia to bear. She felt raw inside and could not seem to get past her sense that her husband had betrayed her. He felt he had convinced Amelia of his innocence and was not concerned anymore that she would question him further about his involvement with the woman.

While Amelia had been away, he had gone to New Orleans and checked into the same hotel. He had met with Sam again, spending the better part of the day going from one cattle buyer to another, verifying information that Sam had furnished him. Then, he had hired a carriage and traveled to the outskirts of town, driving through the gate of an imposing mansion sitting in the middle of lush gardens and fountains. When he was admitted by the butler, he was immediately shown to the huge library, where he was left alone for quite some time. Finally, the door opened and Hannah Wilson entered. She smiled smugly as she crossed the room to him. "Matthew, I've been waiting for you." She attempted to embrace him but he grabbed her arms, holding them in a vice-like grip, his face furiously angry.

"I hear you paid my wife a visit, Hannah. Just what are you trying to prove?" she tried to free herself from his hands, but he only tightened his grip. You may as well relax. You'll listen to every word I say, then, when I'm ready, I'll let you go." his handsome features were contorted by suppressed rage and suddenly, she was afraid. She winced as his hands bit into her arms, bruising them, she knew.

"If you ever, I mean ever, contact my wife in any way again, I will choke the life out of you with my bare hands. Do I make myself clear? He shook her then, trying to control his desire to hit her." He saw her fear and he laughed, an ugly sound, for it was without humor. How he despised her. How he despised them all. They were all the same. He shook her again, trying to get an answer.

"Alright, Matthew, let me go." Her look of submission was replaced by anger, then, for when he finally released her arms, she drew back her hand, slapping him across his face as hard as she could. Without conscious thought, he struck her across the face, watching as she spun away from him and landed on the floor, striking a chair as she tried to catch herself.

"You should know better than to hit me, Hannah. Nobody hits me and gets by with it. I've been hit all my life. I'm a big boy now. Be sure to remember what I told you about my wife." he picked up his hat and walked to the door.

Her voice reached him as he opened the door. "I'll kill you, Matthew Carlisle. I'll kill you for what you've done to me." Then he heard her sobbing as he crossed the wide foyer and let himself out the front door. That was the end of the affair, as far as he was concerned.

He had been involved with Hannah Wilson for several years and it had gotten out of hand. After their initial meeting all those years ago, he had totally forgotten all about her. Then, unexpectedly, they had met again, in New Orleans, where she had built an imposing mansion, entertaining important people connected with the business empire she had built from her daddy's original beginning as a rancher in Texas.

She had never married, because she felt no man would rule over her. When she saw Matthew again, she felt the same desire to have him as she had the first time they had met. The problem was that he had changed. She found out immediately that she was no longer dealing with a shy, inexperienced boy. The violent emotions that ruled him enticed her and gave her a thrill of danger. She was looking for excitement and Matthew provided it. She found herself in love with him. Wanting to draw him away from his wife, who must surely be an idiot, to allow such a man to be away from her so often. She used her wealth and power as a drawing card, buying him expensive gifts, fine clothes, and a carriage, which was kept in town for his use. The relationship began as an attraction to beauty, forbidden pleasure, on Matthew's part. Her weakness and obvious attraction for him excited him and filled him with self-confidence in his ability to control women. Underneath it all, however, was the desire to punish all women for the offenses he had suffered as a child growing up in a house full of women. Humiliating her, finally, he felt glad to be rid of her, for she had become possessive, and dominating, trying to force him to leave Amelia and move in with her. She promised him wealth, power, anything his heart desired, even as Bethany had, so many years before.

When he compared these women to his wife, Matthew had to acknowledge the difference. He never wanted to marry Hannah Wilson. He wanted to stay married to Amelia, with her sweetness, honesty, and faith in God, her devotion to see their children grow up and live clean lives. He just had been drawn to Hannah, with her green eyes and beautiful face, her way of making him feel that she would die without him. She had forced his hand, though, for now, he was through with her.

Chapter 29

Sam Reynolds had known Matthew for ten years, now. He had worked for him off and on, doing whatever needed to be done on a large spread, such as Matthew had managed to build up over the years. He had no family and had grown attached to Matthew's children. He admired Matt Carlisle. His smart mind and seemingly effortless way of accomplishing whatever he wanted to do earned him Sam's respect and loyalty. So, when Sam began to get a word here and there of a rustling operation going on, he immediately made Matthew aware of it. They had noticed a discrepancy in the number of cattle they began with and the final count when they reached the buyers. Somehow, the brands were being changed or altered and cattle sold under someone else's brand.

Matthew decided to take care of his problem himself. He and Sam had been conducting an investigation of their own, now, for a year or more, never having been able to pinpoint the exact time and place that the altered branding was taking place. All he knew was that he had been losing money for quite some time, but had not realized how much until he had begun to keep a tally himself. He and Sam had traveled to New Orleans separately, hanging around the places frequented by sellers and buyers. Sam frequented the shipyards, hiring out as a roustabout on the docks, hoping to catch a word here and there that would lead them to the source of the thievery.

Matthew had begun to worry about Sam, for he had not contacted him since he had met with him while Amelia had visited her parents. He usually heard from him at least every month, where he would exchange information and get orders and money from Matthew. Since the problem with Hannah, Matthew had been sticking close to home, trying to allay Amelia's suspicions of him. He knew that she did not wholly believe his story, but hoped in time they could be close again. Finally, he realized that he would have to go and try to find out what had happened to Sam. He dreaded telling Amelia, for he knew her reaction already. He was torn between his need to see about his friend and having peace with his wife. It never occurred to him to take Amelia into his confidence, to let her know what was going on around her home. He was so used to keeping things from her that the truth was something he didn't consider.

Matthew had become an accomplished liar during his involvement with Hannah. He couldn't seem to break the pattern, now. It was so much easier for him to make up a story, preventing a scene, than to face the truth and endure the consequences of his actions.

Travel had greatly improved in the twenty years since Matthew had settled in Louisiana. Trains had increased the speed at which people could move themselves and their products across the country. New inventions have made work easier and faster on all levels, from the housewife to the cattle rancher. So, Matthew could easily travel to New Orleans or other parts of the state rather quickly, now. He decided to check the last place Sam had hired on, one of the loading points where cattle were transported, held in pens and then shipped out to all points of the country. Telling Amelia that he needed to purchase a new piece of equipment, he felt he was then free to travel in any direction he desired. She received the news calmly, but he saw a flicker of doubt in her eyes.

"How long will you be gone, Matt? It's almost Christmas, you know. I had hoped you and I might make a trip to Baton Rouge or New Orleans, together. We haven't been anywhere together in a long time." her tone was wistful and he suddenly felt regret for his treatment of her. She had been a good wife, he realized. A good mother. He felt dirty and low down, suddenly, lying to her.

"Not more than a few days, I hope. We'll try to get a trip in before Christmas, Amelia, I promise." He had put his arms around her and held her close.

When she lifted her head and looked up at him, he was reminded of that long ago night on the trail to Ian's when she had done the same thing, telling him she loved him for the first time. Contrition swept through him and he kissed her gently and lovingly, as he had done the first time. Held in his arms, she tried to put all the bad out of her heart and mind. 'Faith is the substance of things hoped for; the evidence of things not seen.' Her faith will prevail and someday Matthew will turn to God and become the man she knows he could be, she reminded her heart.

Before he could leave, he received a telegram that changed his plans. It was from Sam. He had gotten the information they had needed. He wanted Matthew to meet him in New Orleans. The trail of the stolen brands had led to a person who would shock him, he knew. He could not put the information in the telegram. As soon as he could pack, Matthew left, reaching the city in the early afternoon. He checked into the hotel, had something to eat, and then waited in his room for Sam to appear. He waited all night.

No Sam. The next morning, after a restless night, he descended to the dining room. Drinking coffee, he ordered breakfast, watching the doorway intently.

While Matthew sat in the dining room having breakfast, Sam was in a bad situation. He had sent the telegram, then, returning to his room, had met with trouble in the form of two individuals who escorted him out of the hotel. They carried him to a small house, tied him up and left him there, without a word as to why. Later that night, they had returned, untied him, blindfolded him and put him in a carriage, which traveled for quite some time, it seemed, before stopping. Still blindfolded, he was jerked roughly from the carriage and led into some kind of building.

"I guess you're wondering what's going on, Sam." the voice sounded vaguely familiar, but Sam could not put a name to it. "Well, you've gotten yourself mixed up in something that's too big for you, that's what's going on. Now, I know you're working for Matt Carlisle. I know you've planned to meet him. I want you to tell me the information that you planned to give him. If you cooperate, you won't suffer any harm. That's why the blindfold. You won't have any way of identifying us, so you won't be a danger. That's the only way we can allow you to go free. Just give me the name of the person you've been following." the voice was educated sounding, not the rough, coarse talk of a cowhand, Sam thought.

He wasn't about to give his information to the man behind the voice, Sam decided. He had no idea who these people were. He tried to think of a name that would get him off the hook, but his mind wasn't working too well. Finally, trying to gain time, he gave them the name.

"I found out that Matthew's cattle are being rustled by his own neighbor. A friend, in fact. Nathan Scarbrock, that's the one that has been stealing the cattle. Dirty and low down, that's what I call it. Taking your own neighbor's cattle." Sam pretended indignation at Nathan's seeming betrayal of Matthew.

The man laughed, then. He needed not to worry about Sam, after all. He motioned to the men to take him back to a place where they could leave him, and then he quickly exited the building.

Across town, Matthew was becoming concerned about Sam. He had no way of tracking him down, even. Leaving the hotel, he hired a horse, then rode out of town, following a road leading to a large holding area for incoming shipments of cattle, After Matthew left the hotel, a heavily veiled woman dressed in the black of mourning, also left, climbing into a carriage, which followed the same road toward the cattle pens. As the carriage neared the end of the road, it stopped and a black-gloved hand moved the curtain aside just enough to watch the road. In a short while, Matthew galloped past the carriage, giving it a cursory glance, wondering what a fine carriage was doing out here.

One of the workers at the yard had given him information about Sam. Sam had worked there just two days ago, but had not returned. He had mentioned that he might be leaving for home, somewhere in the central part of the state, but had not returned for his pay. Matthew hurried back to the hotel, where he checked his room, hoping Sam might have contacted him by now. Sure enough, the clerk informed him that someone had inquired for him about an hour before and was waiting in his room for his return. Taking the stairs two at a time, Matthew opened the door to his room, and then halted in surprise.

"Hannah! What do you want?" his voice was suddenly wary, though hard.

She smiled, but her green eyes were dangerously bright in her beautiful face. "Well, Matthew, I want you." She came close to him, then and he remembered the scent she wore, expensive, alluring. "Why Matthew, I believe you still love me." her voice was soft, as she lifted her face, her eyes expecting his kiss.

He was tempted to take up her challenge, but instead, he placed his hands on her shoulders, holding her away from him. "What do you really want, Hannah. You didn't come here to seduce me, I know that."

"Could I seduce you, Matthew? Or have you become suddenly a holy man? Maybe that's it, your wife has converted you." she put emphasis on the word, showing her scorn for Amelia. Seeing his eyes darken, she shook off his hands and walked across the room to look out of the window. When she turned to face him, she was smiling again. Matthew saw her intent as she walked toward him again but knew he could not give in to her. A wild excitement gripped Hannah as she looked at Matthew. She wondered again what attracted her to him, even though he had rejected her. Why did he stay with that plain little wife when he could have her, she could not fathom.

"I have some information you have been wanting. I've discovered that I have a gang of thieves working for me." At his expression, she laughed. "Oh, not with my consent, believe me. In fact, they have been stealing my cattle, along with yours and anyone else's they can manage to get access to during shipment to market. Your man, Sam, was snatched from the hotel just before you arrived. They tried to get him to give them the name of the person behind it all. Sam thinks I'm the one behind the gang. I'm not, but my manager at the ranch is the boss of the whole operation. He has built up quite an empire for himself while I've been away so much. I've notified the authorities and they are arresting him, along with about a hundred others, scattered around the country. I was told of this by one of my men who remained loyal, and who has been with me since my Daddy died. He risked his life to let me know, for these men have a lot to lose by being exposed." she walked to the window, looking out as she talked. "Well, well, what an opportunity," she realized, as her eyes lighted on a figure approaching the hotel entrance.

Suddenly, a little smile touched her lips, which Matthew could not see. Malice filled her eyes and she felt a moment of triumph.

"Well, Hannah, I'm certainly glad to hear what you've told me. I'm just wondering where Sam could be. I need to try to find him." He could not believe Hannah was interested in helping him. It was not like her to be concerned about anyone. He was suddenly on his guard, for he remembered her parting words when he had slapped her down and left her.

Hannah had turned from the window and he thought she was about to leave. Instead, she suddenly rushed over to him and threw her arms around his neck. Pulling his head down to her, she kissed him, clinging to him so tight, that he couldn't get free.

That was the scene that Amelia witnessed when she quietly opened the door of Matthew's room. She stood in the doorway, swathed in black, a veil covering her face. She saw the gloating green eyes of the woman and she was filled with rage. Trembling from head to foot so hard, she could hardly stand; she knew then how it would feel to kill someone. She felt a desire to lash out, wipe that triumphant smile off her face, claw that perfect face so that it bled, as her heart was bleeding now.

Then, Matthew turned partially around, having heard some sound. She saw the confusion on his face. He didn't recognize her through the veil, she realized, so she lifted it from her face. Then his expression changed to dismay and surprise, for he realized what Hannah had done to him. She had seen Amelia and timed her little act just right. Angrily, he turned from her grasp, wanting to choke her until she begged for mercy. She had her victory. She had paid him back. Her laughter mocked him as he hurried after his wife.

Matthew reached the lobby but could not see Amelia. She must have had a carriage waiting at the door. She would be headed for the train station, he decided. Not taking time to hail a carriage, he began to run toward the train station. When he arrived, out of breath, he could not find her. Puzzled, he sat down on a bench, trying to catch his breath.

He waited for almost an hour, but she never appeared. He returned to the hotel, retrieved his bag and was walking out the door when Sam came rushing into the hotel. He grabbed Matthew by the arm and began to tell him all that had happened to him that day.

Amelia watched her husband hurry down the street, then turned back into the room she had rushed into after leaving Matt's doorway. She didn't want to hear any of his lies, ever again. She could not allow him to touch her, or get close to her. He would somehow cause her to doubt the scene she had witnessed a few moments ago. He would have such a plausible explanation, that he would convince her. Then, she would be right back where she started, again. She could not continue this life she had been living. She felt herself dying inside. She did not know herself anymore. If she had carried a weapon, she could have murdered them both. A horrible revulsion caused her to shudder with fear that she could even entertain such a thought. She fell to her knees beside the chair and began to repent for the terrible thoughts that had taken her over at the sight of her husband in that woman's arms. Jealousy surged through her like fire and she tried to pray, to rid herself of what she felt were her sinful thoughts toward Matthew and that woman. Dry-eyed, for the rage had dried her tears, she lay on the bed, staring at the ceiling, trying to make some kind of a plan as to what she should do next.

"I'll stay here, in the room, until I know he's left town. Then, I'll go and have something to eat." She suddenly realized she had not eaten since morning. After that, she was blank. Her thoughts could carry her no further. Finally, hunger drove her to the dining room. She had divested herself of her widow's clothes, feeling no need for concealment, now that Matthew had left.

Matthew and Sam rode down the trail after leaving the train. Darkness was falling and Matthew wondered what arrangements Amelia had made for Jonathan when she had left to follow him. For he realized now, that she had followed him to New Orleans. In spite of her seeming acceptance of his explanation, she had not believed him. Well, he really couldn't blame her. "If I can only get to her, he thought, I'll make her see the truth."

The house was dark and empty. Matthew could not remember ever coming into such emptiness, not even when Amelia had been away visiting her parents. He realized, suddenly how tired he was, drained of strength. Sam had gone on to his own little cabin, where he had lived since he came to work for Matthew.

He stood in the middle of the big kitchen, wondering what he could find to eat.,. He found some leftover biscuits and filled them with blackberry jam, which he ate standing up at the window. He had suddenly felt too tired to cook even eggs.

Afterward, he wandered through the house, opening and closing each door, as though expecting to find someone. Finally, he went to their bedroom, undressed in the dark and fell into bed. He thought he would sleep immediately, but once he lay down, his eyes were wide open. As though the ceiling was a canvas, Matthew began to see scenes he thought were long forgotten. He saw himself, the day he walked down the road, leaving Aunt Martha calling to him from the porch. He saw Amelia the first time they met. He smiled at the picture of her, freckles covering her face, blue eyes big and inquisitive. She was about twelve then, he thought. How strange, how their lives had come together, separated, then merged, flowing together after all those years. He saw himself, with his baby daughter, Sara, riding his big horse; she was just a tiny little thing, with dark hair so like his. One after another, they had come, his five children.

All beautiful, healthy, strong. He wondered when their loving dependence on him had changed. He had worked hard to make their lives better. They seemed not to appreciate all his hard work over the years, just like Katherinend Millie. Matthew felt deep loneliness, a little boy's pain when he realized for the first time that he was unloved, rejected as a true son and only tolerated for his work.

What is love? Amelia, how do you feel when you love someone? He had asked her that. She seemed to know. Was it the feeling that filled him when he held his son in his arms for the first time? Or was it that surge of emotion, that painful yearning that he felt now, for his absent wife? God is love. She said that to him. She said so many things to him. Ian tried to help him, but he didn't listen.

"Matthew, if you would just let Jesus into your heart, you wouldn't have all that hate and anger. Matthew, how can you say you love me and your children and talk with such hatred in your eyes?"

He had gotten angry when she told him that. The darkness was always there, inside, crouching, waiting for an outlet, a victim. He knew it. He hadn't wanted Mark to go. What had made him so angry with his son that he lost control? He didn't remember now. He had always shouted them into submitting to his will. Now, they were gone. Even his mother. She said she loved him. His daddy is gone now, too. He felt the loss of unsaid words, unfulfilled needs, and vague yearnings, now never to be realized.

He reached for the lamp, turning it up. Then he pulled out the fragile piece of paper that tied him to the past. It is the bridge that could carry him back to his beginning. He read the words again. It seemed important, suddenly, that he solve the mystery. He must find the name. Maybe the answer would come if he could hold the stone in his hand. Something always seemed to happen when he held the stone. Turning the lamp low, he lay back on the pillow, the letter still held in his hand. He didn't know that he slept.

He was dreaming. In his dream, Matthew stood at the edge of a field, looking into the distance. He could see familiar faces all around him. They were going away from him, though. There was his beautiful Indian princess. She beckoned to him, a look of longing on her face, but then she began to move away, almost as though her feet did not touch the ground. One after the other, he saw them. His daddy joined hands with the princess, his face happy, carefree and young again.

Then, there was Mark, a sad expression on his face. He looked at Matthew, held out his hands, and then he too, began to move away, looking back over his shoulder at his daddy. Felicity, then Hope, Jonathan, Sara and last, with terrible fear piercing his heart, he recognized Amelia. She started walking away, but stopped and turned, as though to come back. He could almost reach her outstretched hand, but suddenly, she disappeared and there was only emptiness where she had been. A hole seemed to exist inside him, as though he had become an empty shell and would crumble into dust, fragile and defenseless. He awoke with tears wet on his face and his heart pounding as though he had been running. The room was cool, but he was wet with perspiration. He had been dreaming. Relief made him weak, and he shivered at the coolness on his hot skin. He turned up the lamp and checked the time. Four o'clock. He got up, poured water into the basin and began to wash his face with the cool cloth, wiping the perspiration from his skin. He stared at himself in the mirror. Haunted eyes looked back at him from a face strangely pale, unlike himself. What a dream!

He went to the kitchen, built a fire in the stove, put the coffee pot on and then stared out the window into the still dark morning. Where is Amelia, he wondered. What would happen to her, alone, without him to protect her? She couldn't just wander around alone. It wasn't safe for women. The bubbling coffee brought his mind back to the present and he inhaled the aroma as he poured himself a generous cup. Opening the back door, he walked out onto the porch. No light in the sky yet. He sipped his coffee. He had to find out about Jonathan, and then he had to find Amelia. Would she go home to her parents? He discarded the thought of contacting them. They would worry if she didn't come, then question him as to why he didn't know her whereabouts. He had such an insistent urging inside to find her, hold her. Without her, there would be no light in him at all. He felt torn, for something still nagged at his mind. There was something else, just as urgent as his need to find Amelia. He had come to a decision last night; he remembered, before he dropped off to sleep. The white stone. His cave and the box with the white stone. He needed to go to the cave and hold the stone in his hand. For some unexplainable reason, the stone beckoned to him. Why did the name in the stone seem to offer him hope for all the despair of his life? He couldn't say. He only knew he would go. He went back into the house, poured himself another cup of coffee, and carried it into the bedroom, where he quickly dressed in riding clothes. He didn't take time to cook breakfast, but went on down to Sam's cabin, for he knew he would be up. Sure enough, he saw the smoke rising from the roof and a light through the one window.

Sam was cooking bacon and eggs and the little cabin smelled cozy and homey to Matthew. His stomach growled so loudly that Sam laughed, placing a plate on the table in front of him.

"I guess you didn't cook yourself any breakfast. A man can't think on an empty stomach, you know. Here, fill up that growling hole with this." Sam's grin seemed to bring the morning into perspective, somehow, and Matthew began to feel better. He gave Sam instructions as he ate, telling him he would be gone several days and he was leaving him in charge. He told him to go over to Nathan's, fill him in on all that had happened, and check on Jonathan.

"If he's there, see if he can stay until I get back. If he's not, find out where he is and bring him here to stay with you. I know I can trust you, Sam. You're a good man." Matthew slapped Sam on the shoulder as he finished his food and rose to go.

He was back at the train station by six. He bought his ticket, and then paced impatiently up and down until the train pulled in. Quickly boarding and taking a seat by the window, he watched as others climbed aboard and soon the car was almost full. Finally, the whistle blew its last warning and the wheels began to turn. Matthew was going back in time, he realized. He never dreamed he would want to go back, but he knew now that only by going back could he rid himself of the past and turn finally toward the future with Amelia and his children.

He had a long ride, even on the train. Then, he had a long horseback ride. He hired a horse at the livery stable for the last leg of his journey. Even though it was late afternoon, he felt driven to go on to the cave that day. He forced his common sense to prevail, though and checked into the hotel and had a good hot meal. Then he slept soundly for ten hours. He woke at his usual time, around four. He tried not to think about Amelia and what she might be enduring, for he could do nothing about that right now. He could only believe that she would be alright until he could find her and bring her home. If she would come home. She had to come home. He needed her, he admitted to himself. How could he allow her to know how much, for then he would be in her power and he did not know if he could go that far, with any woman. They could not be trusted.

After a huge breakfast and two cups of strong black coffee, Matthew rode out of town, fortified for his expedition to the cave. As he slowed his horse to a walk, once out in the open country, memories flowed through his mind like smooth running water in the clear little creeks that were everywhere. He stopped and got down on his knees, scooping the cold water in his big hands and drinking thirstily, while his horse drank too. He felt strange, disconnected from the home he had left and the past he was about to face. As though he were in some neutral place, neither here nor there, a traveler between what was and what was to be. He met no one and that made his journey even more ethereal, as though all of this scenery was just for his eyes and for his senses to feel and experience.

The sun was warm on his back and a feeling of well-being stole over him as he rode along. He noticed the magnolias were blooming here. He remembered Amelia's face when he had returned to the wagon that day with the news that they would be leaving the wagon train. He had given her the huge magnolia blossom. You would have thought he had given her the moon, for her eyes had drawn him into her soul, it seemed. They were so blue and clear, loving him. He knew she would cry. She always cried when he gave her a gift, no matter how small. It could be a wildflower that he had picked on a whim and she would have tears in her eyes when he presented it to her. Why did she cry? He had never thought about it, he realized. A revelation came to Matthew, then.

After so many years of marriage, he did not know his wife. Was she so glad for the gift that she cried? No, that didn't sound right. It never had occurred to him before, but could Amelia still wonder if he loved her? Did she cry because each small gesture on his part was a sign to her that his love was real? Matthew felt himself receiving answers to questions he had never taken the time to ask before today. Why now, today, he wondered. He realized he was near Uncle James's old place. He didn't know what he would find there, so he skirted around it and went through the woods, as he had done since he was a small boy here in this very place.

His horse splashed through the creek, narrow here, then the trees closed over his head and he was on thick pine straw and fallen leaves. Amazingly, the place where the cave was located had hardly changed at all. More trees had slid into the gully cut by the water, but Matthew could see the cave opening. He moved down the bank, the sand soft and moist. As he struggled through fallen branches, he realized he was no longer the skinny little boy he used to be. The entrance was smaller than he remembered and he had to move some of the debris to make the opening larger so he could finally crawl in on his hands and knees. Inside, damp and musky smelling, he realized that there was no telling what kind of animal he could encounter, for this would make a nice den for the winter. He had nothing with which to build a fire, he realized.

Then he remembered the fire-making tools he had left here. Was it possible he could still remember how to build a fire the Indian way? Gradually his eyes became accustomed to the gloom and he found his box and everything just as he had left them. Soon, he sat cross-legged on the floor of the cave, twirling the fire stick between his fingers, the small pile of dried leaves and straw clustered around the base, waiting to be ignited by the spark from the flint stone. When he got the fire going, gradually adding sticks, the cave became cozy instead of dismal and he held his hands over the flame. The small space was soon feeling drier and by the light of the fire he opened the box. Yes, there it is. He smiled to himself. Lifting the eagle feather in his hand, he suddenly untied his bandana from around his neck and tied it around his head.

Then, he stuck the eagle feather in the bandana. He removed the coin that Annie had returned to him. He held it in his hand. Then, without thought, he laid the coin in the fire. He watched the flames rise up around it. He wasn't sure what prompted his action. He had a sense that he was being watched and that everything he did was very important. Then, almost reverently, he picked up the white stone. Holding it close to his eyes, he examined the strange sign on its surface. Since he had read the letter, the stone looked different. He knew it held a secret that he must somehow unlock. It is a message that would change his life, as his mother had told him. He closed his eyes as he used to do as a child. He saw the pictures again, though his eyes were closed. The Indian princess, the hawk nosed Indian chieftain. Something was different, though. Now, there was a little boy with them. He knew it was him as a child, looking up into the old Indian's face. The Indian pointed up into the sky and then at the white stone the boy held in his hand. The little boy shook his head. The Indian disappeared into the air, like the smoke that rose from the fire. He saw the little boy look at the stone, smile, and hold it up toward the sky, as though offering it to someone. Then, he, too, disappeared into the smoky air. Matthew sat still, mesmerized by the vision he has seen. He is stunned at such an occurrence in his life. He felt the presence of the man on the creek bank. It flowed all around him, through his body, as though he is without flesh. Tenderness enveloped him, as though he is being held in the arms of someone who truly loves him.

He crawled out of the cave, mounted his horse and rode away, carrying the white stone with him.

Chapter 30

Amelia had remained in the hotel for two days and two nights, venturing out to sightsee in the mornings, then returning at noon. She ate nothing after that first day. She spent her time praying, trying to decide what to do with the rest of her life. She knew no one in the city, so felt totally alone and aimless. With no beds to make, dishes to wash, or husband to cook for, she realized, time moved very slowly. She had been waiting for some sign that she should return home, go to her parents, or maybe try to find some type of employment for herself and just remain in the city. She dreaded meeting Matthew. She dreaded having to pit her will against his, for she always came out the loser in their conflicts.

Finally, on the third morning, she felt an urge to go home. It was the first time she had felt that way since she had last watched Matthew leave town. She believed it to be the sign she had been waiting for, so she packed her bag and took the train. She knew there would be no one to meet her at the station. She would have to hire a buggy. Well, she could do that, she decided, finally feeling a sense of direction. She reached home late that afternoon. It was nearly dark, so she decided to stay at the hotel and hire a buggy the next morning.

She woke up before daylight and was fully dressed when the light first streaked across the sky. She immediately went to the livery stable, hired a buggy and started home, not even taking time to eat breakfast. She knew Matthew was not there the moment she saw the house through the trees. There was no smoke coming from the kitchen stove and no light showing anywhere. It looked so peaceful and welcoming, she thought. How deceiving looks can be from the outside, she realized, thinking of all the conflict within its walls.

She had made arrangements with Nathan and Lillibeth for Jonathan to remain with them until she came for him. She had not told them the true nature of her trip, but she wondered if they guessed at the problem. Now, she went to the kitchen, built up the fire and soon had coffee made and her breakfast cooked. As she bowed her head and prayed, she wondered where Matt was at that moment. The thought of his being with that woman sent fresh anger coursing through her whole body, causing her to tremble, her hand shaking as she tried to hold her fork. As soon as she had eaten, she began to feel she needed to leave the house. Not understanding this, she went into the bedroom. The bed was unmade, so he had been here since she left. Something was on the floor beside the bed and she picked it up, curious. It was the letter from Matt's mother.

'*Strange,*' she thought, for it to be lying on the floor. Maybe he had dropped it from wherever he had been keeping it and didn't know. She placed it carefully in the dresser drawer. Still feeling she needed to leave, but not knowing where she should go, she stood still, waiting.

Finally, she just walked out of the house and stood on the porch. The roses were in full bloom in her garden. The gazebo Matthew had built for her, just like the one back home, looked lovely with the morning glory vines she had trained trailing up the posts and across the roof. Before she realized what was happening, she had descended the steps and started across the yard toward the little white building, set amid the flowers. She sat down on the bench her husband had built, folded her hands and became very still. She knew the voice of the Lord would speak to her heart and lead her, as he had always led her.

She felt it deep inside her soul at first, and then it rose up within her spirit and spilled over, even as the bubbling spring spilled over and became a stream. The desire to give thanks to God and to praise Him. She didn't feel it in her mind, but she knew it in her heart. So, she began to thank the Lord for filling her husband with His love and His spirit.

"Oh, Lord, you are great and mighty. Only you know the heart, only you can save us, not we ourselves. You are King of Kings and Lord of Lords. You are the Rose of Sharon, the Lily of the Valley. I see you high and lifted up. I exalt you, Oh, my God, for you are worthy to be praised." Amelia lifted her voice into the still morning air and her praises rang out in a declaration of her faith in a faithful God. "There is none like you, Oh Lord, for you have done marvelous things and are even now working in our lives to bring us closer to your perfect plan for us."

Her heart felt light and she laughed out loud with expectation and excitement, for she knew, suddenly, that morning was coming into her life, after a long period of night. She had seen no change in her situation, in her marriage, but there was a certainty born of faith in an all-powerful God, that the nothing she was holding to would soon become a reality.

Later that day, she thought of going to fetch Jonathan home, but something told her to wait. She felt as though she is an actor in a play and her cue was soon to be given. All day, she had debated whether to leave or not to leave. She needed to return the buggy to the livery stable. She had not seen anyone working around the barn or stables, so guessed that Matthew had either not planned to be gone this long, or had left Sam in charge and that he was tending to everything. She felt like walking down to Sam's cabin, so off she went. He was sitting on the little porch, rocking. He was surprised to see her.

"Mrs. Carlisle, to what do I owe this pleasure, mam? Is everything alright up at the house?"

"I'm just taking a walk, Sam. I haven't seen you in a while, so thought I would stop by. I need to return a hired buggy to the livery stable. I thought perhaps you could have one of the men return it for me."

"I'm the only one here, Mrs. Carlisle. The other men are way on the other side, building fences along the property line. Matthew is planning on moving some stock over there as soon as they finish with the fences. He ain't back yet?" his eyes were sharp, as though he knew something she didn't.

"No, he hasn't returned." she didn't volunteer any information, although she felt he expected more from her. "I'll finish my walk now, Sam. Take care of that buggy as soon as you can. The horse needs tending if we don't get it back to the stable today." Amelia waved her hand and went on toward the woods and creek.

Sam watched her speculatively. That's mighty peculiar, her coming down here. What's going on, I wonder. Strange goings on, I say. He knew Jonathan was over at Nathan's for he had checked, like Matthew told him to. Nathan said Mrs. Carlisle had brought him over and said for him to stay until she came to get him. Wonder why she hadn't brought the boy home. Something else strange. None of his business, though. Sam continued rocking and thinking. That Wilson woman had fooled Matthew, for sure. He frowned, remembering the men who had kidnapped him, then let him go. Matthew believed her, saying she had too much money to be involved in any such scheme as stealing cattle. Why she had thousands of cattle. Why would she want to steal his? Sam knew why.

"Hell hath no fury like a woman scorned." That's what the Good Book said. She wanted Matthew and couldn't have him. She didn't steal anyone else's stock except his, but her manager had seen an opportunity to make himself rich. So, under cover of obeying her orders, he filled his own pockets. It was as clear as day to Sam, but he couldn't convince Matthew. He was rid of her, he said. Sam wasn't so sure of that. No sir, he had a bad feeling about that woman.

Amelia returned to the house, having walked until she was tired. She still didn't know what to do. She had no mind for much of anything, she admitted. Finally, she put a pot of dried black-eyed peas on to cook and went and lay down across her bed. She must have fallen asleep, for she came to herself and remembered the peas. When she checked them, they were not done, but she mixed up some cornbread and sliced some tomatoes she had picked a few days ago. She knew she would be hungry later. The day wore on into the evening. Amelia ate the peas with the cornbread and sliced tomatoes, then made herself some coffee and carried it out to the porch. How many nights such as this had she sat here, she wondered.

The summer had lasted long into what should have been fall. Thanksgiving was only a month away and the days were still warm. Her heart sank when she thought of having to deal with the holidays in the midst of all that was wrong with her and Matt. The children would be expecting her to have the food and be there, as always. How could she fail them? She noticed the buggy was gone, so Sam must have decided to take it into town himself.

The next morning, Amelia decided to ride over and bring Jonathan home. Then, she realized he would be in school that day, so she would have to wait until the afternoon to go. She cleaned an already clean house, dusted, swept, shook out rugs, cleaned windows, scrubbed floors, and made a pie. The day had turned cool, so she built a fire in the fireplace and lit the candles and lamps early. With a sense of having accomplished something worthwhile at last, she saddled her horse and rode over to Nathan's. They greeted her with questioning looks and she felt that she owed them an explanation. Jonathan and Carlyss had been no trouble at all, Lillibeth told her, with a warm hug. In fact, they were glad to have him. "He's a sweet boy, Lilli told her."

"Yes," Amelia agreed. "He surely is." He was glad to see his mother, though, for he allowed her to hug him, even in front of Carlyss. "Are you ready to come home?" She questioned, teasing him, "Or do you want to be adopted by Nathan and Lilli?"

"Mama, you know better than that." he scolded her and then went to get his things.

Carlyss complained about his going, but Amelia felt she had imposed on Nathan and Lilli enough.

When they reached home, Jonathan was ready to eat, so they ate together in the kitchen, warm and happy to be together again. He complimented her on the pie and cleaned his plate with a smile for the good food she had prepared. He even helped her clear the table before going to his room to do his homework. He didn't ask about Matthew and Amelia didn't offer any explanation for his absence. She went to bed with an air of expectancy and knew Matthew was on his way home.

The next afternoon, Amelia looked up from her sewing at the sound of a horse. She looked out the window and saw Matthew ride in and go to the barn. She suddenly wanted to find a place to hide. She didn't want to face him. She didn't know what possessed her to stay until he came back, anyway. She should have packed some clothes, taken Jonathan and left for good. Now, she was sick to her stomach with nerves. Her legs were trembling so she had to sit down. She didn't know what would happen when she told him her plans. Oh, God, please help me, she silently cried. She pictured his rage boiling over on her and she grew panicky, her hands shaking as she clasped them together in her lap.

Then, he was striding across the yard, up the steps he came, pausing to wash up on the porch, and then he was there, looking at her, as though he had never seen her before that moment. His eyes were dark, but shining with hope.

"Hello, Matthew." Her voice shook despite her effort to appear in control.

"Hello, Amy." The sound of her family's name for her surprised her, for he seldom called her Amy. He noticed she avoided looking at him and he was suddenly afraid he could not win her back.

"I have food cooked if you're hungry." She began to take down silverware and reached for a plate and a glass.

"Don't bother with that now. I'll eat later." He kept his voice low, and soft, for she looked as though she was ready to run away from him at any moment.

"I'll get back to my sewing, then." She turned to leave the kitchen, but had to pass close to him and she suddenly stopped as though she didn't know what to do.

He wanted to take her in his arms and kiss her until she loved him again, but he stepped aside and let her pass. Her skirts brushed his legs and she smelled of gardenias and sunshine. He stood there after she went back to her sewing room. He heard the door close behind her. He would rather she had screamed and cried and beat him with her little fists, called him names, anything other than this polite, distant coldness. He didn't know what he could do to get close to her. He knew she had shut him out just as surely as she shut the door to that room. He would have to wait for her to open the door and let him in. His way would not work anymore. A little voice of fear nagged at him. Had he finally gone too far?

He left the house and went to see Sam, to find out what was going on. He felt totally out of touch with everything and everybody. Routine chores seemed unimportant. He knew he had to tend to his place, though, in spite of his feelings being in a mess.

Amelia was not sewing. She was staring out the window. She would not get into a shouting match with him. She would not allow Jonathan to be subjected to that again. She wondered why he did not try to explain himself to her.

She had expected him to tell her some lie about that woman. Well, she would not have believed him, anyway.

Jonathan came home from school and the first thing he noticed was that his daddy was home. His heart sank. Maybe they wouldn't fuss. He sure hoped they didn't. He hated it when they argued. His daddy always got too mad, cursing and yelling, scaring him half to death. He had decided that as soon as he got sixteen, he would go live with Mark. He had already told his brother all about it. Mark had left and he would too. He hated to leave his mother. He was afraid that his daddy might hurt her sometimes when he was mad. He greeted Matthew with a cautious smile and was surprised when his daddy came to him and hugged him.

"What have you been up to, Jonathan? You and Carlyss have a good time?" He sounded like he really wanted to know, not just making conversation. Jonathan watched him, wondering at his good humor, for he knew more than his mother realized about the situation between them.

"We went down to that swimming hole and killed two squirrels. I killed two. Carlyss didn't kill any. His mom cooked them for us. They were some good, too." Jonathan grinned proudly.

"You're just like I was when I was a boy, son. Old Eagle Eye, that's what they called me. I brought home the meat for the whole family. You should have seen that big buck I killed one winter, with the snow on the ground." Matthew told Jonathan all about his experiences as a young boy out hunting for the family's winter supply of fresh meat.

After supper that night, Matthew went out onto the porch while Amelia cleaned up and Jonathan did his homework. He waited for her to join him like she always had, but she never did come. When he finally went in, he found that she had moved her things into the spare room. For a moment, he felt anger and he wanted to go get her and make her come back into their room, back to sleep in their bed. He remembered why she was there and his anger died, for what would he have done had he caught her in the arms of another man? He would probably have become a murderer, he admitted. So, he went to bed and lay awake. Maybe he could get her to go on a trip with him. He remembered he had promised he would take her before Christmas. He suddenly realized that Thanksgiving was a little over three weeks away, and then Christmas would be so close. How he could manage it, he didn't know. She probably wouldn't go now, anyway.

Just before he fell asleep, for some reason, he remembered the Christmas play that year that he and Millie were Mary and Joseph. He smiled when he thought of the little boy who had been the angel, Gabriel. He had lost his tooth and had a space where his front teeth should have been. He had a really hard time getting out the words. "And his name shall be called Jesus." He was supposed to say, but without his teeth, it sounded quite different. All the "s'es" were missing. Everyone laughed, but that was expected in a school play with little kids. Surprisingly, he slept soundly. That night, though, he dreamed again. This time, he was back at the cave in the woods. He was a little kid again and he saw himself, so real, sitting beside the fire, holding the white stone in his hand. Then, strangely, he saw an old Indian outside the cave.

When the little boy Matthew crawled out of the cave, he spoke to the old Indian, the white stone still in his hand. The Indian pointed up into the sky, then at the white stone. As little Matthew shook his head, the old Indian disappeared into the air, like smoke rises from a campfire. Then the little Matthew looked at the stone and with a smile, held it up toward the sky, as though offering it to God. Then, he, too, disappeared into the air.

Even in sleep, Matthew was puzzled, it seemed. The meaning of the dream eluded him when he awoke the next morning. Unusual for him, he lay in bed; his head pillowed on his folded arms, watching the sun slip into the room and push aside the shadows. Struck by an impulse, he opened the drawer of the table beside the bed. Pulling out a brand-new Bible, he looked at it with helpless frustration in his eyes. Amelia had given it to him years ago. He had never opened it, other than his initial examination when she had presented it to him one Christmas. Her eyes had been expectant, as though he would be glad, or show some emotion, but she had been disappointed, for he looked puzzled at the gift. Now, he had no idea why he was even holding it in his hand, for he didn't have enough knowledge of its contents to find what he needed to know. He looked for the letter, but couldn't remember where he had put it. He needed to read it again so he could look up the scripture in his bible. Throwing aside the covers, he decided to ask Amelia if she had put the letter away.

She was awake, but not up when the door suddenly opened and Matthew stood there, she felt her heart begin to pound and hated her weakness for him. He didn't come near her, though, but stood near the open doorway.

"Amelia, did you put my mother's letter away? I can't seem to find it."

"I found it on the floor. It's in the dresser drawer." her eyes were questioning, curious as to what was going on in his mind.

"Thanks." he turned to go, then paused, looked back at her. "Do you want me to make coffee?"

"Whatever you want to do." she was as polite as he, her eyes saying more than she realized, for she could never hide her feelings. Her eyes always gave her away.

He resisted what he saw in her eyes, for he knew if he approached her, she would push him away. His power over her emotions was something he had always used against her. Once he had realized how her feelings for him overcame her anger at his treatment of her, he never worried about losing her love. Now, he was coming to realize that he had pushed her beyond her weakness for him. Love and physical attraction were not the same in his mind anymore. When he realized that fact, he couldn't say. He just knew it. A beautiful face sometimes hid an evil heart.

After he left, she threw aside the covers and went to the window, welcoming the bright sunshine, seeing a sign in its appearance. No matter how dark it seemed she had the promise of another morning.

The door opened again. Matthew was bringing her coffee, the steam rising up from the cups as he handed it to her. He knew her so well, she realized. He is trying to break down my resistance to him. He thinks he can manipulate me like he's always done. Well, it won't work this time,

Matthew. It won't work. She moved away from him, then, climbing back into bed, she placed the pillows behind her back, pulled the covers up and watched him as she began to sip her coffee.

He sat down on the edge of the bed. "Amelia, I want to ask you something. I don't want you to start preaching to me. I just want an answer to my question." He waited for her response. She waited for him to continue, her eyes questioning his motive.

"Will you tell me where in the bible it talks about the angel coming to tell Mary that she was going to have a baby? You know, it says he told her his name would be Jesus." He was sincere, she could tell and her eyes began to shine with excitement. He saw the excitement and wondered, waiting for her answer.

"That verse is in Matthew, the first book of the New Testament. It's in the first chapter, the twenty-first verse."

"Oh, that's the one where my mother got my name. How about that!" His face was childlike, amazed at such a coincidence. "Could that be the name she wanted me to find, you think? My own name?" He looked puzzled again. "Where is that other scripture, you know, the one in Revelation, the last book in the bible."

"Revelation 2:17, Matthew. The last book in the bible." She could hardly sit still, praying for the light to break through in his mind. She felt like jumping out of bed and shouting for joy, but she forced herself to remain still, drinking her coffee and watching his struggle.

"Amelia, does that mean anything? You know, the first book and the last book. I wonder about that. My name is Matthew and that's the first book. His name is Jesus and the angel told Mary about his name in the first book, too." He still couldn't see what his mother wanted him to see about the white stone.

He's almost there, Lord, she laughed inside. Almost there.

"What do you think, Matthew?" She could hardly stand it, she thought. "Come on my love. Think! Her heart cried.

He suddenly stood up and left the room, returning with the bible. Reseating himself on the bed, he opened it, finally finding the scripture he wanted. He read Matthew 1: 21, then his eyes followed down to the next verse and the next. When he looked at Amelia, she saw the light break through. He grinned, for the first time since he had returned home, and she grinned back.

"God with us. His name shall be called Jesus, Emanuel, God with us. Is that it, Amy? Jesus is the name of God? Jesus means that God is with us?" He knew there was more, but her face was lit up like it had been that night at Ian's house when she and Belle had prayed with Penelope. He couldn't help himself. She looked so appealing. He had to gather her into his arms and feel her nearness. He almost did. But with an effort he didn't know he had; he knew he had better wait.

Then he turned to the last book, Revelation and began to read the verse again that his mother had told him was so important. The white stone with the name on it. All this stuff about names, he thought. What is the connection? It still eluded him, like trying to catch smoke. It looked substantial, but when you thought you had it, it slipped away, leaving your hand empty. He suddenly closed the bible and her heart sank. Surely, he wasn't going to give up now, she thought. He was so close. She started to encourage him but felt restrained, so she kept silent. He looked at her then and she read his mind. He wanted to explain what she had seen at the hotel. She didn't want to hear that now. She wanted him to pursue the course God had him on right now. She felt impatient at his unawareness of the spiritual miracle within his reach.

Matthew didn't want her to know that he just could not seem to understand what he had read. Her knowledge of the bible intimidated him. He felt ashamed that his wife knew more than he did about anything. So, he closed the bible. He would think about it by himself, so she could not see how ignorant he was. He suddenly remembered all those years ago talking with Ian and how eager he had been to learn how to understand the Bible.

"Would you believe me if I told you that things were not as they appeared?" He leaned toward her, as though to take her in his arms, but she stiffened immediately, and he felt her resistance. She could not let him get by with his lying and mistreatment of her any longer. She knew it. If she accepted his explanation, he would only do it again, she was certain.

"Matthew, I don't want to talk about it. I'm sorry, but I cannot believe anything you tell me at this point. Let me up. I've got to get Jonathan up for school. He'll be late." Because of his softness of the morning, she forgot how quickly he could change.

"What if I don't let you get up?" His smile was deceiving, for he suddenly leaned toward her, his weight pinning her under the covers.

"Please, Matthew, I have to get Jonathan up for school." her voice betrayed her fear and he felt it then, the need to control her, to prove his superior strength. To show her she was really in his power. He couldn't take a chance on her leaving him for good. If he could break her down, she would give in just like she always had before. In spite of his good intentions of the morning, the need to be in control asserted itself, then, and the ugliness that was still there rose to the surface. His arms were around her and his eyes were close to her face. She looked into their darkness and hated what she saw. He smiled because he knew his strength was greater than hers. He could do whatever he wanted with her. She could not help herself. She turned her head away from his lips and felt them on her face and neck. She could not get her arms free. Then she began to cry in helpless frustration at her inability to free herself. She lay her head back in surrender and the tears rolled down her face. She hated him at that moment. She hated the demon that ruled him. All the beauty of the morning dissipated into ugliness and she wept in despair. Matthew kissed her, then abruptly stood, releasing her legs from the confining covers. Her eyes flew open and she tearfully climbed out of bed, grabbed her robe and fled to the kitchen.

After she left, he sat down on the bed again, retrieving the bible where it had fallen to the floor.

Later after Jonathan left for school, Matthew left the house to see to the chores. Amelia dragged her bag down and began to gather up items of clothing, packing them carefully. She would be gone when he returned, she told herself. She wrote Jonathan a note, telling him that she would return for him. She begged him to understand that she could no longer live with his daddy, but she was not forsaking him. He would be all right. His daddy would see that he was fed and got to school. She would come and get him, she promised.

She was dressed in riding clothes, going to the barn to get the buggy, when she saw him coming back. She panicked, then, hid in one of the stalls, waiting for him to go into the house. Then, instead of getting the buggy, she saddled her horse, her hands shaking so hard she couldn't manage it. Her heart was threatening to choke her breath off for it was pounding so hard. If he caught her, he would force her to stay, and she knew she had to get away from his domination, his cruelty. He caused her to hope one minute, then her hopes were dashed the next. She could not endure this emotional destruction inside herself. She feverishly tried to get the girt tight under the horse's belly, feeling she had no strength left.

Matthew stood and watched her for several minutes, trying to decide what to do. He knew she was trying to leave him, for he had read the note she had left for Jonathan. He knew his action that morning had been wrong. He always seemed to mess up, but he knew he couldn't let her go. Without her, he would have nothing to work for, no one who cared for him. Finally, he walked over to where she struggled with the saddle. She jumped in alarm, her gasp of fear making him ashamed. He said nothing, just began to finish the job for her. He offered her the reins. She looked like a lost child, then. Her face had a hopeless look that pierced his heart.

"Baby, you don't have to go, you know. I won't bother you if you don't want me to." I never loved that woman. I want you to know that. I can't tell you why I got involved with her. I've never loved any woman except you. What you saw at the hotel was her last effort to divide us, you and me. She was so mad at me for dumping her that she swore to get even with me. She saw you from the window and timed it so you would catch her kissing me. That's all I can tell you." He still held the reins in his hand. She made no effort to take them from him. Instead, she turned and walked back to the house, not once looking back.

After that day, and through Thanksgiving they appeared to be a normal couple, enjoying their children and little grandson. Matthew felt that Amelia believed his explanation, for she moved back into their bedroom. She no longer resisted his embraces and seemed to welcome their times of intimacy. Deep within her heart, she knew, though, that all was not well with them. She knew it was only a matter of time until the thing that lived inside Matthew, that spirit that hated her and all she represented, was once more aroused and rose up to manifest itself in rage.

Little Mattie, almost two, was a source of delight and joy to them both. Matthew had to get him up on his horse, proudly reminding everyone how he resembled his grandpa. Sara and John smiled at her daddy, glad to see his affection for Mattie. Amelia was so thankful that they were all together for the first time in quite some time. Her heart dared to hope again, in spite of her awareness that her husband had not completed his journey to God.

Christmas was to be a big event, with Hope coming home and Amelia prayed that Mark and Joy would make an appearance. She had three weeks to make her preparations and welcomed the activity, for she had no time to dwell on the past. Matthew had asked her if she wanted to go on a short weekend trip, just to Baton Rouge, or New Orleans, perhaps Lafayette before Christmas.

"I would love to go shopping for gifts. I can just go to Alexandria. I think I can find what I need there."

She waited until the last minute to approach him with what was on her mind. The Christmas play and supper at the church was an event to which he seldom went. She planned to ask him to go with her this year. Finally, one day, they walked down to the creek, enjoying the balmy weather, even though it was the middle of December. The leaves had all fallen, but the grass had hardly turned brown. They had only had a couple of early morning frosts the whole winter.

He held her hand and her heart was light and full of hope for the future, for she was full of faith. Deciding this was a good time to bring up the subject, she told him about the play and supper.

"Matt, you know every year there is a play and supper at the church. I wish you would go with me this year." They were standing at the edge of the creek, watching the water glide along the sandy bottom. They could see every grain of sand, almost, it was so clear.

"I don't see why not, Amy. I wouldn't mind seeing the Christmas play. It's been a long time since I've seen a Christmas play. You know, one year I was Joseph. Would you believe that?" His grin was appealing and she put her arms around his waist, laying her head against his chest, as she had done for so many years.

"I bet you were the most handsome Joseph they had ever seen." She squeezed him, and then laughed, looking up, her head thrown back in that same gesture he remembered so well. He kissed her, just as he had done then and they clung to each other, savoring the sweetness of the moment.

Chapter 31

Jonathan was so happy. His mother and daddy seemed to be on good terms again. They held hands a lot and laughed and it made him laugh. They had gone looking for a Christmas tree together. Then they decorated it, together. His daddy placed the ornaments on the top branches and he did the lower part. Then, they stood back and admired their work. There were already some presents underneath and he wondered if they were for him. He decided that maybe he would not leave home after all, since things seemed to be going so well.

Matthew looked so handsome, Amelia thought. His hair had a touch of gray, but she loved it. He was still trim and fit, due to his constant activity and the years of manual labor on the place. She didn't look bad, herself, she decided. After giving birth to five children, her figure was still girlish and slender. Her hair had darkened to a deep auburn, as she got older, but the ends were sun-bleached, almost strawberry blond. They made a nice-looking couple, she felt, as they reached the church. She was delighted that everyone was so welcoming to Matthew. The men all came and shook his hand, glad to see him there with her. He wasn't aware of the prayers that had been prayed for him over the years, she knew.

He seemed to enjoy himself. All the ladies had brought a covered dish and there was an abundance of good food, which he always relished. The sweet, innocent faces of the children representing angels and shepherds were beautiful in the candlelight. Matthew was very attentive tonight, she noticed. His eyes were bright with some emotion she could not name, as she stole glances at him during the play.

The peace and joy of the season seemed to remain with them as they reached home and Jonathan hugged them both before going to bed.

Amelia felt overwhelmed by love and gratitude that night. She lay beside Matthew after he slept and prayed and gave thanks to the Lord until sleep finally came.

"What is the name?" Matthew came awake with a start. Who said that? His mind was playing tricks on him. He could have sworn someone asked him a question. He had gone to sleep thinking about that name business again; the play had brought it all back to him. Closing his eyes once more, he dozed off, to find himself involved in a dream in which he was both an observer and a participant.

He was walking through the woods, his gun in his hand. As was his custom, he had sat down at the base of a tree, waiting for a squirrel to appear. Seeing something white in the distance, he looked intently, trying to make out what it was. To his astonishment, it was a man, walking toward him, through the trees. As he drew nearer, he held out an object for Matthew to see. In the dream, Matthew could see it looked like his white stone. As the man held it out, a ray of light touched it and he saw the writing. But the writing was not just a sign like his stone had on it. He could see, as plain as day, the stone had "Jesus" written on it. He stared at the man, for his eyes were the eyes of the man who had touched him that day on the creek bank. He stood there, the stone lying in his hand, holding it toward Matthew, his eyes full of such compassion that Matthew felt his heart melt, overcome by such feeling directed toward him. He finally reached out his hand to take the stone and realized that he also held a stone. Then the man spoke.

"What is the name?" As he looked at the stone in his hand, Matthew saw his own name written on its surface.

"My name is Matthew." He replied. He felt as though the eyes of the man could see past his flesh and knew his thoughts. Suddenly, he felt naked, ashamed for the world to see the darkness that dwelt within him.

"I will give you a new name. You will be my son. You shall bear my name." the man said, and then he took Matthew's stone from his hand and left it lying on Matthew's palm. He then turned and walked away through the trees.

In his dream, Matthew watched the man disappear in the light of the sun. He looked at the stone lying in his hand, the stone the man had given him. Who was it? Then, he knew. The last book. The last book said He would give the over comers a stone with a name. The name in the white stone. He began to weep, then, as the revelation hit him. He had to have that name. He had to have Jesus within him. Then, he would be a son. His mother was right. Suddenly, he was weeping out loud, clutching the stone to him. His heart felt as though it was full of tears that had been dammed up forever, from the beginning of his life.

"Forgive me, Jesus. Forgive me of all my sins. I repent. I want your presence. Fill me with your spirit."

The prayers of his mother rained down upon him and the darkness resisted. He felt the stone pressing into his chest, the stone with the name that he wanted to be his. Over and over, he cried that name, waking Amelia, then himself, saying that name, as though he couldn't stop. His body was racked by sobs, his face contorted with desperation. Again he cried out. "I'm a sinner, Jesus, I need you to change my heart and save me from my sinful ways."

Amelia sat up in bed and saw her miracle being born right before her eyes.

"His name is Jesus. He said his name is Jesus. He gave me the stone. His name is Jesus. Matthew's voice was broken; unlike anything she had ever heard or seen since she had known him. She began to thank God, then. Her body rocked back and forth in the bed as she praised and worshiped the Lord.

"Oh God, your name is Jesus," she heard Matthew's voice filled with awe at the revelation he had finally received from the Lord, himself. Then his voice changed and words poured from his lips that Amelia could not understand. She knew then, that her prayers were being answered, for Matthew's face was alight with Godly joy and the beauty of the Holy Ghost was upon him.

When they talked about the events of that night in the years following, it seemed that life did not begin for them until after that unbelievable night in December. There was no more sleep, but rejoicing filled the house and Jonathan awoke, to be drawn into the circle of their praise.

Later, they went into the kitchen, made coffee and cooked breakfast, but hardly knowing what they were doing, they were so elated and filled with excitement. They didn't even realize the time of the night that all of this had occurred, but it didn't really matter. For, just as Amelia had believed for so long, through the long dark night, their morning had come. After Jonathan had gone to bed, Matthew led Amelia to their room. He knew there was something he had to do to complete the ending of the old man he was to becoming the new man in Christ he is. He directed Amelia to sit down in the chair and then knelt down on the floor before her. Before he said a word, tears threatened behind her eyes, but he took her hand and looked into her face. "Amelia, Will you be able to trust me and believe that I am no longer the Matthew that has been so cruel and unfeeling to you and our children? Will you be able to see me as a new man and believe that the love I have for you is the love of God and not the selfish kind that I called love? I know now that only by being filled with God's spirit can a man have pure love for others. All my life I've been seeking to know how love feels. I felt loved at Aunt Willie's and Uncle Buck's house and when I met you and your family.

I saw love, real love in the lives of all of you. I've asked the Lord to forgive me and I know He has, but I have to ask you to forgive me. My heart is full of sorrow at the way I have treated you and our children and even others for all my life. I cannot go back and change or erase from your memory the terrible things I have said and done in anger. When I repented, the Lord forgave me and the Bible says that he blots out even the record of our transgressions and does not remember them ever again. But I know that no one can forget like God, even when we forgive. I have to forgive Uncle James, Aunt Martha, Millie, my dad and all the people in my life that I have hated for the way I was treated. I have to love them all like Jesus loves me and forgives my sins. I hope you see me as a new man and I pray the betrayal of my vows does not come to your mind to remind you of the sin I committed. I know how love feels now. God's love is not selfish, but thinks of others and cares for others more than self. I love you and I will show you my love in action for the rest of our lives, for you have shown me love even when I treated you so shamefully and wounded you over and over. You never gave up on me, Amelia. That is the love of God you have shown me and I don't know what would have happened to me without your prayers. I want you to know I am so thankful for you and our children and I promise with God's help to be the husband you deserve and the daddy our children deserve from this day forward. Can you forgive me?" Matthew clasped her hands in his and laid his head in her lap as he wept for all the wrong he had done to her. Her tears fell upon his bowed head. "I have already forgiven you, my love. I see you as the man I have always known you were meant to be. Weeping endures for the night, but our morning has come and with it, God has given us joy unspeakable and full of glory for Him. Let's give him praise." Amelia lifted their hands together to the Lord.

They stood on the porch as the morning began to push back the shadows of night. The sun rose in unbelievable splendor, the shining on their faces reflecting its glory.

Oh, God, he thought, how I love this woman that you have given me. He turned her gently to face him. His eyes were so clear and washed clean of all darkness that she could see his soul reflected in their depths. His love filled his eyes and his face was changed. Her arms were around him, her head thrown back. Her eyes were so blue, her love for him shone so brightly, that he was dazzled by the intensity and force of it. He pulled her close to him, lifting her slight body off the floor. Their lips met in joy and promise for the years ahead. The morning of the white stone had broken upon them and the glory of the Lord filled their house.

EPILOGUE

Christmas came with anticipation unexcelled by anything they had ever known. All their children, even Felicity, big with child, timidly at first, then with joy, celebrated the birth of their daddy into God's family, while they celebrated the birth of their Savior. Jonathan couldn't seem to stop smiling. Happiness glowed on his face.

Mark came, bringing his Joy. Hope came too. She was in awe at the change in her dad. She wept in joy and thanksgiving for the miracle. She introduced her to Joel, a friendly young man with a sense of humor that kept them all laughing through the Christmas celebrations. Amelia saw the happiness in Hope and Sara with John and little Mattie, now laughing and clapping his little hands with excitement. Thank God, for your love shed abroad in our hearts, she whispered, for we have become one at last.

Matthew stood before all his children and with tears running down his face, asked for their forgiveness for all the years he had been such an angry man. "I cannot take back all the wrong and hurt I've caused all of you, who have loved me in spite of my unworthiness to be loved. I can only show you that I love you and asked you to forgive me and see me as a new man, for the old Matthew Carlisle died" All the children gathered around him, hugging him and kissing him, tears running down their faces for the miracle of seeing their prayers answered in their daddy.

Amelia's heart was full of joy as she watched her children and grandbabies altogether at last.

Her eyes turned to Matthew. She would never forget that day she first saw him and lost her head and her heart over a tall, dark-haired young man. He felt her eyes on him and met her gaze, his eyes speaking volumes across the room. The little grin that made her heart respond like a silly girl lifted his lips as he started toward her. Her lips formed the words "I love you."

She saw the promise in his eyes as they twinkled in response. "I love you, too." he sent the message back to her.

THE BEGINNING